Embedded Systems

Embedded Systems
ARM Programming and Optimization

Second Edition

Jason D. Bakos

Professor of Computer Science and Engineering
University of South Carolina
Columbia, SC

ELSEVIER

Morgan Kaufmann is an imprint of Elsevier
50 Hampshire Street, 5th Floor, Cambridge, MA 02139, United States

Notices

Knowledge and best practice in this field are constantly changing. As new research and experience broaden our understanding, changes in research methods, professional practices, or medical treatment may become necessary.

Practitioners and researchers must always rely on their own experience and knowledge in evaluating and using any information, methods, compounds, or experiments described herein. In using such information or methods they should be mindful of their own safety and the safety of others, including parties for whom they have a professional responsibility.

To the fullest extent of the law, neither the Publisher nor the authors, contributors, or editors, assume any liability for any injury and/or damage to persons or property as a matter of products liability, negligence or otherwise, or from any use or operation of any methods, products, instructions, or ideas contained in the material herein.

British Library Cataloguing-in-Publication Data
A catalogue record for this book is available from the British Library.

Library of Congress Cataloging-in-Publication Data
A catalog record for this book is available from the Library of Congress.

ISBN: 978-0-12-822575-2

For Information on all Morgan Kaufmann publications visit our
website at https://www.elsevier.com/books-and-journals

Acquisitions Editor: Steve Merken
Editorial Project Manager: Helena Beauchamp
Publishing Services Manager: Shereen Jameel
Senior Project Manager: Mani Chandrasekaran
Design Direction: Mark Rogers

Printed in India

Last digit is the print number: 9   8   7   6   5   4   3   2   1

Contents

Preface

The content of this book is adapted from the "CSCE 313: Embedded System Design" course that I developed at the University of South Carolina in 2010–2011 and then taught until 2019. Since this was my first embedded systems course, I began my planning for it by surveying other embedded systems courses. I noticed that Carnegie Mellon University was offering no less than six courses with "Embedded System" in the title or description, with each course focusing on a unique aspect of embedded systems, such as applied control theory, robotic control systems, low-power mobile systems, and real-time systems. Since my department was planning to offer only one embedded systems course, it was left to my discretion on which topics to cover.

At the same time, smartphones were just beginning to proliferate the market, with the iPhone having been introduced 3 years earlier and the first Android phone having been introduced 2 years earlier. When I purchased my first Android smartphone in 2009, I immediately noticed a striking difference between the Android user interface and the iPhone user interface. Swiping left and right on the iPhone produced a smooth, continuous transition between pages, while swiping left and right on the Android produced a jerky, discontinuous transition. This was in spite of the fact that both phones had nearly identical hardware capabilities, being based around 32-bit ARM CPUs. This inspired me to consider how programming methodologies from high-performance computing, such as low-level programming and use of data quantization, must impact the degree to which performance can be extracted from limited hardware capabilities. I also noted that the apparent high frame rate of the iPhone interface produced a visceral level of satisfaction as compared to the sluggish experience offered by Android, and it might be possible to leverage this as a way to capture the interest of students in working on course projects involving code optimization. Thus, I decided to focus the course on performance optimization with an emphasis on graphics.

The first edition of this book, written in 2016, primarily targeted the 32-bit ARMv6 and ARMv7 CPUs in the first-generation Raspberry Pi and first-generation NVIDIA Jetson using Linux and the GCC compiler. At that time, it was possible to achieve a substantial speedup using hand-crafted assembly language over compiler-generated code for the example applications highlighted in the book. When updating the text to the second edition to target the 64-bit ARMv8 CPU of the fourth-generation Raspberry Pi, I was surprised to see that it was now significantly more difficult to write low-level code that outperformed the compiler-generated code. This is due to both improvements in the GCC compiler's ability to utilize the ARM NEON instructions and the dropping of certain ARMv6 and ARMv7 features, such as predicated instructions and vector floating-point instructions, as the compiler support for these features was poor. For this reason, this edition of the text places less emphasis on low-level programming and more on ways to structure high-level code to produce high-quality executable code.

Using This Book

This book is intended for use in a junior- or senior-level undergraduate course in a computer science or computer engineering curriculum. While other topics in embedded system programming are strongly represented in the corpus of textbooks on the subject, this book focuses on performance-oriented programming for lightweight system-on-chip embedded processors. This book should accompany an embedded design platform such as a Raspberry Pi, on which the student can evaluate the practices and methodologies described.

When using this text, students are expected to know the C programming language, have a basic knowledge of the Linux operating system, and understand basic concurrency such as task synchronization.

Instructor Support

Lecture slides, exercise solutions, and errata are provided at the companion website: textbooks.elsevier.com/9780128225752

Acknowledgments

Several students assisted me in the development of the first edition of this book. **Benjamin Morgan**, **Jonathan Kilby**, **Shawn Weaver**, **Justin Robinson**, and **Amadeo Bellotti** learned how to access the performance monitoring unit (PMU) on the Raspberry Pi's Broadcom BCM2835 and the Xilinx Zynq 7020. **Daniel Clements** helped develop a uniform approach for using the Linux perf_event on the ARM11, ARM Cortex A9, and ARM Cortex A15. Daniel also evaluated Imagination Technology's OpenCL runtime and characterized its performance on the PowerVR 544 GPU on the ODROID XU Exynos 5 platform. **Friel "Scottie" Scott** helped evaluate the Mali T628 GPU on the ODROID-XU3 platform and proofread Chapter 5. Much of my insight about memory optimizations for computer vision algorithms was an outgrowth of my graduate student **Fan Zhang**'s dissertation on auto-optimization of stencil loops on the Texas Instruments Keystone Digital Signal Processor architecture.

I would like to thank the following reviewers, who provided feedback, insight, and helpful suggestions at multiple points throughout the development of the book:

- **Miriam Leeser**, Northeastern University
- **Larry D. Pyeatt**, South Dakota School of Mines and Technology
- **Andrew N. Sloss**, University of Washington, Consulting Engineer at ARM Inc.
- **Amr Zaky**, Santa Clara University

I would like to thank Elsevier and specifically **Helena Beauchamp**, **Stephen Merken**, and **Nate McFadden** for their encouragement and patience throughout the writing. I also wish to thank **Mani Chandrasekaran** and **Shereen Jameel** for their detail-oriented editing and **Mark Rogers** for designing the cover.

CHAPTER 1

The Linux/ARM embedded platform

Chapter Outline

Our culture is becoming increasingly inundated with mobile and wearable devices that can deliver snappy touch-based user interfaces, immersive gaming applications, virtual and augmented reality, high-speed wireless broadband connectivity, and high-resolution real-time sensing and image processing. These devices owe their existence to two crucial technologies.

The first is ARM processor technology, which powers virtually all mobile devices. ARM processors were introduced into customer electronics in the 1980s and have grown to become the *de facto* mobile processor architecture.

ARM processors are not manufactured as standalone chips, but rather as components integrated into a diverse and heterogeneous embedded *system-on-chip* (*SoC*) that is customized for each specific product. An embedded SoC is a collection of interconnected hardware modules on a single chip, including one or more ARM processor cores, a set of memory interfaces (for SDRAM, flash memory, etc.), a set of communications interfaces (for USB, Bluetooth, WiFi, etc.), one or more graphical processor units (GPUs), and sometimes one or more neural processor units (NPUs), image processor units (IPUs), security and/or cryptographic processors, and real-time processors. The primary ARM processor cores serve as the "host" or "master" of the whole SoC and are responsible for running the operating system, implementing the user interface, and coordinating control of all the peripherals and special-purpose coprocessors.

Figure 1.1 shows a photo of the Apple A15 SoC, the processor inside Apple's iPhone 13 (photo courtesy of TechInsights). The chip contains 15 billion transistors over an area of 107.7 mm^2 and is manufactured in the TSMC 5 nm N5P process. The areas identified as "CPU 1" and "CPU 2" comprise a six-core ARM processor. The areas identified as "GPU" comprise the Graphical Processor Unit, a set of special-purpose processors used for video and graphics. The areas identified as "NPU" comprise the 16-core Neural Processor Unit. Not labeled is the Image Processor Unit (IMU) used for computational photography. The large unlabeled area contains additional modules used for various other peripherals to support the iPhone's functionality.

In the sense of being capable of executing any program written in any programming language, the ARM processors comprise the "computer" part of the SoC. However, embedded ARM processors are generally less sophisticated than modern desktop and server processors because their design emphasizes power consumption over performance.

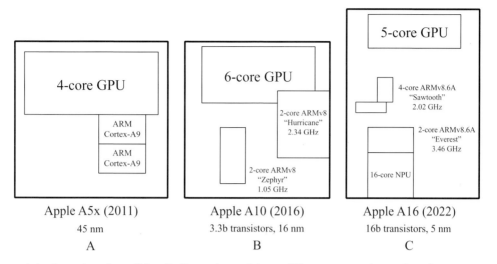

Figure 1.1: An estimation of the die floor plans of three different generations of Apple's System-on-Chip designs, based on die photographs. Note that these are not to scale. As shown, the portion of the die allocated to both the CPU and GPU cores has trended down, while later generations allocate an increasing portion to specialized processors like the Neural Processor Unit (NPU) and, not shown, the Image Processor (ISP) on the Apple A16 designed for computational photography and the Display Engine on the Apple A16 designed for a low-power "always on display" feature. Also note how the Apple A5x used a 32-bit ARM Cortex-A9 CPU, designed by ARM, while later generations used an Apple-designed ARM processor with various codenames, such as "Hurricane," "Zephyr," Sawtooth," and "Everest". Additionally, the ARM cores on the A10 and A16 are of two designs, one for lower-performance and lower-power, and one for higher-performance and higher-power.

The second technology that enables modern consumer electronics is the Linux operating system (OS), which is run on nearly all ARM processors. Due to its free availability, success, and widespread adoption on desktop and server computers, Linux has grown to become the universal standard embedded OS. As an embedded OS, Linux greatly facilitates code development and code reuse across different embedded platforms.

1.1 Performance-oriented programming

Since mobile embedded processors emphasize energy efficiency, writing highly performing code for embedded processors generally requires more effort on the part of the programmer as compared to writing code for desktop and server processors.

This is because desktop and server processors are designed to extract maximum performance from both *legacy code*, code written and compiled long ago for a previous version of the processor, and *processor agnostic code*, code that was not written with any specific target processor in mind. They achieve this by devoting much real estate and energy consumption to two specific features, given as follows.

1. **Automatic extraction of instruction-level parallelism:** The processor attempts to (1) maximize the number of instructions executed per clock cycle, (2) rearrange the

execution order of instructions as compared to their program order to minimize the impact of dependencies between instructions, and (3) predict execution behavior and speculatively execute instructions before knowing if they are needed, throwing away unneeded results when necessary. This allows the processor to sustain high instruction throughput even when the native program order of the instructions in the code would not otherwise permit this.

2. **Large, complex caches:** The processor attempts to maximize memory system performance even when the program accesses memory in a non-ideal access order for the attached memory. This involves intelligent data pre-fetching, memory access scheduling, and high associativity, allowing the cache to minimize repeated accesses to the same memory location.

Embedded processors, on the other hand, generally forego these features. Although some embedded processors can execute multiple instructions per clock cycle, the instructions are executed in program order, meaning that instructions that are ready to execute cannot "cut in line" to execute before a previous instruction that is waiting for its inputs. Likewise, embedded processor caches are generally less sophisticated than desktop processor caches in that they have fewer levels in their hierarchy. Additionally, embedded processors generally have around ten times less bandwidth than their primary system RAM.

This makes embedded processors exhibit a wider performance gap between programs that are "performance tuned" and those that are not. This difference is most noticeable for *compute bound* and *memory bound* programs, which are programs whose speed or response time is determined by the processor or memory speed as opposed to input and output speed. For example, an embedded processor will certainly require more time than a desktop processor to encode a video, since this waiting time is determined by the processor and memory speed.

On the other hand, the performance of an *I/O bound* program is determined by the speed of communication channels or other peripherals. For example, a program that forces the user to wait for data to be downloaded would not complete any earlier, regardless of the processor technology. In this case the response time is determined by how fast the device can complete the download.

As mentioned, video encoding is generally compute bound, but since it relies on rarely changing standards (e.g., the H.264 or H.265 encoding format), most SoC vendors offload these tasks to special-purpose hardware that can encode and decode video faster and more efficiently than could be achieved on the ARM processor cores.

However, emerging embedded applications, especially those that have rapidly evolving algorithms, do not—at least initially—have the benefit of dedicated coprocessors. For these, a potential application developer may need to target the CPU cores or the GPU cores, or even another specialized processor that was not originally intended for the task.

This textbook provides a general overview of some of the methods of how program design can influence processor performance—methods in which a programmer can make changes to code without impacting program functionality but improving code performance.

These techniques generally require that the programmer write his or her code in such a way as to expose specific features in the underlying microarchitecture. In other words, the programmer must write code at a *low abstraction level* in such a way that the program is aware of the underlying processor technology. This is often referred to as *performance tuning* or *code optimization*.

The techniques covered in this text are common tools in *high-performance computing* and are presented in the context of embedded processors, and ARM processors in particular. They will provide insight into computer architecture, application design, and embedded systems, as well as allow the reader to gain practical knowledge in embedded software design for modern embedded systems. This book also introduces methodologies for programming mobile general-purpose GPUs (GPGPUs) using the OpenCL programming model.

In describing these methodologies, the textbook will use several example applications, including image transformations, fractal generation, image convolution, and several computer vision tasks. This textbook will take advantage of the system facilities offered by the Linux OS, including Linux's GCC compiler toolchain and debug tools, performance monitoring support, OpenMP multicore runtime environment, video frame buffer, and video capture capabilities.

This textbook is designed to accompany and work with any of the many low-cost Linux/ARM embedded development boards currently on the market, notably the Raspberry Pi. The Raspberry Pi is notable in that it presents the programmer with an interactive login session to compile, debug, and characterize code, eliminating the need for complex cross-compilers, remote debuggers, and/or architectural simulators.

1.2 ARM technology

ARM processor technology is controlled by ARM Holdings. ARM stands for "Advanced RISC Machine", and RISC stands for "Reduced Instruction Set Computer." RISC is a design philosophy developed in the 1980s at the University of California, Berkeley, where the native language of the processor, or *instruction set*, is deliberately designed to be a small repertoire of extremely simple instructions in the sense that the amount of work performed by each individual instruction, in terms of fundament memory, computational, or decision operations, is minimized. This means that the processor must execute a large number of these simple instructions when executing a program. The advantage of this approach is that—even if a program requires the execution of N times more simple instructions as compared to a processor having individual instructions that perform more work—simple instructions can be made to execute more than N times faster on average than complex instructions. This provides better overall performance while also making it easier for the compiler to utilize a large portion of the available instructions.

RISC instructions are generally divided into three main types: *arithmetic instructions*, *memory instructions*, and *control instructions*. Arithmetic instructions, which also include Boolean logic and bit manipulation operations, are the only type of instruction that performs any actual "number crunching" computations, while memory and control instructions are necessary overheads required to exchange data with an external memory and allow the program to perform data-dependent behaviors. Memory and control instructions on average take more time than arithmetic instructions. Memory instructions are up to *10–20 times slower* than arithmetic instructions, although this depends on the program's *memory access pattern* and the achieved performance of the processor's *memory hierarchy*. Together, these factors determine the *average memory access time* for a particular program with a particular input data set, which in turn determines the cost of the memory instructions.

The ARM instruction set architecture (ISA)—the standardized machine and assembly language used to interface software with hardware—was originally developed in the 1980s by the British company Acorn Computers for their ARM1, ARM2, and ARM3 CPUs. These CPUs were intended to be used as desktop personal computer CPUs, but after unsuccessfully competing against the Intel x86 and Motorola 68000 CPUs of the time ARM changed its business model from selling physical CPUs to selling the rights to use its processor design and/or ISA. Their first major customer was Apple, who used an ARM processor for their Newton PDA released in 1993, which had the result of cementing ARM's place as the *de facto* embedded processor for consumer electronics.

Today, ARM processors are sold as a reusable *macrocell*, a pre-made design to be incorporated as one of the many modules that comprise a system-on-chip (SoC), alongside coprocessors such as GPUs, memory controllers, and I/O controllers. In other words, a pre-designed ARM macrocell is inserted into an existing design with other pre-designed macrocells to form a customized, heterogeneous SoC, as is the case with the Broadcom chips used in the Raspberry Pi.

Additionally, the macrocells themselves are customizable, allowing the customer—in this case, an original equipment manufacturer (OEM) for an ARM-based SoC—to choose which features of the ISA to support in hardware (i.e., floating point, hardware multiply, single-instruction multiple data [SIMD] instructions, superscalar execution width, virtualization features, security features, etc.), as well as the size of the caches.

Alternatively, ARM allows its instruction set architectures to be licensed, allowing the implementation of the ISA to be designed from scratch by the licensee, as is the case with Apple Cyclone (starting with the Apple A7 SoC) and Nvidia Project Denver. In this case, ARM requires that the processor design be tested for compliance with the ARM ISA before being sold to consumers.

In either case, the widespread use of a consistent instruction set architecture allows programmers to leverage mature development tools such as compilers, debuggers, and code libraries.

There are several different versions of both ARM instruction set architecture and the macrocell, but none of them alone can deliver real-time HD, 4 K, or 8 K video encoding and decoding; 3D graphics rendering; computer vision; computational photography; augmented reality; or low-latency machine learning that customers have come to expect from modern phones and tablets. For this reason, ARM processors are almost always combined with specialized coprocessors that perform these workloads.

1.3 Brief history of ARM

The ARM instruction set architecture is constantly evolving, but we will pick up ARM development starting with version 6 of the ARM ISA (ARMv6), released in 2002, because it was used for the ARM11 processor core that gave birth to both the first generation of hobbyist single board computers including the original Raspberry Pi, Beagle Bone, and PandaBoard and the first generation of smartphones.

Two years after the ARMv6 ARM11 processor, the ARMv7 ISA was announced in 2004 and then subsequently forked into different versions optimized for specific use cases, such as for microcontrollers (ARMv7-M) and real-time processors (ARMv7-R) that have restricted versions of the instruction set, are limited to physical memory addressing, and have hardware exception handling, as well as a version optimized for general-purpose applications (ARMv7-A) that includes support for modern operating systems using a pipelined architecture for performance.

ARMv6 and ARMv7 are very similar but have two important differences that are relevant to the material in this book. The first is the addition of the NEON instructions in ARMv7, which are a family of 128-bit wide Single Instruction, Multiple Data (SIMD) instructions. With the addition of NEON, ARMv7 dropped vector processing support in the Vector Floating Point (VFP) unit, though the VFP unit was retained to support scalar floating-point operations. The second is the addition of the Performance Monitoring Unit (PMU), which greatly expanded performance instrumentation.

1.3.1 64-bit ARM (ARMv8)

ARMv8 was released in 2013 and introduced significant changes from ARMv7. The most notable was the change from 32-bit to 64-bit. Also, NEON instructions were expanded into "NEON Advanced SIMD", adding new instructions and doubling the number of registers but retaining the 128-bit width. Some of the new features include new reduction operations that can, for example, sum the individual elements contained within a SIMD register (which previously required multiple pairwise add instructions), 64-bit arithmetic operations, an insert instruction (ins) that can transfer scalars between SIMD lanes, expanded support for saturating arithmetic, table lookup capability, and extensions to cyclic redundancy check and cryptography instructions.

ARMv8 also added the AArch32 and AArch64 execution modes (also called A32 and A64, along with the existing 16-bit instruction encoding mode Thumb, called T32, retained from ARMv7). This new execution mode allows 32-bit ARMv7 code to run on an ARMv8 processor. However, when using A64 mode there are significant changes to the ISA, such as the loss of the conditional execution field for most instructions and preventing most instructions from modifying the condition flags in the status register,[1] removal of the program counter (PC) as a general purpose register, dropping of the load multiple and store multiple instructions, expansion of the general purpose register set from 16 to 32 registers, the addition of a hardware divide instruction, and the addition of the branch-if-equal and branch-if-not-equal instructions.

The ARMv9 architecture was released in 2021 and added features for artificial intelligence and security. Unfortunately, at the time of this writing there are no available ARMv9 single board computers.

1.3.2 ARM CPUs

The ARMv6 ISA was deployed in a series of ARM CPU designs, the ARM1136J(F)-S in 2002, ARM1156T2(F)-S and ARM1176JZ(F)-S (in 2003), and the ARM11MPCore in 2005. The first three of these are *single-core* designs, with the ARM11MPCore design being the only multi-core design. A variant of ARMv6, ARMv6-M, was also implemented as the ARM Cortex-M0 and ARM Cortex-M1 CPUs. These are simple microcontroller processors that have even lower power consumption than the ARM11 processor and have increased execution time determinism.

For ARMv7, the ARMv7-M ISA was deployed in the Cortex-M3 to Cortex-M7 CPUs, the ARMv7-R ISA was deployed in the Cortex-R4 to Cortex-R8 CPUs, and the ARMv7-A ISA was deployed in the Cortex-A5 to Cortex-A17 CPUs. Each of these CPUs has varying levels

---

[1] ARMv8 supports a small set of conditional data processing instructions, including conditional branch, add/subtract with carry in, conditional select with increment, negate, or invert, and conditional compare.

of features and performance. The Cortex-M and Cortex-R designs are single core and the Cortex-A designs are multicore.

Beginning with the ARMv7-A, ARM developed a technology called "big.LITTLE" and the later version "DynamIQ", in which lower-power Cortex-A processor cores, such as the Cortex-A7 or Cortex-A53, to be paired on the same SoC with more powerful processor cores such as the Cortex-A15 or Cortex-A72, allowing the operating system to schedule workload onto the lowest-power processor core that meets the performance requirements and shut down higher-power cores when not needed. This allows the system to run with higher energy efficiency as compared to homogeneous sets of cores.

Starting with ARMv8, the number and diversity of deployments increased substantially, especially for Cortex-A, which spans the Cortex-A32 to Cortex-A78.

1.3.3 The Raspberry Pi

This edition of the book covers the ARMv6, ARMv7, and ARMv8 architectures, each of which can be found in the single-board computer market, as shown in Table 1.1.

Table 1.1: Raspberry Pi models and specifications.

Model	Architecture	Release date	Processor	CPU cores	Floating point support	GPU/features
Raspberry Pi 1	ARMv6 32-bit	2012	ARM11 700 MHz	1	VFP	Broadcom VideoCore 4 H.264 1080p30 decode at 40 Mbits/s OpenGL ES2.0 and OpenVG @ 1.5 Gtexel/s, 1 Gpixel/s 24 Gflops general-purpose compute
Raspberry Pi Zero		2015	ARM11 1 GHz			
Raspberry Pi 2	ARMv7-A 32-bit	2015	Cortex-A7 (V1.1) 900 MHz	4	VFP (no vector support) + NEON	
	ARMv8-A 64-bit	2016	Cortex-A53 (V1.2) 900 MHz			
Raspberry Pi 3		2018	Cortex-A53 1.4 GHz			
Raspberry Pi 4		2019	Cortex-A72 1.5 GHz			Broadcom VideoCore 6 H.265 4K60 decode OpenGL ES 3.1, Vulkan 1.0

Continued

Table 1.1: Raspberry Pi models and specifications.—cont'd

Model	Architecture	Release date	Processor	CPU cores	Floating point support	GPU/features
Raspberry Pi Pico	32-bit	2021	Cortex-M0+	2	No floating-point, DSP, vector, or SIMD instructions	None
Raspberry Pi Zero 2	ARMv8-A 64-bit	2021	Cortex-A53 1 GHz	4	VFP (no vector support) + NEON	Broadcom VideoCore 4 H.264 1080p30 decode at 40 Mbits/s OpenGL ES2.0 and OpenVG @ 1.5 Gtexel/s, 1 Gpixel/s 24 Gflops general purpose-compute

This textbook is not intended to be a thorough treatment of either ARM assembly language or ARM microarchitecture. However, to understand and improve code performance, it is often necessary to interpret assembly code that is generated by the compiler. In many cases it is also necessary to write snippets of code in assembly language to describe a particular operation more efficiently than the compiler. Note that this hand-written assembly language can be embedded into a program written in high-level language.

1.4 ARM programming

ARM processors can be programmed using virtually any high-level programming language. Some ARM processors can even natively execute Java bytecode. Since this textbook is primarily concerned with code performance, it uses C, which is a performance-oriented programming language.

The two most popular open-source C/C++ compiler toolchains, GCC and Clang, include a backend for ARM processors. This allows full C/C++ development, library support, and debugging. ARM Holdings, Keil, and Texas Instruments also offer commercial compiler toolchains for ARM. Commercial compilers may generate faster object code than the open-source compilers but this book will use Linux's official compiler GCC for characterizing high-level code.

RISC architectures like ARM were originally designed with a small, simple instruction set. This allowed compilers to efficiently utilize the available instructions. However, most modern instruction set architectures, including those from ARM and Intel, have added *complex instructions* such as those for media, digital signal processing. Many of these instructions allow a single instruction to process multiple inputs (single instruction, multiple data, or SIMD). Today's compilers can't always make efficient use of these instructions without the programmer explicitly invoking these instructions using *intrinsics*, inline assembly language, or libraries that utilize these instructions through one of these approaches. Intrinsics are functions that resolve to specific instructions when compiled. Intrinsics are easier to use than assembly language, but some optimization techniques require assembly language.

1.5 ARM architecture set architecture

ARM is a *"load-store" architecture*. This means that the programmer must explicitly *load* input data from memory into registers before the data can be processed. Likewise, the programmer must explicitly *store* output data to memory after it has been processed. All arithmetic instructions use the contents of registers as both their inputs and results. Registers can also be used to store temporary or intermediate results, such as loop counters or subexpression values. The programmer (or compiler when using a high-level language) has control of the state of the registers. For example, when adding two values, the programmer must decide which register to temporarily assign to each value and the computed sum. Registers can be arbitrarily reused when their previous contents are no longer needed.

1.5.1 ARM general-purpose registers

ARM is a *three-address architecture*, meaning that a single instruction can reference up to three register addresses. For example, an arithmetic instruction such as "add" can specify two registers from which to read the input values and one register to store the calculated sum. When using gcc's assembler, the destination register is listed first.

1.5.1.1 ARMv6/ARMv7 integer registers

ARMv6 and ARMv7 have sixteen 32-bit user-accessible integer registers named **r0** through **r15**. Only registers r0 to r12 are available for general-purpose use, but some registers have special roles:

- register **r13** holds the stack pointer (SP), which is written by compiler-generated code when calling and returning from functions;
- register **r14** holds the link register (LR), which is written by the hardware when executing a branch-and-link (**bl**) instruction; and
- and register **r15** holds the program counter (PC), which is written by the hardware at the same rate as it issues instructions.

Thus programs can freely use any of the registers without inference from the hardware, except for r14 and r15.

When writing inline assembly language or an assembly language routine—especially one that is embedded in or callable from C code—the programmer should be careful when using certain registers that have special meaning, as defined under the *ARM Procedure Call Standard* (*APCS*). Caution is needed because these registers may be arbitrarily changed by code generated by the compiler or by code written by other programmers.

These registers are comprised of the following:

* Registers **r0** and **r1** are used for function return values. *Unlike other RISC instruction sets, register **r0** is not "hardwired" to contain a zero value.*
* Registers **r0** through **r3** (also called **a1–a4**, for *argument* registers) are used for passing arguments to functions. The programmer can freely use these registers as "scratch registers" but should be aware that their state may not be preserved across function calls.
* Registers **r4** through **r11** (also called **v1** through **v8**, for *variable* registers) are generally safe to use, except that some obscure compilers may use **r9** as the *static base register* (also called **sb**, **SB**, or **v6**) and **r10** as the *stack limit register* (also called **sl**, **SL**, or **v7**).
* Compilers such as gcc use **r11** as the *frame pointer* (also called **fp**, **FP**, or **v8**) to point to the base of the current *activation frame*. The activation frame contains local subroutine data such as the local variables.
* Register **r13**, the *stack pointer* (also called **sp** or **SP**), is used to point to the top of the activation stack.

1.5.1.2 ARMv8 integer registers

ARMv8 has thirty-one 64-bit user-accessible integer registers named x0 through x30, which can also be used as 32-bit registers w0 through w30. The w-registers point to the lower 32 bits of the x-registers and, when written, zero-out the upper 32 bits. Shift instructions on w-registers treat bit 31 as the MSB and sign bit when performing shifts and rotations. In some cases, the register prefix alone cannot distinguish between 32- and 64-bit operations. For example, there are separate 64-bit and 32-bit bitwise-OR instructions.

Like ARMv6, register 0 does not contain a constant value of 0. Instead, register 31 serves that role, but it also serves as the stack pointer. When used as a load or store base register, register 31 reads as the stack pointer. When used in a small selection of arithmetic instructions, register 31 provides read/write access to the stack pointer. For all other instructions, register x31/w31 reads as the value zero and discards any results written to it.

Unlike ARMv7, the PC is not a numbered register. Register 30 is the link register (LR), meaning that it is replaced with the return address on the execution of a jump-and-link instruction.

1.5.1.3 Flexible second operand

One unique feature of ARM is a *flexible second operand*, meaning that arithmetic instructions allow the second operand register to be shifted or rotated prior to being used in the instruction's execution. For example, the instruction

```
add r1,r2,r3, lsl #2
```

… left-shifts the contents of register r3 before adding it to the contents of register r2, and

```
add r1,r2,r3, asr r4
```

… arithmetically right-shifts the contents of register r3 by a number of bits as specified by the low-order byte of the contents of register r4 before adding them to the contents of register r2.

The list of valid shift operations is given as follows.

- `asr`: arithmetic shift right, store the last bit shifted out in the carry flag (if instruction uses the S suffix);
- `lsl`: logical shift left, store the last bit shifted out in the carry flag (if instruction uses the S suffix);
- `lsr`: logical shift right, store the last bit shifted out in the carry flag (if instruction uses the S suffix);
- `ror`: rotate right, place original bit $n - 1$ into the carry flag (not available in ARMv8 for add/sub instructions);
- `rrx`: rotate right exactly one bit; this operation does not accept a shift amount, treat the register as a 33-bit register with the carry flag acting as the LSB (not available in ARMv8).

These operations also have their own corresponding instructions, but when using these as instructions the flexible second operand is not available. In other words, the following instruction is not allowed:

```
asr r1,r2,r3, asr #4
```

1.5.1.4 Floating point registers

ARMv6, ARMv7, or ARMv8 CPUs with floating point support have a separate set of floating-point registers. ARMv7 and ARMv8 CPUs that include NEON support share the floating-point registers with the NEON instructions. ARMv6 offers sixteen 64-bit floating point instructions (named v0 to v15), ARMv7 offers sixteen 128-bit floating point registers (named v0 to v15), and ARMv8 offers thirty-two 128-bit floating-point registers (named v0 to v31).

Like the integer registers, instructions can refer to a portion of a floating-point register by using a specific prefix before the register number. As shown below, the prefix **b** accesses the lower 8 bits as an integer value, **h** accesses the lower 16 bits as an integer or a half-precision value, **s** accesses the lower 32 bits as an integer or a single-precision value, **d** accesses the lower 64 bits as an integer or a double precision value, and **q** accesses all 128 bits as an integer (only on ARMv7 and ARMv8, as ARMv6 is limited to 64 bits).

127:64	63:32	31:16	15:8	7:0
				b0
			h0	
		s0		
	d0			
q0				

In ARMv7 and ARMv8 the floating-point registers can also be referenced as a multielement vector by using a v prefix, followed by the register number, followed by a period, a vector width, and an element size. For example, register v0.4s refers to four 32-bit elements in register 0 and register v2.16b refers to sixteen 8-bit elements in register 2 (either way, the total vector size is 128 bits). Individual elements within a vector register can be referenced using square brackets, so register v4.s[0] refers to element 0 of register 4 assuming it is comprised of four 32-bit elements.

For example, the following sequence:

```
ldr  s0,[sp]
dup  v0.4s, v0.s[0]
```

will load a 32-bit value from the stack as a scalar into the lower 32 bits of the floating-point register 0 and then duplicate this value into the other three 32-bit elements in the register. Note that in this sequence, **s0** and **v0.s[0]** refer to the same location but different prefixes are used due to their context. This two-instruction sequence is needed because there is no version of the load instruction that will broadcast a 32-bit value into four elements of a floating-point register.

It is possible to copy values between individual vector elements and integer registers. For example, the instruction "umov w1, v0.s[0]" will copy from 32-bit element 0 from floating point registers 0 to the lower 32 bits of integer register 0, zero extending due to the use of the unsigned version of the mov instruction.

1.5.2 The status register

ARM v6/v7 maintains a status register called the **CPSR** (current program status register) that holds four condition bits, negative (N), zero (Z), carry (C), and overflow (O). These bits can be used for conditional instruction execution.

The condition bits are set according to the most recently executed ALU instruction that includes the special "s" suffix. For example, the "adds" instruction will modify the status bits but the "add" instruction will not. There are fewer such instructions in ARMv8 as compared to ARMv6/7.

Some instructions can include an optional *condition code* that determines if the instruction will be executed or skipped over. In other words, an instruction whose condition code is evaluated to false will not change the state of the processor, such as writing a result register to changing the PC. Again, there are fewer instructions that allow condition codes in ARMv8 as compared to ARMv6/7.

1.5.2.1 ARMv6/7 condition codes

For example, the ldreq instruction will only execute if the Z-bit in the CPSR is set, which will be the case if the most recent computational instruction resulted in a result of zero.

For example, the sequence:

```
subs r2,r2,#1
streq r3, [r0]
```

…will decrement register r2 and store r3 only if the new value of r2 is zero.

The compare (cmp) instruction can be used to set the status bits without any other side effect.

For example:

```
cmp r2,r3
streq r4, [r0]
```

…will store register r4 only if the contents of registers r2 and r3 are equal.

When combining the condition code and the "s" suffix, the condition code comes first, for example:

```
addeqs r0,r0,r1
```

The complete list of conditional suffixes is shown in Table 1.2.

1.5.2.2 ARMv8 condition codes

In ARMv8, instructions that support condition codes use a period before the condition code, such as "b.eq".

1.5.3 Memory addressing modes

Like other load-store architectures, the only ARM instructions that access off-chip memory are load and store instructions. For load and store instructions, there are several available

Table 1.2: Condition codes.

Suffix	Flags	Meaning
eq	z set	Equal
ne	z clear	Not equal
hs	c set	Unsigned $>=$
lo	c clear	Unsigned $<$
mi	n set	Negative
pl	n clear	Positive or zero
vs	v set	Overflow
vc	v clear	No overflow
hi	c set and z clear	Unsigned $>$
ls	c clear and z set	Unsigned $<=$
ge	n and v the same	Signed $>=$
lt	n and v different	Signed $<$
gt	z clear, or n and v the same	Signed $>$
le	z set, or n and v different	Signed $<=$

addressing modes, or ways that the off-chip memory address can be specified by the programmer or compiler.

Let us begin by examining the format of load and store instructions.

To load from memory, use the `ldr` instruction *mnemonic* followed by the target register and the memory address:

```
ldr < register >, < memory address >.
```

To store to memory, use the `str` instruction mnemonic followed by the source register and the memory address:

```
str < register >, < memory address >
```

Notice that, unlike most instructions, in the store instruction the destination location (the memory address) is given second.

The `ldr` and `str` instructions can also exchange non-32-bit values (such as bytes and halfwords) in memory by using an optional type modifier following the mnemonic:

`ldrd/strd`	load/store double (64 bits)
`ldrsh`	load signed halfword (16 bits)
`ldrh/strh`	load/store halfword (16 bits)
`ldrsb`	load signed byte (8 bits)
`ldrs/strb`	load/store byte (8 bits)

In ARMv7, load and store instructions can also be conditional. For example, `ldreq` only loads if the z flag is set. This feature is not available in ARMv8.

The memory address is specified using register in square brackets. An optional constant offset, index register, and scaling factor can be specified. ARM also supports auto-incrementing of registers.

Table 1.3 summarizes the memory addressing modes.

1.5.4 The GNU ARM assembler

This textbook uses the GNU assembler to illustrate the ARM instruction set architecture. The GNU assembler uses a different assembly language than other assemblers including ARM's own assembler.

For example, in the GNU assembler syntax:

- labels that denote instruction locations for branch targets end with a colon (e.g., "`loop: ldr r2,[r3]`"),
- assembler directives begin with a period (e.g., "`.text`"), and
- comments begin with "//" (e.g., "`// outer loop`").

Other notable characteristics of ARM assembly code include:

- for ARMv6/7: destination registers are generally listed to the left of source registers and are named r0 through r15 (e.g., "`add r1,r2,r3 // add contents of r2 and r3 and store sum in r1`");

Table 1.3: ARM memory addressing modes.

Example instruction	Effective address calculation
`ldr r0, [r1]`	address = R[r1]
`ldr r0, [r1, #4]`	address = R[r1] + 4
`ldr r0, [r1, #4]!`	*preincrement:* address = R[r1] + 4 R[r1] = R[r1] + 4
`ldr r0, [r1], #4`	*postincrement:* address = R[r1] R[r1] = R[r1] + 4
`ldr r0, [r1, r2]`	address = R[r1] + R[r2]
`ldr r0, [r1, r2, #4]`	address = R[r1] + R[r2] + 4
`ldr r0, [r1,r2, lsl #2]`	address = R[r1] + R[r2] × 4 (shift the address left 2 bits)
`ldr r0, [pc, #8192]`	address = R[PC] + 8192

- for ARMv8: destination registers are generally listed to the left of source registers and are named x0 through x31 (e.g., "`add x1,x2,x3 // add contents of x2 and x3 and store sum in x1`");
- immediates, which are constant values encoded directly within an instruction, are denoted with a hash symbol (e.g., "`add r1, r2, #12`"); and
- constants that are defined using the ".equ" directive are preceded by an equal sign when used (e.g., "`add r1, r2, = N`").

1.6 Assembly optimization #1: sorting

The next two sections walk through ARM assembly programming, optimization, and performance analysis for two examples. The first example is a bubble sort.

1.6.1 Reference implementation

Begin by writing a *reference implementation* in C in the file `bubble_sort.c`:

```c
#define N 32768
int data[N];
int main () {
  for (int i=0;i<(N-1);i++)
    for (int j=0;j<(N-1);j++)
      if (data[j]>data[j+1]) {
        int temp=data[j];
        data[j]=data[j+1];
        data[j+1]=temp;
      }
  return 1;
}
```

The first three lines allocate an array of 32 K integers in global memory. For now, the program will not initialize this array.

Recall that the bubble sort compares each consecutive pair of values $n - 1$ times, where n is the number of elements. After each comparison, the values are swapped if they are in non-sorted order. Each individual value can move at most one position toward the beginning of the array per iteration of the outermost loop, which can be thought of as bubbles slowly rising to the top of a liquid.

Save this file as bubble_sort.c and compile with gcc, using the "-O3" flag to tell the compiler to use maximum optimization:

```
gcc bubble_sort.c -O3 -o bubble_sort
```

Execute and time the program using:

```
time ./bubble_sort
```

On an ARM Cortex-A15 (on the ODROID-XU platform), the program requires 4.0 s of user CPU time to execute. On an ARM Cortex-A72 (on the Raspberry Pi 4) this program requires 2.4 s of user CPU time to execute. Note that your results may vary depending on your platform and compiler version.

From this it is possible to make rough estimations regarding the efficiency of the compiler.

The program compares $n^2 = 2^{15} \times 2^{15} = 2^{30}$ pairs of values, meaning the Cortex-A15 needs approximately $4.0/2^{30} = 3.7$ ns per comparison and the Cortex-A72 needs approximately $2.4/2^{30} = 2.2$ ns per comparison.

The maximum clock rate on the Cortex-A15 is 2.3 GHz and on the Cortex-A72 is 1.8 GHz (found in `/sys/devices/system/cpu/cpu0/cpufreq/cpuinfo_max_freq` or `/sys/devices/system/cpu/cpufreq/policy0/cpuinfo_max_freq`).

Note that these processors can dynamically adjust their clock frequency. You can find the available frequencies in `/sys/devices/system/cpu/cpufreq/policy0/scaling_available_frequencies` and the current frequency in `/sys/devices/system/cpu/cpufreq/policy0/cpuinfo_cur_freq`.

You can also view a histogram of the time spent with each clock rate in:

```
/sys/devices/system/cpu/cpufreq/policy0/stats/time_in_state.
```

On the Raspberry Pi, you can also determine the current CPU clock rate using the command

```
vcgencmd measure_clock arm
```

and the current GPU clock rate using the command

```
vcgencmd measure_clock core
```

Note that the "vc" in these commands is for "VideoCore", which is the name of the GPU on the Broadcom SoCs that are used in the Raspberry Pis.

Assuming the CPU executed the bubble sort code at the maximum clock rate, the CPUs required.

$$2.3e9 \frac{cycles}{second} \times 3.7e-9 \frac{seconds}{comparison} = 8.5 \text{ cycles per comparison on the Cortex-A15 and}$$

$$1.8e9 \frac{cycles}{second} \times 2.2e-9 \frac{seconds}{comparison} = 4.0 \text{ cycles per comparison on the Cortex-A72.}$$

This includes both the cycles required to execute the comparison instructions and the time needed for the transactions with memory (cache miss stalls). Can we do better than the compiler?

To find out, let us write a pure assembly implementation in the file bubble_sort_asm.s.

1.6.2 Assembly implementation

Create a new file bubble_sort_asm.s. In it, use the ".equ" assembler directive to define the constant N:

ARMv6/7	ARMv8
.equ N,32768	.equ N,32768

Use the ".comm" assembler directive to allocate space for the data array. This creates the array with name "data", size N*4, and whose starting address is aligned on the 4-byte boundary (i.e., evenly divisible by 4).

ARMv6/7	ARMv8
.comm data,N*4,4	.comm data,N*4,4

Next, use the ".global" directive to tell the assembler to export the main function (defined later) so that it can be statically linked and called by Linux's runtime environment:

ARMv6/7	ARMv8
.global main	.global main

Finally, use the ".arch" directive to tell the assembler to generate ARMv7-A or ARMv8-A machine language:

ARMv6/7	ARMv8
.arch armv7-a	.arch armv8-a

Begin the main function with the "main" label, using the first instructions to set register **r1** up to be the *iteration limit* for both the outer and inner for-loops. Our first instructions will perform the following:

1. load the value defined as N into register r1 and
2. decrement this register by 1

ARMv6/7	ARMv8
`main: ldr r1,=N` `sub r1,r1,#1 // r1 = N-1`	`main: ldr w1,=N` `sub w1,w1,#1 // r1 = N-1`

Notice above that we use 32-bit registers for both the ARMv6/7 and ARMv8 code, which require different prefix letters, r for ARMv6/7 and w for ARMv8.

Begin the outer for-loop by assigning the outer loop counter—the *i* variable—to register 5 and initialize it to 0:

ARMv6/7	ARMv8
`mov r5,#0 // i = 0`	`mov w5,#0 // i = 0`

Both the outer and inner loops are for-loops. For-loops are *pretest* loops, so they begin with a test to determine if the loop body should be executed. In this case, compare the value of the outer loop counter to the limit, which is assigned to registers 5 and 1, respectively. If these values are equal, exit the loop.

ARMv6/7	ARMv8
`oloop:cmp r5,r1 // i == N-1`	`oloop:cmp w5,w1 // i == N-1 ?`

Note that the branch-if-equal instruction has a different mnemonic on ARMv6/7 and ARMv8 (beq vs b.eq).

ARMv6/7	ARMv8
`beq exito`	`b.eq exito`

The outer loop body will consist of the inner loop, which can be set up exactly as for the outer loop. Use register 3 for the inner loop counter:

ARMv6/7	ARMv8
`mov r3,#0 // j = 0`	`mov w3,#0 // j = 0`

In addition to initializing our loop counter to 0, initialize a base register for the array:

ARMv6/7	ARMv8
`ldr r2,=data // r2 = &data`	`ldr x2,=data // r2 = &data`

Note above that we must use a 64-bit register for address values in ARMv8, necessitating the use of the x-prefix.

In a literal translation of the C code, the inner loop will load elements j and $j + 1$ into two registers, compare them, and store them back in reverse order if necessary. But every iteration of the inner loop needs only to load element $j + 1$, since element j would have been available in the previous iteration (the compiler might have also used this optimization).

The inner loop allocates register 11 for element j and register 10 for element $j + 1$. The register numbers are in reverse order, so use a store-multiple (stm) instruction to store the registers in order when swapping the values in memory (a requirement of the stm instruction).

Before starting the inner loop the program must pre-load the first element.

ARMv6/7	ARMv8

`ldr r11,[r2]`	`ldr w11,[x2] // note that`
	`// addresses must be stored in`
	`// 64-bit register`

Add our inner loop exit test:

ARMv6/7	ARMv8
`iloop:cmp r3,r1 // j == N-1 ?` `beq exiti`	`iloop:cmp w3,w1 // j == N-1 ?` `b.eq exiti`

The inner loop body loads one value from the array (corresponding to element $j + 1$), compares it with element j, and stores them back to the array in reverse order if necessary.

Use register 2 as the base register for the current position in the array. When loading element $j + 1$, use the pre-indexed addressing mode that will load the second value and update register 2 to the address of the second value:

ARMv6/7	ARMv8
`ldr r10,[r2,#4]!`	`ldr w10,[x2,#4]!`

Compare these values. On ARMv7, the condition of element j being greater than the element $j + 1$ value will serve as the predicate for storing the values back in reverse order. Use the store-multiple instruction when storing the elements. On ARMv8 we cannot perform a conditional store multiple, so we must skip this instruction if the condition was less-than.

ARMv6/7	ARMv8

`cmp r11,r10 // compare values`
`stmgt r2,{r10,r11} // store`
`// multiple in reverse order`
	`cmp w11,w10 // compare values`
	`b.le skip1`
	`stp w10,w11,[x2,#-4] // store`
	`// in reverse order`
	`b skip2`

If the program stored the values back in reverse order, the current value of register 11, which originally represented element *j*, will now have moved up one position in the array to become element *j* + 1. This value will be treated at element *j* in the next iteration so that the program can leave it in register r11 for the next iteration.

If the values were not swapped, copy the value in register 10 to register 11 for the next iteration of the loop. The condition for this is less than or equal (le), the logical complement of greater than. Note that ARMv8 does support conditional move, so we can use this to update the value of r11 if we did not swap the elements in the array (note, however, the different syntax needed for the ARMv8 conditional move instruction).

ARMv6/7	ARMv8
`movle r11,r10`	`skip1: mov w11,w10`

After the inner loop body, increment the inner loop counter and then branch back to the beginning of the loop.

ARMv6/7	ARMv8
`add r3,r3,#1 // j++` `b iloop`	`add w3,w3,#1 // j++` `b iloop`

Upon exiting the inner loop, do the same for the outer loop:

ARMv6/7	ARMv8
`exiti:add r5,r5,#1 // i++` `b oloop`	`exiti:add w5,w5,#1 // i++` `b oloop`

Upon exiting the outer loop, return from the main function by jumping to the location stored in the link register:

ARMv6/7	ARMv8
`exito:bx lr`	`exito:br lr`

Assemble this code using gcc and time its execution by:

```
gcc bubble_sort_asm.s -o bubble_sort_asm -O3
time ./bubble_sort_asm
```

On the Cortex-A15, the time required by this assembly implementation requires 3.6 s, a speedup of 11% over the compiler-generated version.

On the Cortex-A72, the time required by this assembly implementation requires 2.4 s, matching the compiler-generated version. In this case, four cycles are required for each comparison, which corresponds to the workload of the innermost loop, which is comprised of either eight or nine instructions in the ARMv8 version depending on the outcome of the element comparison:

```
iloop:   cmp     w3,w1

         b.eq    exiti

         ldr     w10,[x2,#4]!

         cmp     w11,w10

         b.le    skip1

         stp     w10,w11,[x2,#-4]

         b       skip2

skip1:   mov     w11,w10

skip2:   add     w3,w3,#1

         b       iloop
```

If we assume the outcome of the comparison is true 50% of the time, this implies that the CPU is executing approximately $8.5/4 = 2.125$ instructions per cycle in steady state.

1.6.3 Result verification

Assembly code is less readable than C code, making it more prone to programming errors. As such, when testing an optimized implementation, you should always validate its results against a second, *reference implementation* and compare the results. Executing both implementations provides the ability to perform performance comparisons, and bugs are revealed by mismatches in the output data.

To link both the C-based reference implementation and assembly-based test implementation into a single executable, convert the reference implementation into a function. This requires changing the return type, deleting the code relating to the array and the value of N, changing the name of the function from main to "bubble_sort", and using arguments to pass in the pointer to the array and its size (i.e., change "N" to "n" in the for-loops):

```
void bubble_sort (int *data,int n) {

  for (int i=0;i<n-1;i++)

    for (int j=0;j<n-1;j++)

      if (data[j]>data[j+1]) {

        temp=data[j];

        data[j]=data[j+1];
```

```
        data[j+1]=temp;

    }

}
```

Next, convert the assembly implementation into a function. To do this, remove the ".equ" and ".comm" directives, change the name of the exported symbol to "bubble_sort_asm", add a new directive that specifies this as a function, and change the name of the function from "main" to "bubble_sort_asm":

```
.global bubble_sort_asm
.arch armv7-a // or armv8-a
.type bubble_sort_asm, %function
bubble_sort_asm: …
```

The function arguments, the pointer to the array and its size, will arrive in registers 0 and 1, respectively. As such, remove the instruction "ldr r1,=N" or "ldr w1,=N" for ARMv8 that initializes the size of the array. Also, change the instruction that **initializes** the base register for the array in the outer loop body from "ldr r2,=data" to "mov r2,r0" for ARMv7 or "mov x2,x0" for ARMv8.

Lastly, set the return value in register 0 just before returning to the caller, using "exito: mov r0,#1" for ARMv7 and using "exito: mov w0,#1" for ARMv8.

Now write a *driver* named "driver.c" that will call both functions. The driver will also be responsible for allocating the arrays and verifying the results.

```
#include <stdio.h>
#include <stdlib.h>
#define N 32768

int bubble_sort (int *data,int n);
int bubble_sort_asm (int *data,int n);

int main () {
  int *data1,*data2;

  data1 = (int *)malloc(N*sizeof (int));
  data2 = (int *)malloc(N*sizeof (int));

  srand(11);
  for (int i=0;i<N;i++) data1[i]=data2[i]=rand();
```

```
bubble_sort(data1,N);

bubble_sort_asm(data2,N);

for (int i=0;i<N;i++)

  if (data1[i] != data2[i]) {

    fprintf(stderr,"mismatch on element %d\n",i);

    return 0;

  }

  return 1;

}
```

Compile this code with gcc:

```
gcc driver.c bubble_sort.c bubble_sort_asm.s -o main
```

If the program runs without validation errors, it is reasonable to assume that the assembly implementation is functionally correct and implements the same algorithm as the compiler-generated code. But what accounts for the performance difference?

Recall that performance is impacted by many factors, including:

- number of instructions executed,
- stalls from data dependencies and branch mispredictions,
- data dependencies and resource constraints that prevent multiple-issue, and
- stalls from cache misses.

All of these factors, including the cache miss rate, can potentially be changed in a way that improves performance by changing the assembly code implementation of the algorithm.

1.6.4 Analysis of compiler-generated code

In order to explore how assembly implementation affects these performance factors, examine the compiler-generated assembly (using) and compare it with the hand-written assembly. Use gcc's "-s" switch to generate the assembly and the "-03" switch to enable maximum compiler optimization. Use gcc's "-c" switch to compile only, which causes the compiler to generate an object file (.o) instead of an executable file.

The bubble sort function begins with r0/x0 containing the address of the data array (data) and r1/w1 containing the size of the array (n).

Compute $n - 1$ and exit the function if the result equals 0.

ARMv6/7	ARMv8
| ```
sub lr, r1, #1
cmp lr, #0
ble .L2
``` | ```
sub w6, w1, #1
cmp w6, #0
ble .L1
``` |

Compute the effective address of the end of the array, which is data + n*4. Note that "ip" is register r12, which is defined as the "intra procedure scratch register."

ARMv6/7	ARMv8
| ```
add ip, r0, r1, asl #2
``` | ```
add x4, x0, #2
add x4, x4, x1, uxtw #2
``` |

Set r4 = data + 4 and initialize i = (r0) = 0

ARMv6/7	ARMv8
| ```
add r4, r0, #4
mov r0, #0
``` | ```
add x4, x0, 4
mov w5, #0
``` |

Begin outer loop; reset r3 to point to the beginning of the array:

ARMv6/7	ARMv8
| ```
.L3:
mov r3, r4
``` | ```
.L5:
mov x1,x0
``` |

Begin inner loop; load two elements into r2 and r1. Note that r3 begins at 4 bytes into the array, so the first load offsets by −4 bytes and the second load uses post-increment to increment r3.

ARMv6/7	ARMv8
| ```
.L6:
ldr r2, [r3, #-4]
ldr r1, [r3], #4
``` | ```
.L4:
ldp w2, w3, [x1]
``` |

Compare the values and swap (using the "store multiple" or "store pair" instruction) if necessary.

ARMv6/7	ARMv8
| ```
cmp r2, r1
stmgtdb r3, {r1, r2}
``` | ```
cmp w2,w3
ble .L3
stp w3,w2,[x1]
.L3:
``` |

Compare r3 with the end of the array and loop; if not equal, repeat inner loop.

ARMv6/7	ARMv8
| ```
cmp r3, ip
bne .L6
``` | ```
add x1, x1, 4
cmp x1, x4
bne .L4
``` |

Once finished with inner loop, increment counter, compare counter with n, and if not equal, repeat output loop.

ARMv6/7	ARMv8

add r0, r0, #1
cmp r0, lr
bne .L3
	add w5, w5, 1
	cmp w5, w6
	bne .L5

The ".L2" label is the exit point.

ARMv6/7	ARMv8
.L2:	.L1:

The inner loop is comprised of only six instructions, while ours has nine instructions, so we must assume our inner loop required less than two-third of the cycles as compared to the compiler-generated inner loop.

1.7 Assembly optimization #2: bit manipulation (ARMv6/7)

The code optimizers built into compilers are less effective for codes that cannot be naturally expressed in a high-level language, such as those that involve complex bit manipulation, specialized arithmetic, or high-latency operations such as floating-point instructions or memory instructions having low access locality.

Consider the following simple C loop, which reverses the order of bits within a word. In this code, "in" and "out" are declared as unsigned integers:

```
for (int i=0;i<32;i++) out |= ((in >> (31-i)) & 1) << i;
```

When compiled with maximum optimization (using the "-O3" switch), the compiler generates the following assembly code, where the "in" variable is assigned to register r0:

Compiler-generated assembly code	Purpose
mov r3, #0	**i** = 0
mov r2, r3	**out** = 0
.L3:	loop body begin
rsb r1, r3, #31	**temp** = 31 − **i**
mov r1, r0, lsr r1	**temp2** = **in** << (31− **i**)
and r1, r1, #1	**temp** = **temp** & 1
orr r2, r2, r1, asl r3	**out** = **out** | (**temp2** << **i**)
add r3, r3, #1	**i**++
cmp r3, #32	compare **i** and 32
bne .L3	if not equal, repeat

The compiler-generated assembly code looks reasonable, but it is possible to reduce the number of instructions in the loop body by taking advantage of instruction set features that cannot be described in the C language.

Specifically, recall that when using shift operations, either as standalone instructions or as the flexible second operand, the last shifted-out bit is stored in the carry flag. Also, the rotate right and extend (RRX) operation allows the carry flag to be shifted into a register. This allows us to use the carry flag to transfer each bit between the original and reversed registers while using opposing shift operations. An added benefit is that the program can terminate the loop when all the bits have been shifted out of the source register, eliminating the need for the instruction that increments the **i** variable. This approach is shown below. Note that we assume that original value of "in" is saved prior to executing this loop.

Hand-written assembly code	Purpose
`mov r2, #0`	**out** = 0
`lsls r0,r0,#1`	**in** = **in** << 1, save bit that was shifted out to C flag
`or r0,r0,#1`	set LSB of **in** to 1 to "mark" the 32nd bit to be shifted, to ensure that the value does not become 0 until this final bit is shifted out
`.L3:`	loop body begin
`rrx r2, r2`	out = out >> 1, shift in C flag
`lsls r0,r0,#1`	**in** <<= 1, save bit that was shifted out to C flag
`cmp r0, #0`	compare **in** and 0
`bne .L3`	if not equal, repeat

In this version, the loop body shrinks by two instructions. Assuming the cost of each instruction is the same as in the previous version, this gives a speedup of $7/4 = 1.75$, making the code 75% faster.

1.8 Assembly optimization #2: bit manipulation (ARMv8)

When compiling the bit reversal code for ARMv8 with "-O3" optimization, the compiler makes heavy use of NEON instructions. First, it fully unrolls the loop, meaning that it removes the conditional branch instruction at the end of the loop body and generates a code that can perform the workload of all 32 iterations.

The loop body performs a $(31 - i)$-bit right shift of the original input value, followed by a bitwise AND by 1, followed by an i-bit left shift. All 32 values produced are then bit-wise OR'ed together.

The unrolled ARMv8 NEON implementation performs both shifts and the bitwise-AND operation in each of the four 32-bit elements of a NEON register in parallel.

This is the main workload of the unrolled loop to be completed by eight groups of vector instructions.

These eight 4-element results are pairwise OR'ed into two vectors, and these results are again paired OR'ed into a single vector. The four remaining values, stored in a single four-element vector, are reduced into one 32-bit value using the `ext` instruction, which allows the 16 - N upper bytes of one vector to be concatenated with the lower N bytes of another vector. This instruction allows arbitrary elements within a vector to be used as operands for computational instructions.

1.9 Code optimization objectives

Program execution time can be computed as the product of number of instructions executed, average number of cycles per instruction (**CPI**), and clock period, that is:

$$\frac{\text{seconds}}{\text{program}} = \frac{\text{instructions}}{\text{program}} \cdot \frac{\text{cycles}}{\text{instruction}} \cdot \frac{\text{seconds}}{\text{cycle}}$$

Optimizing code usually involves reducing the first two terms, since the clock period is normally outside the programmer's control. However, reducing the number of instructions executed (the first term) can potentially increase the number of cycles per instruction (the second term), since the new instruction sequence might affect:

- the number of data or control stalls caused by the new sequence,
- the instruction cache miss rate, or
- the data cache miss rate.

To accurately capture the impact of code changes, the programmer must measure the program's runtime behavior using *profiling*. The objective of profiling is to collect runtime information on a processor or using a cycle-accurate simulator. Cycle-accurate simulators are able to associate performance-relevant events to lines or features in the code but are slow and limit the scope of programs and datasets that can be tested. Using a real processor is much faster but information can only be collected in an aggregated way using *performance counters*.

These counters, as well as the associated logic used to program each counter with a specific event, are called the *PMU*.

One way to profile code performance is to use performance counters. Performance counters are a low-level architectural feature and are generally difficult to use without the help of one or more *abstraction layers*. Linux provides a *system-level* abstraction, and this chapter will describe how to build a *user-level* abstraction on top of it.

Profiling often involves counting events in the processor. Often, the number of countable events exceeds the limited number of counters available, so the programmer must choose which events to count. When choosing which events to count, our objective is to identify those that significantly impact program performance but whose occurrence rate can most easily be manipulated through code transformations that do not change program semantics.

1.9.1 Reducing the number of executed instructions

Reducing the dynamic instruction count involves eliminating redundant code. The compiler can eliminate some redundancies in high-level code automatically, usually by eliminating the recomputation of common subexpressions or moving loop invariant code outside of a loop. Even so, compilers will sometimes generate more instructions than necessary when translating high-level code to assembly code. In this case, significant performance can sometimes be gained by writing small segments of assembly code for performance-critical code in the innermost loops.

For this reason, it is important to have a performance counter to count the number of executed instructions. Because most processors use branch speculation, where some instructions are executed before a proceeding branch is resolved, instruction counters are often an estimation rather than an exact number.

1.9.2 Reducing average CPI

An ARM11 processor is only capable of beginning execution, or *issuing*, one instruction per cycle. The ARM Cortex-A53 on the Raspberry Pi 2 and 3 can issue up to two instructions per cycle, and the ARM Cortex-A72 on the Raspberry Pi 4 can issue up to three instructions per cycle. In general, both processors achieve less than their peak issue rate due to dynamic stalls.

Stalls are events caused by an instruction that temporarily prevents the processor from beginning execution (issuing) the maximum number of instructions in subsequent cycles. In other words, most ARM processors have an ideal CPI of 0.5.

There are three major causes of stalls, given as follows.

- *Branch stalls*: Caused by branch mispredictions or branch target buffer misses.
- *Data dependency stalls*: Caused by register read-after-write dependencies and is most serious when involving floating-point instructions that have long latency.
- *Load/store stalls*: Caused by cache misses, requiring off-chip access to external memory.

Branch stalls are caused when the processor fails to accurately predict the outcome of a conditional branch instruction. When this happens, instructions that were speculatively fetched after the branch must be discarded and replaced with stalls.

For example, assume the following instruction sequence:

```
cmp r1,r2
beq target
```
< *n* -1 speculative instructions >

In this case, the `beq` instruction depends on the status register outcome of the `cmp` instruction, which itself may depend on the outcome of previous instructions that compute register r1 and register r2. The processor will continue fetching instructions after the `beq` based on its branch prediction. The number of these speculative instructions will depend on how long the processor must wait for the `beq` instruction to execute the execute stage. If the branch is found to be mispredicted, all these instructions will be converted to branch stalls.

The rate at which this occurs is associated with the rate at which conditional branches are executed, which is higher for programs that contain control-dependent code, code that has unpredictable if-statements in the innermost loops.

One way to reduce branch stalls is to reduce the number of if-statements, but it is often difficult to do this without changing the semantics of the code. Another technique is to replace conditional branch instructions with predicated/conditional instructions, which is only effective when the number of conditional instructions is relatively small, and this can only be done on ARMv6/7 processors.

Data dependency stalls are caused when instructions must wait to execute until the results from previous instructions have been computed. These stalls are most serious in programs that perform floating-point instructions since these instructions have the longest latency of all the arithmetic instructions.

For example, the following sequence of instructions performs a sequence of two dependent double-precision add instructions, because the second instruction cannot begin execution until the value of d0 is computed by the first instruction.

```
faddd d0,d2,d4
faddd d4,d0,d2
```

In this case, the second instruction cannot enter the execute pipeline until the first instruction completes. The time between the completion of the first instruction and the initiation of the second instruction is spent executing stalls. Most floating-point programs contain many of these types of dependencies leading to data dependency stalls and resulting in low utilization of the floating-point functional units.

Reducing the number of these stalls is generally accomplished by rearranging the order of instructions in the code, allowing the latency of floating-point instructions to be "hidden" by executing other, nondependent floating-point instructions in the meantime.

Processors that perform aggressive *dynamic scheduling*—also called *out-of-order execution*—can do this automatically at runtime without the need to change the program code. However, most embedded processors, including those from ARM, cannot afford the cost of this feature in terms of chip real-estate or power consumption, so they generally have limited or no capability for dynamic scheduling.

Chapter 2 describes how to use code optimization techniques to hide the latency of floating-point instructions and reduce the number of data dependency stalls by using *double buffering*, *software pipelining*, and *SIMD instructions*.

Another way to reduce the effect of floating-point latency is to convert floating-point instructions into fixed-point instructions. Fixed-point representation allows the usage of fractional numbers using the lower-latency integer functional units. One drawback of this approach is a reduction in the *dynamic range*, or the ratio between the largest- and smaller-magnitude numerical values that can be represented. Luckily, many graphical computations do not require high dynamic range. Chapter 2 explores this technique as well.

Load and store stalls are linked to the effectiveness of the processor's cache but can be reduced by changing the order in which data is accessed in memory. The goal is to increase the *locality* of the accesses. To do this, the programmer or compiler must arrange the order of load and store instructions such that the resulting sequence of effective addresses is favorable for the cache. This means that whenever the same or nearby addresses are accessed, the time between accesses should be minimized. This often requires changing the structure of nested loops.

The primary method for accomplishing this is through *loop transformations*, such as loop interchange, loop fusion, loop fission, and loop tiling. To track load and store stalls, the programmer must be able to monitor the number of references and misses on the last-level cache.

This chapter describes the use of performance counters to keep track of cycles, instructions, cache references, and cache misses. The cycle count will provide information about execution time, the ratio of instructions to cycles will provide CPI, and the ratio of cache misses to references will provide cache miss rate. Note that the total CPI includes the stall cycles from branches, data dependencies, and cache misses, although there is no way to discriminate each type of stall. There is still enough information to make optimization decisions and understand how our code transformations affect performance.

On a final note: the ARM11 and ARM Cortex-A9 PMUs can count data dependency stalls, but this event is no longer supported in later CPU PMUs.

1.10 Runtime profiling with performance counters

The performance counters are a limited hardware resource that must be shared by all programs and users, so the OS must be responsible for arbitrating access to the counters. In addition, a user may want to count more events than there are physical counters, so the OS must be responsible for multiplexing access to the counters. Also, multicore processors will often have a PMU in each core, so inconsistent results may arise when a program inadvertently reads the counters of different cores. As such, the OS must be responsible for maintaining per-process counter states across all cores. This also includes not incrementing the per-process counters during the times when the process is suspended by the OS, even though the hardware counters would still otherwise be counting.

For these reasons, the OS must manage the PMU on behalf of the users. In fact, the processor will prevent user code from directly accessing the counters (registering as an invalid instruction exception). Users are therefore forced to access the PMU through the OS using system calls.

1.10.1 Linux perf_event

Linux provides an abstraction layer for PMU management called *perf_event*.

To check if your instance of Linux has support for perf_event, type the command:

```
dmesg | grep perf
```

And check for a message similar to the following:

```
[    0.287607] hw perfevents: enabled with armv8_cortex_a72 PM U
driver, 7 counters available
```

In addition to interfacing with the PMU, perf_event is also capable of keeping track of *software events* such as context switches and page faults. Unfortunately, as of this writing, perf_event is not fully implemented for the ARM11 processor of the original Raspberry Pi. Appendix A describes how to patch the kernel to add support.

When more counters are requested than are physically available, perf_event uses a technique called *multiplexing*. In this case, the kernel enables a subset of the requested counters, enabling a different subset at regular intervals. This allows the hardware counters to statistically sample the event counts at various periods throughout the time the user requests the counters to be enabled. When the user requests the results, perf_event will also report the number of cycles since the user enabled the counter and the number of cycles the counter was actually enabled. These values are called time enabled and time running. The user can extrapolate the actual count by scaling the reported count by the ratio of these values.

In order to use perf_event, the user instantiates each counter using the system call named perf_event_open. Once open, the user can use the standard POSIX ioctl() function to enable, disable, and reset it, and the read() function to read its state.

When opening a counter, the user must fill in a "struct perf_event_attr" structure to configure the counter. The two most important fields of this structure are the .type field and .config field. When counting hardware events, there are only two valid types: PERF_TYPE_HARDWARE and PERF_TYPE_RAW.

PERF_TYPE_HARDWARE is a platform-independent mechanism for specifying a set of common events, while PERF_TYPE_RAW allows the user to specify a processor-specific event encoding to count.

1.10.2 Performance counter infrastructure

To use perf_event, it is easy to develop a set of reusable functions to measure the performance of various aspects of program execution. This will include functions for initialization, result printing, resetting the performing counters (named "tick"), and reading the state of the performance counters (named "tock").

Begin by adding the necessary header files and constant definitions of each of our five counters:

```c
#include <stdio.h>          // needed for printf()
#include <stdlib.h>         // needed for malloc() and RAND_MAX
#include <string.h>         // needed for memset()
#include <math.h>           // needed for floating point routines
#include <sys/time.h>       // needed for gettimeofday()
#include <unistd.h>         // needed for pid_t type
```

```
#include <sys/ioctl.h>              // needed for ioctl()

#include <asm/unistd.h>             // needed for perf_event syscall

#include <linux/perf_event.h>       // needed for perf_event

#include <linux/hw_breakpoint.h>

#include <stdint.h>                 // needed for integer types

#include <errno.h>


#define CYCLES                    0

#define INSTRUCTIONS              1

#define CACHEREFS                 2

#define CACHEMISSES               3


#define SIZE                      (128<<20) // 128 MB


#define CLOCK_RATE_FILE           "/sys/devices/system/cpu/cpufreq/
                                  policy0/cpuinfo_cur_freq"
```

Next, write an explicit C wrapper to invoke the system call to open a specific performance counter using perf_event:

```
int32_t perf_event_open(struct perf_event_attr *hw_event,

                        pid_t pid,

                        int32_t cpu,

                        int32_t group_fd,

                        uint32_t flags) {

    int ret;

    ret = syscall(__NR_perf_event_open, hw_event, pid, cpu, group_fd, flags);

    return ret;

}
```

The `pid` argument specifies the Linux process ID for which processes the measurements are made. There are two special values: if `pid` is 0 the measurement is made on the current process, and if `pid` is − 1 the measurement is made on all processes. This code will set this argument to 0 to measure the current process.

The `cpu` argument allows the user to restrict measurements on a single CPU. If `cpu` is -1 then events are measured on all CPUs.

The `group_fd` argument allows event groups to be created, allowing for more than one event to be counted with a single call to `perf_event_open`. The code in this chapter uses separate calls to `perf_event_open` to count each individual event, so set this argument to -1 to measure a single event.

Also needed is a function that will scale the results given by perf_event according to the ratio between *time enabled* and *time running*. Reading a counter opened with perf_event returns an array of three 64-bit integers; the value at index 0 represents the counter value, the value at index 1 represents the time enabled, and index 2 represents the time running.

```
static inline uint64_t perf_count(uint64_t *values) {
        return (uint64_t)((float)values[0] * (float)values[1]/(float)values[2]);
}
```

In perf_event, individual performance counters can be accessed through a file descriptor, so begin by declaring an array of file descriptors:

```
int fd[5];
```

Declare an array to store the information read from each counter:

```
uint64_t cnts[4][3];
```

The following function will open the four counters. Opening the cache miss and cache reference counters is slightly different for the ARM11, so the code assumes that the ARM11 variable is set when compiling for the ARM11 (compile with the –DARM11 option).

```
int cnts_open (int *fd) {
    struct perf_event_attr attr;


    memset(&attr, 0, sizeof(attr));


    attr.type = PERF_TYPE_HARDWARE;
    attr.size = sizeof(struct perf_event_attr);
    attr.read_format = PERF_FORMAT_TOTAL_TIME_ENABLED|
                       PERF_FORMAT_TOTAL_TIME_RUNNING;
    attr.config = PERF_COUNT_HW_CPU_CYCLES;
    fd[CYCLES] = perf_event_open(&attr, 0, -1, -1, 0);
```

```
    if (fd[CYCLES] == -1) {

        perror("cannot open perf_counter for cycles");

        exit(0);

    }


    attr.config = PERF_COUNT_HW_INSTRUCTIONS;

    fd[INSTRUCTIONS] = perf_event_open(&attr, 0, -1, -1, 0);

    if (fd[INSTRUCTIONS] == -1) {

        perror("cannot open perf_counter for instructions");

        exit(0);

    }


#ifdef ARM11

    attr.type = PERF_TYPE_RAW;

    attr.config = 0x9;

    fd[CACHEREFS] = perf_event_open(&attr, 0, -1, -1, 0);

    if (fd[CACHEREFS] == -1) {

        perror("cannot open perf_counter for cacherefs");

        exit(0);

    }


    attr.config = 0xB;

    fd[CACHEMISSES] = perf_event_open(&attr, 0, -1, -1, 0);

    if (fd[CACHEMISSES] == -1) {

        perror("cannot open perf_counter for cachemisses"); exit(0);

    }

#else

    attr.config = PERF_COUNT_HW_CACHE_REFERENCES;

    fd[CACHEREFS] = perf_event_open(&attr, 0, -1, -1, 0);

    if (fd[CACHEREFS] == -1) {

        perror("cannot open perf_counter for cacherefs");
```

```
        exit(0);

    }


    attr.config = PERF_COUNT_HW_CACHE_MISSES;

    fd[CACHEMISSES] = perf_event_open(&attr, 0, -1, -1, 0);

    if (fd[CACHEMISSES] == -1) {

        perror("cannot open perf_counter for cachemisses");

        exit(0);

    }

#endif

}
```

Add the "tick" and "tock" functions, which can be called before and after the code to be measured:

```
void cnts_tick (int *fd) {

    int i,ret;

    cnts_open(fd);

    for (i=0;i<4;i++) {

        ret=ioctl(fd[i], PERF_EVENT_IOC_RESET);

        if (ret==-1) perror ("ioctl() in cnts_tick() failed");

    }

}


void cnts_tock (int *fd, uint64_t cnts[][3]) {

    int i,ret;


    for (i=0;i<4;i++) {

        ret = read(fd[i], cnts[i], sizeof(cnts[i]));

        if (ret!=24) perror ("ioctl() in cnts_tock() failed");

    }

    cnts_close(fd);

}
```

```
void cnts_close(int *fd) {

    int i;


    for (i=0;i<4;i++) close(fd[i]);

}
```

1.11 Measuring memory bandwidth

To begin using perf_event, let us use it to measure the time required for the processor to write a contiguous block data and to read a contiguous block of data. This test will also allow us to measure the processor's memory bandwidth, which is often different for reads versus writes. The programmer can use these values to calculate the upper bound for the performance.

Write a print routine that prints our performance results and calculates memory bandwidth:

```
void cnts_dump (uint64_t cnts[][3]) {

    FILE *myFile = fopen (CLOCK_RATE_FILE,"r");

    if (!myFile) {

        fprintf(stderr,"ERROR opening clock rate file for reading:
        %s\n",strerror(errno));

        exit(1);

    }


    uint32_t clock_rate;

    fscanf(myFile,"%d",&clock_rate);

    fclose(myFile);

    clock_rate *= 1000;

    printf ("current clock rate = %d\n",clock_rate);


    float time = ((float)perf_count(cnts[CYCLES]))/(float)clock_rate;

    float membw_mbs = (float)SIZE/time/(float)(1<<20);

    uint64_t cycles = perf_count(cnts[CYCLES]);

    uint64_t instructions = perf_count(cnts[INSTRUCTIONS]);

    float cpi = (float)cycles/(float)instructions;

    uint64_t cache_misses = perf_count(cnts[CACHEMISSES]);
```

```
        uint64_t cache_refs = perf_count(cnts[CACHEREFS]);

        float cache_miss_rate = (float)cache_misses/(float)cache_refs;


        printf("[perf_event] cycles = %llu (%0.4e s)\n",cycles,time);

        printf("[perf_event] effective memory bandwidth = %0.2f MB/s\n",membw_mbs);

        printf("[perf_event] executed instructions = %llu (CPI=%0.2f)\
                                       n",instructions,cpi);

        printf("[perf_event] misses = %llu, references = %llu (miss rate=%0.4f)\
                           n",cache_misses,cache_refs,cache_miss_rate);



    }
```

Next add defines to specify the size, in words, of the memory block to copy, and the processor clock frequency.

In order to verify our clock frequency setting and that perf_event is reporting correct cycle counts, examine a segment of code using both the performance counters and the Linux system clock using `gettimeofday()`. The system clock measures the "**wall clock time**", while perf_event only counts cycles while the process is running. Because of this, the programmer may observe higher values from the system clock, since it may accumulate time during temporary periods when the process is suspected by the OS.

In order to use `gettimeofday()`, declare two variables to hold the time values that it returns:

```
    struct timeval time1,time2;
```

The timeval struct contains a 32-bit value *tv_sec* that measures seconds and a 32-bit value *tv_usec* that measures microseconds within each second.

You will also need to declare and allocate a test array:

```
    unsigned int *test_array;
    test_array = (unsigned int *)test_array(N);
```

The following code independently tests memory read and write throughput.

When testing reads, make sure you print the final value of sum in order to prevent sum from being optimized out by the compiler.

```
    void main () {
            int fd[5];

            uint64_t cnts[4][3];
```

```
uint64_t us;

struct timeval time1,time2;

int i,j,n,z,sum=0;

uint32_t *test_array = (uint32_t *)malloc(SIZE+16);

// align on 16-byte boundary

uint32_t *test_array_aligned = (uint32_t *)(((uint64_t)test_array & ~
                                Ox1F) + Ox10);

// initialize test_array

for (i=0;i<(SIZE>>2);i++) test_array_aligned[i]=0;

printf("--------------------write test--------------------------\n");

cnts_tick(fd);

gettimeofday(&time1,0);

for (uint32_t i=0;i<(SIZE>>2);i++) test_array_aligned[i]=10;

gettimeofday(&time2,0);

cnts_tock(fd,cnts);

us = time2.tv_sec*1000000 + time2.tv_usec - time1.tv_sec*1000000 - time1.
    tv_usec;

printf("[system clock] time elapsed = %llu us\n",us);

cnts_dump(cnts);

printf("------------------------read test------------------------\n");

cnts_tick(fd);

gettimeofday(&time1,0);

for (uint32_t i=0;i<(SIZE>>2);i++) sum+=test_array_aligned[i];

gettimeofday(&time2,0);

cnts_tock(fd,cnts);

us = time2.tv_sec*1000000 + time2.tv_usec -time1.tv_sec*1000000 - time1.
    tv_usec;

printf("[system clock] time elapsed = %llu us\n",us);

cnts_dump(cnts);
```

```
        printf ("[sum] = %d\n",sum); // used to ensure that test_array isn't
                             optimized out


        free(test_array);

}
```

1.12 Performance results

Compile the code using the -03 flag and run it on your platform.

The report below shows the memory bandwidth results for a Cortex-A72 on the Raspberry Pi 4. The differences in CPI and miss rate shed some light on the reasons for this difference. The higher CPI and miss rate of the read test indicates that the cache does not block the CPU or register a cache miss as often when writing, probably because the cache does not allocate space in the cache on a write miss, and a write miss is only triggered when all the write buffers are full.

```
--------------------------------write test-----------------------------
[system clock] time elapsed = 45539 us

current clock rate = 1800000000

[perf_event] cycles = 82055344 (4.5586e-02 s)

[perf_event] effective memory bandwidth = 2807.86 MB/s

[perf_event] executed instructions = 25312392 (CPI=3.24)

[perf_event] misses = 1280, references = 16837084 (miss rate=0.0001)

--------------------------------read test------------------------------
[system clock] time elapsed = 32887 us

current clock rate = 1800000000

[perf_event] cycles = 59236300 (3.2909e-02 s)

[perf_event] effective memory bandwidth = 3889.51 MB/s

[perf_event] executed instructions = 33675144 (CPI=1.76)

[perf_event] misses = 100828, references = 8437227 (miss rate=0.0120)

[sum] = 335544320
```

1.13 Performance bounds

A program loop or loop nest that comprises a substantial portion of the execution time is referred to as a *kernel*. The runtime behavior of relatively simple kernels can be characterized by *arithmetic intensity*, or number of primitive CPU operations performed per unit of data. Once the kernel's arithmetic intensity is known, it can be used to compute a performance upper bound as a function of a processor's peak memory bandwidth.

The processor's peak floating-point throughput can be estimated by multiplying its clock rate by the number of floating-point operations it can perform per cycle. If, for example, a processor can perform 10 floating-point operations per cycle at 1 GHz, its peak throughput is thus 10 billion floating-point operations per second, or 10 Gflops. Note that the term "*flops*" can be confusing, since it can be used as an acronym for floating-point operations per second or as shorthand for floating-point operations. You can usually determine the intended meaning from its context.

Kernels that have a high arithmetic intensity are said to be *compute bound*, which means that the performance is limited by the number of operations that can be dispatched to the processor's internal functional units. This contrasts with *memory bound*, which means the performance is limited by the memory bandwidth.

The exact arithmetic intensity value at which a kernel goes from being memory bound to compute bound depends on the processor, but in practice, very few kernels are compute bound. Even kernels that seem to have very high arithmetic intensity, such as matrix-matrix multiply that performs $O(n^3)$ flops for every $O(n^2)$ input and output value, are often still performance bounded due to load-store stalls or data dependency stalls. This is seen in cases where SGEMM achieves only 50–75% of the peak theoretical performance for a particular processor.

Arithmetic intensity is measured in floating-point operations per byte (flops/byte). Thus the performance upper bound for a kernel can be computed as $P = A \times B$, where $A ==$ *arithmetic intensity* in flops/byte, $B ==$ *memory bandwidth* in bytes/s, and $P ==$ *performance* in flops/s (flops).

1.14 Basic ARM instruction set

This section provides a concise summary of a basic subset of the ARM instruction set. The information provided here is only enough to get you started writing basic ARM assembly programs and does not include any specialized instructions, such as system instructions and those related to coprocessors. Note that in the following tables, the instruction mnemonics are shown in uppercase but can be written in uppercase or lowercase.

1.14.1 Integer arithmetic instructions

Table 1.4 shows a list of integer arithmetic instructions. All of these support conditional execution, and all will update the status register when the S suffix is specified. Some of these instructions—those with "operand2"—support the flexible second operand as described earlier in this chapter. This allows these instructions to have either a register, a shifted register, or an immediate as the second operand.

Table 1.4: Integer arithmetic instructions. (NOTE: conditional execution not available in ARMv8 except for add/subtract with carry. Likewise, instructions cannot set condition flags in ARMv8 except for add/subtract with carry.)

Instruction	Description	Function
ADC{S}{< cond >} Rd, Rn, operand2	Add with carry	R[Rd] = R[Rn] + operand2 + Cflag
ADD{S}{< cond >} Rd, Rn, operand2	Add	R[Rd] = R[Rn] + operand2
MLA{S}{< cond >} Rd, Rn, Rm, Ra	Multiply-accumulate	R[Rd] = R[Rn] * R[Rm] + R[Ra]
MUL{S}{< cond >} Rd, Rn, Rm	Multiply	R[Rd] = R[Rn] * R[Rm]
RSB{S}{< cond >} Rd, Rn, operand2	Reverse subtract	R[Rd] = operand2 - R[Rn]
RSC{S}{< cond >} Rd, Rn, operand2	Reverse subtract with carry	R[Rd] = operand2 - R[Rn] − not(C flag)
SBC{S}{< cond >} Rd, Rn, operand2	Subtract with carry	R[Rd] = R[Rn] − operand2 − not(C flag)
SMLAL{S}{< cond >} RdLo, RdHi, Rn, Rm	Signed multiply accumulate long	R[RdHi] = upper32bits(R[Rn] * R[Rm]) + R[RdHi] R[RdLo] = lower32bits(R[Rn] * R[Rm]) + R[RdLo]
SMULL{S}{< cond >} RdLo, RdHi, Rn, Rm	Signed multiply long	R[RdHi] = upper32bits(R[Rm] * R[Rs]) R[RdLo] = lower32bits(R[Rm] * R[Rs])
SUB{S}{< cond >} Rd, Rn, operand2	Subtract	R[Rd] = R[Rn] − operand2
UMLAL{S}{< cond >} RdLo, RdHi, Rn, Rm	Unsigned multiply accumulate long	R[RdHi] = upper32bits(R[Rn] * R[Rm]) + R[RdHi] R[RdLo] = lower32bits(R[Rn] * R[Rm]) + R[RdLo]
UMULL{S}{< cond >} RdLo, RdHi, Rn, Rm	Unsigned multiply long	R[RdHi] = upper32bits(R[Rn] * R[Rm]) R[RdLo] = lower32bits(R[Rn] * R[Rm])

1.14.2 Bitwise logical instructions

Table 1.5 shows a list of bitwise logical instructions. All of these support conditional execution, all can update the flags when the S suffix is specified, and all support a flexible second operand.

1.14.3 Shift instructions

Table 1.6 shows a list of shift instructions. All of these support conditional execution, and all can update the flags when the S suffix is specified, but note that these instructions do *not* support the flexible second operand.

1.14.4 Movement instructions

Table 1.7 shows a list of data movement instructions. Most useful of these is the MOV instruction, since its flexible second operand allows for loading immediates and register shifting.

1.14.5 Load and store instructions

Table 1.8 shows a list of load and store instructions. The LDR/STR instructions are ARM's bread-and-butter load and store instructions. The memory address can be specified using any of the addressing modes described earlier in this chapter.

The LDR instruction can also be used to load symbols into base registers, e.g., "ldr r1,=data".

The LDM and STM instructions can load and store multiple registers and are often used for accessing the stack.

Table 1.5: Integer bitwise logical instructions. (NOTE: conditional execution not available in ARMv8. Likewise, instructions cannot set condition flags in ARMv8.)

Instruction	Description	Functionality
AND{S}{< cond >} Rd, Rn, operand2	Bitwise AND	R[Rd] = R[Rn] & operand2
BIC{S}{< cond >} Rd, Rn, operand2	Bit clear	R[Rd] = R[Rn] & not operand2
EOR{S}{< cond >} Rd, Rn, operand2	Bitwise XOR	R[Rd] = R[Rn] ^ operand2
ORR{S}{< cond >} Rd, Rn, operand2	Bitwise OR	R[Rd] = R[Rn] | operand2

Table 1.6: Integer bitwise logical instructions. (NOTE: conditional execution not available in ARMv8. Likewise, instructions cannot set condition flags in ARMv8.)

Instruction	Description	Functionality
ASR{S}{< cond >} Rd, Rn, Rs/#sh	Arithmetic shift right	R[Rd] = (int)R[Rn] >> (R[Rs] or #sh) allowed shift amount 1–32
LSR{S}{< cond >} Rd, Rn, Rs/#sh	Logical shift right	R[Rd] = (unsigned int) R[Rn] >> (R[Rs] or #sh) allowed shift amount 1–32
LSL{S}{< cond >} Rd, Rn, Rs/#sh	Logical shift left	R[Rd] = R[Rn] << (R[Rs] or #sh) allowed shift amount 0–31
ROR{S}{< cond >} Rd, Rn, Rs/#sh	Rotate right	R[Rd] = rotate R[Rn] by operand2 bits allowed shift amount 1–31
RRX{S}{< cond >} Rd, Rm	Shift right by 1 bit The old carry flag is shifted into R[Rd] bit 31 If used with the S suffix, the old bit 0 is placed in the carry flag	

Table 1.7: Data movement instructions. (NOTE: conditional execution not available in ARMv8. Likewise, instructions cannot set condition flags in ARMv8.)

Instruction	Description	Functionality
MOV{S}{< cond >} Rd, operand2	Move	R[Rd] = operand2
MRS{< cond >} Rd, CPSR	Move status register or saved status register to GPR	R[Rd] = CPSR R[Rd] = SPSR
MRS{< cond >} Rd, SPSR		
MSR{< cond >} CPSR_f, #imm	Move to status register from ARM register	fields is one of: _c, _x, _s, _f
MSR{< cond >} SPSR_f, #imm		
MSR{< cond >} CPSR_ < fields >, Rm		
MSR{< cond >} SPSR_ < fields >, Rm		
MVN{S}{< cond >} Rd, operand2	Move one's complement	R[Rd] = not operand2

1.14.6 Comparison instructions

Table 1.9 lists comparison instructions. These instructions are used to the status flags, which are used for conditional instructions, often used for conditional branches.

Table 1.8: ARM load and store instructions. (NOTE: conditional execution not available in ARMv8. Likewise, instructions cannot set condition flags in ARMv8.)

Instruction	Description	Functionality
LDM{cond} < address mode > Rn{!}, < reg list in braces >	Load multiple	Loads multiple registers from consecutive words starting at R[Rn] Bang (!) will autoincrement base register Address mode: IA = increment after IB = increment before DA = decrement after DB = decrement before Example: LDMIA r2!, {r3,5-r7}
LDR{cond}{B|H|SB|SH} Rd, < address >	Load register	Loads from memory into Rd. Optional size specifiers: B = byte H = halfword SB = signed byte SH = signed halfword
STM{cond} < address mode > Rn, < registers >	Store multiple	Stores multiple registers Bang (!) will autoincrement base register Address mode: IA = increment after IB = increment before DA = decrement after DB = decrement before Example: STMIA r2!, {r3,5-r7}
STR{cond}{B|H} Rd, < address >	Store register	Stores from memory into Rd. Optional size specifiers: B = byte H = halfword
SWP{cond} < B| Rd, Rm, [Rn]	Swap	Swap a word (or byte) between registers and memory

1.14.7 Branch instructions

Table 1.10 lists two branch instructions. The BX (branch exchange) instruction is used when branching to register values, which is used often for branching to the link register for returning from functions. When using this instruction, the LSB of the target register specifies whether the processor will be in ARM mode or THUMB mode after the branch is taken.

Table 1.9: Comparison instructions. (NOTE: conditional execution not available in ARMv8.)

Instruction	Description	Functionality
CMN{< cond >} Rn, Rm	Compare negative	Sets flags based on comparison between R[Rn] and −R[Rm]
CMP{< cond >} Rn, Rm	Compare negative	Sets flags based on comparison between R[Rn] and R[Rm]
TEQ{cond} Rn, Rm	Test equivalence	Tests for equivalence without affecting V flag
TST{cond} Rn, Rm	Test	Performs a bitwise AND of two registers and updates the flags

Table 1.10: Branch instructions.

Instruction	Description	Functionality
B{L}{cond} < target >	Branch	Branches (and optionally links in register r14) to label
B{L}X{cond} Rm	Branch and exchange	Branches (and optionally links in register r14) to register. Bit 0 of register specifies if the instruction set mode will be standard or THUMB upon branching

1.14.8 Floating-point instructions

There are two types of floating-point instructions: the *Vector Floating Point* (*VFP*) instructions and the *NEON instructions*.

ARMv6 processors such as the Raspberry Pi (gen1)'s ARM11 support only VFP instructions. Newer architectures such as ARMv7 support only NEON instructions. The most common floating-point operations map to both a VFP instruction and a NEON instruction. For example, the VFP instruction FADDS and the NEON instruction VADD.F32 (when used with s-registers) both perform a single precision floating point add.

The NEON instruction set is more extensive than the VFP instruction set, so while most VFP instructions have an equivalent NEON instruction, there are many NEON instructions that perform operations not possible with VFP instructions.

In order to describe floating point and *single instruction, multiple data* (*SIMD*) programming techniques that are applicable to both the ARM11 and ARM Cortex processors, this section and Chapter 2 will cover both VFP and NEON instructions.

Table 1.11 lists the VFP and NEON version of commonly used floating-point instructions. Like the integer arithmetic instructions, most floating-point instructions support conditional

Table 1.11: Scalar floating-point instructions.

VFP instruction	Equivalent NEON instruction	Description
FADD[S|D]{cond} Fd, Fn, Fm	VADD.[F32|F64] Fd, Fn, Fm	Single and double precision add
FSUB[S|D]{cond} Fd, Fn, Fm	VSUB.[F32|F64] Fd, Fn, Fm	Single and double precision subtract
FMUL[S|D]{cond} Fd, Fn, Fm	VMUL.[F32|F64] Fd, Fn, Fm	Single and double precision multiply and multiply-and-negate
FNMUL[S|D]{cond} Fd, Fn, Fm	VNMUL.[F32|F64] Fd, Fn, Fm	
FDIV[S|D]{cond} Fd, Fn, Fm	VDIV.[F32|F64] Fd, Fn, Fm	Single and double precision divide
FABS[S|D]{cond} Fd, Fm	VABS.[F32|F64] Fd, Fn, Fm	Single and double precision absolute value
FNEG[S|D]{cond} Fd, Fm	VNEG.[F32|F64] Fd, Fn, Fm	Single and double precision negate
FSQRT[S|D]{cond} Fd, Fm	VSQRT.[F32|F64] Fd, Fn, Fm	Single and double precision square root
FCVTSD{cond} Fd, Fm	VCVT.F32.F64 Fd, Fm	Convert double precision to single precision
FCVTDS{cond} Fd, Fm	VCVT.F64.F32 Fd, Fm	Convert single precision to double precision
	VCVT.[S|U][32|16].[F32|F64], #fbits Fd, Fm	Convert floating point to fixed point
	VCVT.[F32|F64].[S|U][32|16],#fbits Fd, Fm, #fbits	Convert floating point to fixed point
FMAC[S|D]{cond} Fd, Fn, Fm	VMLA.[F32|F64] Fd, Fn, Fm	Single and double precision floating point multiply-accumulate, calculates Rd = Fn * Fm + Fd There are similar instructions that negate the contents of Fd, Fn, or both prior to use, for example, FNMSC[S|D], VNMLS[.F32|.F64]
FLD[S|D]{cond} Fd, < address >	VLDR{cond} Rd, < address >	Single and double precision floating point load/store
FST[S|D]{cond} Fd, <address >	LSTR{cond} Rd, < address >	
FLDMI[S|D]{cond} < address >, < FPRegs >	VLDM{cond} Rn{!}, < FPRegs >	Single and double precision floating point load/store multiple
FSTMI[S|D]{cond} < address >, < FPRegs >	VSTM{cond} Rn{!}, < FPRegs >	
FMRX{cond} Rd	FMRX Rd	Move from/to floating point status and control
FMXR{cond} Rm	FMXR Rm	register
FCPY[S|D]{cond} Fd,Fm	VMOV{cond} Fd,Fm	Copy floating point register

execution, but there is a separate set of flags for floating-point instructions located in the 32-bit *floating-point status and control register (FPSCR)*. NEON instructions use only bits 31 down to 27 of this register, while VFP instructions use additional bit fields.

Floating-point instructions use a separate set of registers than integer instructions. ARMv6/VFP provides 32 floating-point registers, used as 32 individual single-precision registers named s0–s31 or as 16 double-precision registers named d0–d15.

ARMv7/NEON provides 64 floating-point registers, which can be used in many more ways, such as:

- 64 single-precision registers named s0–s63,
- 32 two-element single-precision registers named d0–d31,
- 16 four-element single-precision registers named q0–q15,
- 32 double-precision registers named d0–d31, and
- 16 two-element double-precision registers named q0–q15.

In both VFP and NEON, register d0 consumes the same physical space as registers s0 and s1 and register d1 consumes the same space as registers s2 and s3.

Values in floating-point registers can be exchanged with general-purpose registers, and there is hardware support for type conversion between single precision, double precision, and integer.

1.15 Chapter wrap-up

This chapter covered the following topics:

- *ARM + Linux Embedded System Technology*
  The combination of ARM processors with the Linux OS, along with its standardized programming and runtime abstraction layer, has facilitated the development of many consumer electronics that contain powerful embedded computers. ARM + Linux programs can be easily prototyped using low-cost development boards such as the ubiquitous $35 Raspberry Pi education and hobbyist platform.
- *ARMv6 and ARMv7a Instruction Set Architectures*
  While ARM is a RISC ISA, it offers several unique features not found in traditional RISC architectures such as MIPS. This chapter emphasized several of these, such as ARM's flexible second operand, the status register and conditional instruction execution, and ARM's large set of memory addressing modes.
- *The differences between ARMv6/7 and ARMv8 Instruction Set Architecture*
  ARMv8 lacks some instructions and features available in ARMv6/7 such as the conditional execution field for many instructions, but doubles the number and width of the general purpose registers.

- *GNU GCC Toolchain for Assembly Language Programming*
  This chapter covered how to use the GCC compiler, assembler, and linker to write and execute standalone assembly language programs, as well as how to combine C and assembly code into one executable in order to verify the correctness of assembly code subprograms.
- *Using Performance Counters with Linux perf_event*
  This chapter introduced a methodology for using runtime profiling through code instrumentation to measure key system performance metrics, such as instruction and memory throughput. The Linux perf_event functionality provides this ability without needing to drive a custom kernel module.

Looking forward, Chapter 2 uses a specific floating-point subroutine as a running case study to demonstrate how to use assembly language-level code optimizations to substantially improve program performance. Chapter 2 will also describe how to use performance counters to gain more insight into program behavior and how it relates to processor performance.

Exercises

1. For the following kernels, calculate the arithmetic intensity in *flops per byte* and calculate the expected peak performance for a processor that has a peak memory bandwidth of 12.8 GB/s. Assume all arrays are of type float.

    a. kernel 1:

    ```
    for (i=0;i<n-3;i++)

      for (j=0;j<n-3;j++)

        out[i*rs+j] = in[i*rs+j] + in[i*rs+j+1] + in[i*rs+j+2];
    ```

    b. kernel 2: assume the values in array a are uniformly distributed in the range [0,9]

    ```
    val=0;

    for (i=0;i<n;i++)

        val = val + table[a[i]];
    ```

    c. kernel 3:

    ```
    for (i=0;i<n;i++)

      for (j=0;j<n;j++) {

        sum=0;

        for (k=0;k<n;k++)

          sum = sum + a[i][k] * a[k][j];

      }
    ```

2. How many ways can the instructions in the following code sequence be rearranged without violating any data or control dependencies?

```
add r3, r7, #88

subs r3, r3, #72

movs r2, #0

str r2, [r3]

add r3, r7, #88

subs r3, r3, #76

movs r2, #0

str r2, [r3]

b .L4
```

3. Consider the bubble sort code from this chapter, where predicated instructions are used for swapping values in the array:

```
cmp r10,r11 @ compare values

strgt r10,[r2] @ store in reverse order

strgt r11,[r2,#-4]
```

Let us consider an alternative approach:

```
cmp r10,r11 @ compare values

blt skip

str r10,[r2] @ store in reverse order

str r11,[r2,#-4]

skip:
```

a. Assume we discover that for a particular dataset 45% of the cmp tests determine that R[r10] > R[r11]. Assume that the branch is predicted correctly 80% of the time, and a correctly predicted branch has no stalls but a mispredicted branch adds 10 cycles of stalls to the total instruction count.

b. Calculate the number of instructions executed for both versions of the code assuming an array size of 10,000. Count stalls as instructions.

4. Change the following C code to eliminate any unnecessary if-statements that would be encountered during runtime:

```
if ((a[i]<0) || (a[i]>=10)) {

  if (a[i]==0) sum=sum+1;
```

```
    if (a[i]>20) sum=sum+2;
  } else {
    if (a[i]==5) sum=sum+4;
  }
```

5. Translate the following C function to ARM assembly:

```
int reorder (int a) {
    return (a<<24) | ((a<<16) & 0xFF00) | ((a>>16) & 0xFF0000) | ((a>>24) & 0xFF);
}
```

6. Write a short sequence of ARM instructions that add two 128-bit integers. What is the minimal number of instructions required?

7. Write a short sequence of ARM instructions that multiply two 128-bit integers and produce a 256-bit result. What is the minimal number of instructions required?

8. Which instructions shown in Tables 1.4–1.11 are least likely to be generated by a C compiler when compiling a C program? Why?

9. Write a complete program in ARM assembly that computes the double-precision square root of each value in a randomly generated array of double-precision values. Make sure you use double-precision instruction.

10. Compare its performance against a C implement that uses the POSIX **sqrt()** function from the math library to calculate the square root of the same input array. Also, calculate the average relative difference between the elements of two output arrays.

CHAPTER 2

Multicore and data-level optimization: OpenMP and SIMD

Desktop and server processors contain numerous features intended to maximally exploit **instruction level parallelism**, the ability to execute multiple instructions in parallel without changing program functionality, and **memory locality**, which is the tendency for the addresses of memory accesses to be temporally clustered. Their design places highest emphasis on superscalar out-of-order speculative execution, accurate branch predication, and extremely sophisticated multilevel caches. This allows them to perform well even when executing code that was not written with performance in mind.

On the other hand, embedded processor design emphasizes energy efficiency, so designers generally forego these features in exchange for on-chip peripherals and specialized coprocessors for specific tasks. Because of this, embedded processor performance is more sensitive to code optimizations than desktop and server processors. Code optimizations are software features that are intended to improve performance without changing functionality. Such optimizations can be invoked either by the compiler or the programmer, and can be processor agnostic, such as eliminating redundant code, or processor specific, such as substituting a complex instruction in place of a sequence of simple instructions.

Optimizing code often involves starting with a straight-forward serial implementation. Next, the programmer must identify the *kernels*, or portions of code in which the most execution time is spent. After this, the programmer determines the performance bottleneck of each kernel and transforms the kernel code in a way that improves performance without changing the underlying computation. These changes generally involve finding ways to exploit parallelism by taking advantage of hardware features, or by trading numerical accuracy, precision, or dynamic range in exchange for performance.

2.1 Optimization techniques covered

This chapter will cover two programmer-driven optimization techniques:

1. *Using Assembly Language to Improve Instruction Level Parallelism*
    In some situations, hand-written assembly code offers performance advantages over compiler-generated assembly code. You should not expect hand-written assembly to always outperform compiler-generated code. In fact, the automatic optimizers built into modern compilers are often very effective for integer code, but hand-written assembly is often more effective for intensive floating-point kernels.
2. *Multicore Parallelism*
    Even server processors cannot automatically distribute the workload of a program onto multiple concurrent processor cores. The programmer must add explicit support for multicore parallelism into the program code and verify that the code is free from concurrency errors such as race conditions. Even then, achieving high multicore efficiency is difficult, but it is becoming increasingly important in embedded system programming as multicore embedded CPUs become increasingly common.
    The following chapters cover additional topics in program optimization, including:
3. *Fixed-Point Arithmetic*
    Floating-point instructions are more costly than integer instructions in two ways. First, a typical SIMD unit can usually perform less 32-bit floating-point operations in parallel than 8- and 16-bit integer operations. For this reason, a programmer can potentially increase operational throughput by using integer values instead of floating-point values. However, note that emerging embedded processors may adopt 16-bit and 8-bit floating-point formats to solve this problem. Second, floating-point

functional units always have a higher latency than integer units, which may reduce throughput when there are data dependencies between floating-point operations. Using integers as an alternative to floating-point requires the use of fixed-point representation. Fixed-point representation allows integers to represent fractional numbers but with lower dynamic range as compared to floating point. This trade off is acceptable for some multimedia and sensing applications that do not require high dynamic range. Most high-level languages, including C/C++ and Java, lack native language support for fixed point so the programmer must include explicit support for fixed-point operations.

4. *Loop Transformations*

   Cache performance is associated with a program's memory access locality, but in some cases, the program can be changed such that it exhibits locality that is more favorable to the cache without changing the functionality of the program. This usually involves transforming the structure of loops, such as in loop tiling, where the programmer adds additional levels of loops to change the order in which data is accessed.

5. *Heterogeneous Computing*

   Many embedded systems, and even systems-on-a-chip, include integrated coprocessors such as graphical processor units (GPUs), digital signal processors (DSPs), or field programmable gate arrays (FPGAs) that can perform specific types of computations faster than the general-purpose processors. Since the coprocessor is typically treated as a peripheral to the general-purpose processor, the programmer must write special code for the coprocessor and explicitly handle control, interfacing, memory management, and synchronization of the coprocessor.

   These five techniques cannot be performed automatically and generally requires that the programmer begin with functional but nonoptimized code then iteratively modify the code, verify that the modifications do not break the functionality of the original code, measure the resulting impact on performance, and repeat the process to extract more performance.

   Note that the programmer need not optimize the entire program, because typically only a small portion of the code—usually the innermost loops—consumes nearly all the execution time. These loops or loop nests are called the kernels. The programmer needs only to apply the above techniques to the program kernel(s) in order to achieve a significant overall performance improvement.

2.2 Amdahl's law

Amdahl's Law, shown as Equation (2.1), calculates the overall performance impact resulting from optimizing one or more components of a program.

The equation calculates the overall speedup, of the program, $S_{overall}$, as a function of what portion of the execution time corresponds to the code to which an improvement (parallelism) is applied, time$_{optimized}$ and the amount that it is improved ($S_{optimized}$):

$$S_{overall} = \frac{1}{\left(1 - time_{optimized}\right) + \dfrac{time_{optimized}}{S_{optimized}}} \qquad (2.1)$$

Amdahl's Law has several important implications. First is that the overall improvement of a program depends on improving the *common case* in the sense of execution time. In some cases, this may originate from a very small portion of the program code, i.e., the kernels.

A frustrating aspect of Amdahl's Law is that $S_{overall}$ is often lower than expected. For example, if the programmer speeds up the portion of the code that consumes 10% of the execution time (time$_{optimized}$ = 0.10) by a factor of 10,000X ($S_{optimized}$ = 10,000), our overall speedup is only 11% ($S_{overall}$ = 1.11)! In this case, there was very little return from achieving such a large speedup of this one aspect of the execution.

On the other hand, if the programmer speeds up the portion of the code that consumes 99% of execution time (time$_{optimized}$ = 0.99) by a factor of 100 ($S_{optimized}$ = 100), our overall speedup is only 50 ($S_{overall}$ = 50)! In other words, 50% of the performance benefit of the enhancement is lost from only 1% of the execution time that was not subject to the improvement.

Another important practical aspect is the importance of time$_{optimized}$ over $S_{optimized}$. For example, Figure 2.1 plots $S_{overall}$ versus time$_{optimized}$ for two different optimization speedup factors, $S_{optimized}$ = 10 and $S_{optimized}$ = 1000. As shown in the plot, the overall speedup does not diverge

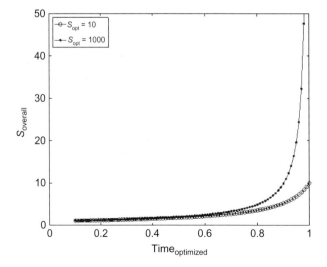

Figure 2.1: $S_{overall}$ versus time$_{optimized}$ for $S_{optimized}$ = 10 and 1000.

significantly until time$_{\text{optimized}} > 90\%$, and the relative difference between the curves is only a factor of $4.1 \times$ when time$_{\text{optimized}} = 97\%$!

2.3 Test kernel: polynomial evaluation

This section introduces a benchmark kernel that is used throughput this chapter and Chapter 5 to describe and evaluate code optimizations. The kernel evaluates a degree-8 polynomial at every point in a vector x:

$$d(x_i) = \sum_{j=0}^{7} a_j x_i^j$$

To implement this, we can use Horner's method. Horner's method evaluates the polynomial iteratively by starting with the highest-degree coefficient and computing each iteration by multiplying the previous iteration's value by x and adding each coefficient in order of degree:

$$d_0(x) = a_7$$
$$d_1(x) = xd_0(x) + a_6 = a_7 x + a_6$$
$$d_2(x) = xd_1(x) + a_5 = a_7 x^2 + a_6 x + a_5$$
$$d_3(x) = xd_2(x) + a_4 = a_7 x^3 + a_6 x^2 + a_5 x + a_4$$
$$d_4(x) = xd_3(x) + a_3 = a_7 x^4 + a_6 x^3 + a_5 x^2 + a_4 x + a_3$$
$$d_5(x) = xd_4(x) + a_2 = a_7 x^5 + a_6 x^4 + a_5 x^3 + a_4 x^2 + a_3 x + a_2$$
$$d_6(x) = xd_5(x) + a_1 = a_7 x^6 + a_6 x^5 + a_5 x^4 + a_4 x^3 + a_3 x^2 + a_2 x + a_1$$
$$d_7(x) = xd_6(x) + a_0 = a_7 x^7 + a_6 x^6 + a_5 x^5 + a_4 x^4 + a_3 x^3 + a_2 x^2 + a_1 x + a_0$$

Begin by implementing Horner's method in C to determine how well the compiler optimizes it automatically. Set the input and output array size to be 128 MB.

```
#define N 128*1024*1024
```

First, inside a function in which you want to evaluate code performance, declare and initialize an array for the polynomial coefficients. Their values will not affect performance assuming they do not cause floating-point exceptions. Assume the coefficients are ordered from highest order to lowest order:

```
static float coeff[8] = {1.2,1.4,1.6,1.8,2.0,2.2,2.4,2.6};
```

Since N represents the size of the dataset in bytes, the array sizes must incorporate the size of a float:

```
static float x[N/4],d[N/4];
```

For this kernel, it is useful to measure performance in terms of floating-point throughput, so we must augment the `cnts_dump()` function from Chapter 1 to calculate floating-point operations per second, or **flops**. For a degree-8 polynomial, there are 14 floating-point operations per input element.

```
float flops; // workload in floating point operation

float mflops; // throughput in megaflops per second

flops = (float)N/4.0 * 14; // 14 ops per output value

mflops = flops/time/1.0e6;
```

Since the floating-point operations are the only operations that directly contribute to progressing the objective of the kernel, it may provide insight to measure code efficiency in terms of number of executed instructions per floating-point operation, which the instrumentation code can compute and print:

```
float ipf; // instructions per floating point operation

ipf = (float)(perf_count(cnts[INSTRUCTIONS])) / flops;

...

printf("[perf_event] mflops=%0.2f, instructions per flop=\
    %0.2f\n",mflops,ipf);
```

Change the memory bandwidth calculation to reflect that the code is now reading and writing the number of bytes specified by N:

```
membw_mbs = (float)N*2.0/time/(1024.0f*1024.0f); // memory bandwidth in MB per second
```

Next, back in the function containing your test code, populate the input array **x** with random numbers. Like the coefficient values, the input values are not important if the values do not cause floating-point exceptions.

First, define a simple function to deal with error returns:

```
void err(const char *msg) {
    fprintf(stderr,"ERROR: %s: %s\n",msg,strerror(errno));
    exit(1);
}
```

Use the performance counter to instrument a naïve version of Horner's method:

```
float *d; // output array

float *x; // input array

int i,j; // loop counters

int fd[5]; // handles to performance counters
```

```
uint64_t cnts[4][3]; // performance counters

float coeff[32] = {1.2,1.4,1.6,1.8,2.0,2.2,2.4,2.6};

d=(float *)malloc(N); // allocate output array

x=(float *)malloc(N); // allocate input array

if (!d || !x) err("malloc()"); // check return of malloc()

// populate input array

for (i=0;i<N/4;i++) x[i]=(float)rand()/(float)RAND_MAX;

cnts_tick(fd); // tick

for (i=0;i<N/4;i++) {        // the outer loop

    d[i]=coeff[0];

    for (j=1;j<8;j++) {     // the inner loop

        d[i]*=x[i];

        d[i]+=coeff[j];

    }

}

cnts_tock(fd,cnts); // tock

cnts_dump(cnts); // dump performance results
```

2.4 Using multiple processor cores: OpenMP

To take advantage of all the processor cores, the programmer must add explicit code to direct the compiler to distribute the workload over multiple cooperating parallel threads that communicate through a shared memory space. The number of threads should equal the number of processor cores so each thread can execute concurrently on its own processor core without needing to share with another thread. **OpenMP** is a convenient method by which the programmer can specify how a kernel should be executed in parallel.

As shown in Figure 2.2, OpenMP assumes a globally sequential, locally parallel approach, where program code executes sequentially until reaching the beginning of a *parallel region*, where multiple child threads are created to cooperatively process a workload. Once all the threads complete, the original thread—or "master" thread—continues executing sequentially at the point immediately following the parallel region. This is called "fork-join" parallelism.

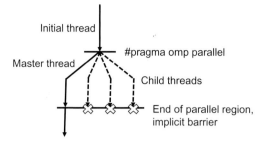

Figure 2.2: OpenMP thread creation. perf_event tracks performance counter events only within the master thread (solid line).

Code-wise, OpenMP involves a combination of "decorating" specific loops and code blocks using preprocessor commands called *pragmas* as well as using a small set of OpenMP library functions.

OpenMP allows the programmer to specify distinct code for different threads, which are defined in a **parallel section**. Often, though, every thread executes the same code. In this case, each thread's behavior is determined by its ability to self-identify its own thread ID and the total number of threads. The OpenMP functions used for this are `omp_get_thread_num()` and `omp_get_num_threads()`. This section provides a short introduction to OpenMP.

2.4.1 OpenMP directives

Most OpenMP directives are meant to mark the next statement or code block as being significant with respect to multithread parallelism (in C/C++, a code block consists of multiple statements enclosed in braces {}), but there are a few directives that stand alone and not used to modify the behavior of following statement or block.

An OpenMP directive is specified using a preprocessor command called a *pragma* using the syntax:

```
#pragma omp < directive name > < directive options >
```

An often-used OpenMP directive is the *parallel* directive, which specifies the start of a *parallel region*:

```
#pragma omp parallel < directive options >
```

As shown in Figure 2.2, in the OpenMP programming model, all programs begin their execution as a single thread called the *master thread*. When the master thread encounters a parallel region, one or more *worker threads* are spawned. Together with the master thread, these worker threads will execute the code inside the parallel region concurrently. The number of worker threads created when the processor encounters a parallel region is determined by the programmer using any of the following methods in decreasing order of precedence:

- using the num_threads() directive option, e.g., `#pragma omp parallel num_threads(4)`,
- through a previous call to OpenMP function `omp_set_number_threads()`, e.g., `omp_set_number_threads(4)`, or
- through the value of the `OMP_NUM_THREADS` environment variable at program launch.

Since the master thread counts toward the total number of threads, the parallel region will cause the OpenMP runtime to create *one less* thread than the number specified by the programmer.

Often, the program will be constructed such that the master thread and worker threads execute the same code. In this case, their behavior will only differ in the ranges of input and output data processed (i.e., their array indices are specified as a function of their thread ID).

In other cases, each thread will execute its own code sections. In yet other cases, the worker threads will execute the same code while the master thread performs special functions. OpenMP includes a directive that allows the programmer to mark portions of the parallel section that should only be executed by the master thread (`#pragma omp master`).

When the master thread reaches the end of the parallel region, it will automatically wait until all worker threads also reach the end of the parallel region. At this point, the worker threads will terminate and the master thread will resume execution. In other words, there is an implicit **barrier** at the end of the parallel region.

The programmer may use nested directives to define separate code blocks to be executed in each thread. Examples of these are shown below:

```
#pragma omp parallel

{


        code to be executed in each thread


}
```

or:

```
#pragma omp parallel

        #pragma omp sections

        {

                #pragma omp section

                {

                        code executed in first thread

                }
```

```
#pragma omp section

{

        code executed in second thread

}

}
```

2.4.2 Scope

By default, variables declared outside the parallel region and used within the parallel region are "*shared*". This means:

- within the parallel region, the variable will inherit its initial state from its state in the master thread just prior to the parallel region,
- any state changes inside the parallel region are visible in all threads, and
- after the parallel region, its value in the master thread will reflect the most recent write among all the threads.

This is illustrated in the following example, in which four threads write the shared variable b.

```
int a=1;

#pragma omp parallel num_threads(4)

{

        a=2;

}
printf ("%d\n",a); // value printed is always 2
```

As is generally the case with parallelism and shared memory, the programmer should use thread synchronization when writing shared variables that are read in another thread. This is described in more detail below.

Alternatively, the programmer can mark an externally declared variable as being *private* in the parallel region using the "private" directive option. Alternatively, the programmer can achieve the same effect by declaring the variable inside the parallel region.

Private variables are local to each thread such that changes to the variable are only visible to the thread making the change and the variable state is destroyed when the thread is destroyed.

Private scope is illustrated in the next example, in which the updates to the private variable are lost after the parallel region.

```
int a=1;

#pragma omp parallel num_threads(4) private(a)

{

      a=2; // a will be destroyed

}

printf ("%d\n",a); // printed value is 1
```

Variables can also be marked as "firstprivate" in which the variable is private but is initialized to its state immediately prior to the parallel region.

```
int a=1;

#pragma omp parallel num_threads(4) firstprivate(a)

{

      a+=omp_get_thread_num(); // initial value of a=1

      printf ("%d\n",a); // prints thread number + 1

}
```

The programmer can also instruct the OpenMP runtime to retain the variable state in each individual thread, even between parallel regions, using the **threadprivate** direction option. Threadprivate variables must be allocated as global or static variables, and the threadprivate directive must be used as a standalone directive. For example:

```
static int a;                                   // threadprivate
                                                //variables must be
                                                //global

#pragma omp threadprivate(a)                    // threadprivate() must be
                                                //used as a

                                                //standalone OMP directive

#pragma omp parallel num_threads(4)             // first parallel region
                                                // sets four

                                                //separate "versions" of
                                                //a variable

{

      a=omp_get_thread_num();

}
```

```
#pragma omp parallel num_threads(4)              // second parallel region
                                                 // recalls the

                                                 //four "versions" of a
                                                 //variable
{

        printf ("%d\n",a);

}
```

Threadprivate variables can be initialized using the "copyin" directive option, as shown below.

```
a=1;

#pragma omp threadprivate(a)

#pragma omp parallel num_threads(4) copyin(a)

{

        a+=omp_get_thread_num(); // initial value of a=1

}
```

A variable can also be specified as a **reduction** variable, which is a private variable, but at the end of the parallel region, its final value in each thread is combined using a specific operation such as summation and assigned to the variable in the master thread after the parallel region. For example:

```
int a;

#pragma omp parallel num_threads(4) reduction(+:a)

{

        a=omp_get_thread_num();

}

  printf("%d\n",a); // printed value is 0+1+2+3=6
```

A variable can also be marked as **lastprivate**, in which the variable's state in the last loop iteration in parallel-for or the last section in the parallel region is assigned to the variable in the master thread after the parallel region. **Parallel-for** loops will be covered in more detail below.

For example:

```
int a,i;
#pragma omp parallel for num_threads(4) lastprivate(a)
for (i=0;i<16;i++) {
      a=omp_get_thread_num();
}
  printf("%d\n",a); // printed value is 3, since iteration 15 is
                    // performed in thread 3
```

In the next example, there are two parallel regions. In the first parallel region, three threads are created. The `default(none)` option changes the default scope for all externally declared variables from *shared* to *none*. This is a safety feature that causes the compiler to generate an error on any line in the parallel region that changes an externally declared variable whose scope was not explicitly specified in the directive options.

Also note the shorthand notation for the parallel region sections, in which the "`omp parallel`" and "`omp sections`" directives are combined into a single directive "`omp parallel sections`". Thread groups within each parallel section are numbered starting at 0. As a result, the `omp_get_thread_num()` function would return 0 in each thread so individual content of each section differentiates the behavior of each thread.

The final state of variables *a* and *b* in each thread are 10, 11, and 12, respectively, demonstrating the initialization of the variable *a*. The printed value of *b* is 12, as assigned in the last section.

Four threads are spawned in the second parallel region. The final state of variable *c* in each thread is 0, 1, 2, and 3. Because *c* is marked as a summation reduction variable, the printed value of *c* is 11, calculated as the sum of these values as well as the initial value of *c*.

```
int a=10,b=1,c=5;
#pragma omp parallel sections firstprivate(a) lastprivate(b) default(none)
{
      #pragma omp section
      b=0+a;
      #pragma omp section
      b=1+a;
      #pragma omp section
      b=2+a; // final value of b is 12
}
```

```
#pragma omp parallel num_threads(4) reduction(+:c)

c=omp_get_thread_num(); // final value of c = 5+0+1+2+3 = 11

printf("a=%d, b=%d, c=%d\n",a,b,c); // a=10, b=12, c=11
```

2.4.3 OpenMP synchronization

Nested pragmas are also used when a section within a parallel block must be executed in a special way, such as when:

(1) a section must be executed in sequential order among the threads (the **ordered** pragma),
(2) a section must be executed only on the master thread (the **master** pragma),
(3) a section must be executed atomically (the **atomic** pragma),
(4) a section should only be executed in one thread (the **single** pragma), or
(5) a critical section that can only be executed by one thread at a time (the **atomic** pragma).

Other synchronization operations are specified using OpenMP function calls, such as omp_ set_lock() and omp_unset_lock().

2.4.3.1 Critical sections

Critical sections are implemented as pragmas. Only one thread can execute code in a critical section at any time, meaning that a thread that encounters a critical section will wait to enter until all threads executing or waiting on the critical section have exited it. This creates a serialization effect and corresponding loss in parallelism, so the use of critical sections should be minimized to maximize performance.

Critical sections are necessary when threads perform read-modify-write operations on shared variables. In the following example, the parallel region manipulates a shared variable named "place" that is used to determine the order in which each thread reaches that place in the code. Since the shared variable is incremented, this section is marked as a critical section. This way, only one thread can execute this code at one time, avoiding any data-sharing errors. In this example, the entire parallel section is in a critical section, which makes the use of the parallel region redundant since this would not allow any of the threads to execute in parallel.

```
int place=0;

#pragma omp parallel

{

        #pragma omp critical (mycritsec)

        {

                place++;
```

```
              printf ("thread %d finished in position %d\n", omp_get_thread_num(),place);

      }

}

printf ("parallel region ended\n");
```

Compile this example with the option "-fopenmp". When executed, the master thread, thread 0, always reaches the critical section first but the worker threads reach the print in different orderings each run. Also notice that the print statement that is immediately after the parallel section will always print after all worker threads finish.

Run 1:

```
thread 0 finished in position 1

thread 2 finished in position 2

thread 3 finished in position 3

thread 1 finished in position 4

parallel region ended
```

Run 2:

```
thread 0 finished in position 1

thread 3 finished in position 2

thread 2 finished in position 3

thread 1 finished in position 4

parallel region ended
```

Run 3:

```
thread 0 finished in position 1

thread 1 finished in position 2

thread 3 finished in position 3

thread 2 finished in position 4

parallel region ended
```

2.4.3.2 Locks

Locks provide a similar functionality as critical sections. Locks are specified as functions, so the programmer calls omp_set_lock() to mark the beginning of a critical section and omp_unset_lock() to mark its end. Locks have an associated handle that the programmer must declare and initialize in the master thread before use.

For example:

```
int a=0;

omp_lock_t mylock;

omp_init_lock(&mylock);

#pragma omp parallel num_threads(4)

{

        omp_set_lock(&mylock);

        a++;

        omp_unset_lock(&mylock);

}

printf("%d\n",a); // printed value is always 4
```

2.4.3.3 Barriers

A barrier is a point in the parallel region in which all threads must reach before any thread may proceed further. Barriers are useful for splitting up dependent phases of a parallel operation.

For example, in a video processing application, multiple threads will process the pixels in the frame in parallel, but all threads must complete before moving to the next frame.

Barriers are specified as pragmas, as shown in the example below:

```
int a;

#pragma omp parallel num_threads(4)

{

        a=omp_get_thread_num(); // note that variable a is shared

        #pragma omp barrier

        if (omp_get_thread_num()==2) a=omp_get_thread_num();

}

printf("%d\n",a); // printed value is always 2
```

2.4.3.4 Atomic sections

An atomic operation is guaranteed to be performed on one thread at any moment in time. In concept, they are identical to critical sections, but atomic sections can only ensure exclusivity for a *single assignment operation*, so they are used only for single statements. Their advantage is that they have lower overhead than critical sections.

Atomic operations are specified as pragmas, for example:

```
int a=0;

#pragma omp parallel num_threads(4)

{

      #pragma omp atomic

      a++;

}

printf("%d\n",a); // printed value is always 4
```

2.4.4 The OpenMP parallel-for pragma

Kernels are usually comprised of a for-loop containing nested for-loops. OpenMP offers a simple way to automatically distribute the iterations of a for-loop to multiple threads using the **for** directive. The directive can be written as

```
#pragma omp parallel

#pragma omp for

for (...)
```

or as a shortcut:

```
#pragma omp parallel for

for (...)
```

The parallel for directive requires that the termination condition be a single less-than, less-than-or-equal, greater-than, or greater-than-or-equal comparison with the loop variable, the increment operation must not be dependent on code in the loop body, and no break, goto, or throw statements are allowed in the loop body.

By default, the loop variable is treated as private. This is important since each thread will be simultaneously working on a different set of loop iterations and so the value of each thread's i variable will have different values at the same time.

Consider the following example:

```
#pragma omp parallel for num_threads(4)

for (int i=0;i<12;i++)

      printf ("iteration %d, thread %d\n",

          i,omp_get_thread_num());

      printf ("master thread completed\n");
```

When executed, the new code will produce something similar to the following output:

```
iteration 0, thread 0

iteration 1, thread 0

iteration 2, thread 0

iteration 9, thread 3

iteration 10, thread 3

iteration 11, thread 3

iteration 6, thread 2

iteration 7, thread 2

iteration 8, thread 2

iteration 3, thread 1

iteration 4, thread 1

iteration 5, thread 1

master thread completed
```

As shown by our output, three iterations are assigned to each thread. Since the threads are executing in parallel, the print statements from all the threads are shown interleaved in the console. The print message after the parallel region from the master thread always appear at the end of the console output due to the barrier after the parallel region.

OpenMP supports several policies for assigning iterations to threads. By default, the assignment is *static*, meaning that each thread executes approximately the same number of loop iterations. Since all threads must finish their assigned set of iterations before the program moves beyond the for-loop, threads whose assigned set of iterations finish faster than other threads will experience a longer waiting time than other threads.

To avoid this problem, OpenMP supports *dynamic scheduling*, in which a smaller batch of loop iterations, called a *chunk*, is assigned to each thread. A new chunk is assigned in turn to each thread that completes its previous chunk. This allows for *load balancing* and is best when the execution time varies between iterations. By default, parallel for loops are scheduled statically. A directive option can turn on dynamic scheduling. For example, "`#pragma parallel for schedule(dynamic)`" turns on dynamic scheduling with automatic chunk size; "`#pragma parallel for schedule(dynamic,chunksize)`" allows the programmer to specify a chunksize, which is the number of iterations assigned at one time to a thread.

2.4.5 OpenMP with performance counters

Perf_event only records events in the master thread so the programmer must account for this when calculating metrics that incorporates values not reported by the performance counters, such as the number of floating-point operations. For example, the cnts_dump() from Chapter 1 will only count the number of instructions executed by the master thread. To calculate the number of instructions per flop, multiply the instruction count by NUM_THREADS.

2.4.6 OpenMP support for the Horner kernel

Consider the example where Horner's method is used to evaluate a degree-8 polynomial over each element of an input array. In this case, the outermost loop contains no loop-carried dependencies between iterations, allowing the iterations to be distributed onto different threads. Add the OpenMP header file and set the number of threads to the number of cores on your system:

```
#include <omp.h>

#define NUM_THREADS 4
```

Specify the size, in bytes, for the input array. For this we can set it to 2^{20}, or one MB.

```
#define     N    (1<<20)
```

Specify the number of threads in the initialization section of the code:

```
omp_set_num_threads(NUM_THREADS);
```

Finally, tell the OpenMP runtime to parallelize the outer Horner loop:

```
#pragma omp parallel for
     for (i=0;i<N/4;i++) {
          d[i]=coeff[0];
          for (j=1;j<8;j++) {
               d[i]=d[i]*x[i];
               d[i]=d[i]+coeff[j];
          }
     }
```

2.5 Performance bounds

A processor's peak theoretical floating-point performance is generally at least $2 \times cores \times frequency \times ops\_per\_cycle$, assuming that fused multiply-accumulate instructions are supported and counted as two operations. For single-precision floating point, $ops\_per\_cycle = 1$ for Raspberry Pi Gen 1 and $ops\_per\_cycle = 4$ for Raspberry Pi Gen 4.

This gives a peak capacity of $2 \times 1 \times 700 \,\text{MHz} \times 1 = 1.4$ Gflops for the Raspberry Pi Gen 1 and $2 \times 4 \times 1500 \,\text{MHz} \times 4 = 48$ Gflops/s for the Raspberry Pi Gen 4.

In practice, processors do not achieve peak floating-point performance since it would require that the processor provide inputs to all its floating-point units every cycle, hide all sources of latency between dependent instructions, avoid any branch stalls, and avoid any memory system stalls.

One significant source of latency is the average memory access time, meaning that the floating-point units would need to be kept busy during the time required to access the data needed for the computation. Since the floating-point units can achieve higher throughput than the off-chip memory, their effective performance depends on the degree to which the kernel reuses data during its execution. This reuse rate is usually characterized using a metric called **arithmetic intensity**, which expressed the average number of floating-point operations performed per byte of data.

Every CPU has a theoretical arithmetic intensity threshold, under which the kernel's performance is bound by memory bandwidth, and over which is usually bounded by computational throughput. Arithmetic intensity provides a tighter upper performance bound than peak floating point-performance. This bound can be computed as:

$$\text{Upper bound} = \min \begin{cases} 2 \times \text{cores} \times \text{frequency} \times n \\ \text{intensity} \times \text{peak memory b/w} \end{cases} \text{floating point operations per second}$$

Our benchmark kernel performs two floating-point operations (multiply, add) per iteration of the inner loop, which iterates seven times for every iteration of the outer loop, giving 14 floating-point operations.

The body of the outer loop references one element of **x**, one element of **d**, and all eight coefficients. Since the coefficients are reused across iterations of the outer loop, the processor would maintain their state in the registers or cache, so this analysis only considers the 8 bytes that comprise each element of **d** and **x**. This gives an arithmetic intensity of $14/8 = 1.75$ flops per byte.

This analysis computes the peak memory bandwidth as a weighted average of read bandwidth and write bandwidth for each platform as measured in Chapter 1. This kernel reads and writes the same amount of data—4 bytes read and 4 bytes written on each iteration of the outermost loop—so in this case, the weighted average is $0.5 \times (\text{read b/w}) + 0.5 \times (\text{write b/w})$.

The performance upper bound is thus 1.75 multiplied by the average bandwidth since this is always less than the peak floating-point throughput on all three CPUs.

The *efficiency* is the ratio of actual performance and the resulting performance bound. This efficiency is determined by factors such as:

- the overheads in the generated assembly code (in terms of *instructions per flop*),
- the *instruction and data cache miss rate*, and
- *cycles per instruction* (*CPI*), which is largely determined by memory performance and stalls caused by data dependencies.

2.6 Performance analysis

Table 2.1 shows the performance results of our kernel implementation on all three platforms. Even when using maximum compiler optimization, the compiler can only achieve approximately 20 to 30% of the peak performance as predicted by the performance bound. The performance counters can provide some insight into the program's implementation problems.

- *Memory bandwidth*: Since the kernel is bounded by memory bandwidth, the performance efficiency will match our memory bandwidth efficiency, so the effective memory bandwidth is not shown in subsequent tables.
- *CPI*: The ideal CPI is 1 for the ARM11, 0.5 for the Cortex A53, and 0.33 for the Cortex A72. Our observed CPIs are substantially higher for the Cortex A53 and A72. This may be caused by unsatisfactory cache performance or unsatisfactory instruction scheduling the compiler, processor, or both.
- *Cache miss rate*: Miss rate measures cache performance and determines the average latency of a memory instruction. As such, it gives an idea of how much the CPI is influenced by cache performance. Miss rate is determined by the locality of the kernel's access pattern. Both the d and x arrays are accessed with both spatial and temporal locality (each element is accessed repeatedly and consecutively), so it is reasonable to expect the data cache to perform well for this kernel.
- *Instructions per flop*: This metric is another way to express the number of instructions executed and is affected by how efficiently the compiler translates the high-level code.

In order to improve the kernel, the programmer requires more control over its implementation.

2.6.1 Cortex-A53/A72: single instruction multiple data with NEON

Nearly all modern processors can perform multiple independent operations using one instruction. These are called *Single Instruction, Multiple Data (SIMD) instructions*, or *vector instructions*. SIMD instructions decrease the number of instructions per operation, which increases floating-point throughput and decreases instruction cache miss rate.

Some processors, such as the ARM Cortex A9 and A15, provide the ability to issue a SIMD instruction in less cycles than an equivalent number of scalar instructions. These processors have multiple *SIMD lanes*, in which there are multiple independent parallel functional units as well as a register file that can provide simultaneous access to all the necessary input and output registers. In this case, using SIMD instructions allows multiple operations to be performed in a single clock cycle as compared to using scalar instructions.

ARM Cortex processors support SIMD floating point with *NEON instructions*. NEON instruction mnemonics begin with the letter V. When compiling code with NEON instructions, you may need to use the "-compile with mfpu-neon" GCC compiler flag.

In Cortex-A53/72 processors, there are 32 64-bit d-registers and 16 overlapped 128-bit registers q0-q15 that each overlaps a pair of d-registers. The vector length of each NEON instruction is determined through a combination of an operand type after the mnemonic and the register size of the operands.

The vector length is implied by dividing the size of the operand register by the size of the type. For example, the instruction **vadd.f32 q4, q5, q6** would perform four floating-point additions because four 32-bit single-precision floating-point values, or lanes, can fit inside of a single 128-bit q-register. In other words, the ".f32" mnemonic suffix specifies the datatype of single precision, while the q-register prefix specifies 128-bit registers, so the vector size is implied by $128/32 = 4$.

There are also several NEON instructions that allow for manipulation of individual subfields within a register, such as **vext**, **vmov**, and **vmvn**.

The NEON load and store instructions use a different method to specify their width, because they support a memory access stride of 1, 2, 3, or 4 values and allow for a list of destination registers. They use the format:

```
vld<stride>.<element size><destination registers>,<base register>
```

For example, the instruction **vld2.8 {d0,d1}, [r0]** would load every other 8-bit value beginning at the address in r0 into d0, and every other 8-bit value beginning at address r0 + 1 into d1.

NEON load and store performance can be improved by using **aligned addresses**—memory accesses that are evenly divisible by 16, 32, 64, 128, or 256 bytes. In addition to ensuring that the addresses are aligned, the alignment must be explicitly given in the instruction by adding suffix such as @64 to the end of the instruction.

While ARM11 short vector instructions support a length of eight single-precision operations, NEON are limited to four. As such, make the appropriate adjustment to the coefficient array. In order to align the coefficient array, use the C **aligned attribute** as shown below:

```
float __attribute__((aligned(16))) coeff_4vector[32] = {1.2,1.2,1.2,1.2,
                    1.4,1.4,1.4,1.4,
                    ...
                    2.6,2.6,2.6,2.6};
```

2.6.2 NEON intrinsics

Unlike VFP short vector instructions, the programmer can use SIMD NEON instructions without using inline assembly language. The header file `arm_neon.h` provides a set of preprocessor wrappers around built-in compiler expressions that allow the programmer to use C-style semantics to invoke specific NEON instructions. These are called **intrinsics**.

Intrinsics allow the programmer to use a C-style function call to generate a specific instruction, meaning that the compiler is forced to use a specific instruction corresponding to the intrinsic. Like inline assembly, intrinsic calls sometimes generate additional auxiliary instructions to allocate C variables, arrays, and pointers into registers.

Intrinsics are only necessary in cases where the compiler is unable to infer the most appropriate instruction from the high-level code. Modern compilers are quite effective at automatically converting simple scalar loops to vector-based loops and using the appropriate SIMD instructions for the target architecture. Additionally, the programmer can use **SIMD datatypes** such as float32x4_t in the high-level code, which increases the likelihood that the compiler can generate efficient instructions. We will use this technique below.

2.7 ARM Cortex-A53/A72: minimizing instructions per flop

The ARM NEON unit can perform four 32-bit floating point multiply-accumulate operations in one instruction when using quad-word (128-bit) registers, ideally providing 0.25 instructions per flop or, 0.125 instructions per flop if we recall that our workload calculation, 14 flops per iteration of the innermost loop, assumes separate floating-point operations for the multiply and add components.

Our performance instrumentation shows an achieved instructions per flop of approximately 0.6 on the Cortex A53 and A72 on the Raspberry Pi Gen 3 and 4.

The compiler generated the following 19 instructions for the innermost loop, showing that it unrolled the 7-iteration loop and performs 7 `fmla` instructions, each of which performs four multiply-accumulates, each for different elements of the outer loop, as indicated by the increment-by-16 loop counter, which increments the inner loop by four 32-bit floats. This would give $\dfrac{19 \text{ instructions}}{7 \times 4 \times 2 \text{ flops}} = 0.34$ instructions per flop.

```
.L42:
    mov v1.16b, v16.16b
    ldr q0, [x21, x0]
    mov v2.16b, v8.16b
    fmla v1.4s, v0.4s, v17.4s
    fmla v2.4s, v1.4s, v0.4s
    mov v1.16b, v7.16b
    fmla v1.4s, v2.4s, v0.4s
    mov v2.16b, v6.16b
    fmla v2.4s, v1.4s, v0.4s
    mov v1.16b, v5.16b
    fmla v1.4s, v2.4s, v0.4s
    mov v2.16b, v4.16b
    fmla v2.4s, v1.4s, v0.4s
    mov v1.16b, v3.16b
    fmla v1.4s, v2.4s, v0.4s
    str q1, [x22, x0]
    add x0, x0, 16
    cmp x0, x1
    bne .L42
```

Is the code above an efficient implementation? To determine this, first let us examine the primary instruction being generated, fmla, the only instruction used in the loop body aside from move, load, store, and branch instructions. The fmla v1, v2, v3 instruction performs:

$$R[v1] = R[v1] + R[v2] \times R[v3]$$

where $v1$, $v2$, and $v3$ are 128-bit four-element vectors and the multiply operation is an element-wise multiply, as opposed to an inner or outer vector product. Each of the fmla instructions performs both the multiply and the add operations in the inner loop in the C code. Each fmla instruction multiplies against v0 (as the second operand), which corresponds to a block of four elements of input array x. The first vector operand must therefore correspond to the coeff array and the destination register corresponds to the d array.

Recall the original high-level code:

```
for (i=0;i<N/4;i++) {
    d[i]=coeff[0];
    for (j=1;j<8;j++) {
        d[i]=d[i]*x[i];
        d[i]=d[i]+coeff[j];
    }
}
```

The inner loop can be unrolled as shown below:

```
d[i]=coeff[0];
d[i]=d[i]*x[i];
d[i]=d[i]+coeff[1];
d[i]=d[i]*x[i];
d[i]=d[i]+coeff[2];
d[i]=d[i]*x[i];
d[i]=d[i]+coeff[3];
d[i]=d[i]*x[i];
d[i]=d[i]+coeff[4];
d[i]=d[i]*x[i];
d[i]=d[i]+coeff[5];
d[i]=d[i]*x[i];
d[i]=d[i]+coeff[6];
d[i]=d[i]*x[i];
d[i]=d[i]+coeff[7];
```

We can convert this code to **single-static assignment** form by replacing all the writes to the d array with temporary values that are written once.

```
T0=coeff[0];
t1=t0*x[i];
t2=t1+coeff[1];
t3=t2*x[i];
```

```
t4=t3+coeff[2];

t5=t4*x[i];

t6=t5+coeff[3];

t7=t6*x[i];

t8=t7+coeff[4];

t9=t8*x[i];

t10=t9+coeff[5];

t11=t10*x[i];

t12=t11+coeff[6];

t13=t12*x[i];

d[i]=t13+coeff[7];
```

We can group the multiplies and adds into single lines of code by substituting each write with its subsequent use.

```
T2=coeff[0]*x[i]+coeff[1];

t4=t2*x[i]+coeff[2];

t6=t4*x[i]+coeff[3];

t8=t6*x[i]+coeff[4];

t10=t8*x[i]+coeff[5];

t12=t10*x[i]+coeff[6];

d[i]=t12*x[i]+coeff[7];
```

For each line that performs a multiply-accumulate, we must ensure that the destination and third operand match to satisfy the behavior of the `fmla` instruction. This can be achieved by making a simple transformation of using the coefficient array as the destination of the fused-multiply accumulate operation:

```
coeff[1]=coeff[0]*x[i]+coeff[1];

coeff[2]=coeff[1]*x[i]+coeff[2];

coeff[3]=coeff[2]*x[i]+coeff[3];

coeff[4]=coeff[3]*x[i]+coeff[4];

coeff[5]=coeff[4]*x[i]+coeff[5];

coeff[6]=coeff[5]*x[i]+coeff[6];

coeff[7]=coeff[6]*x[i]+coeff[7];
```

In this code, the result—a block of four elements of the d array—is stored in `coeff[7]` and the loop body would only require only seven `fmla` instructions. However, this code will destroy the original coefficient values after each iteration of the loop. To address this, we must copy the original values before each `fmla` instruction, as shown below:

```
t0=coeff[0];

t1=coeff[1];

t1=t0*x[i]+t1;

t0=coeff[2];

t0=t1*x[i]+t0;

t1=coeff[3];

t1=t0*x[i]+t1;

t0=coeff[4];

t0=t1*x[i]+t0;

t1=coeff[5];

t1=t0*x[i]+t1;

t0=coeff[6];

t0=t1*x[i]+t0;

d[i]=coeff[7];

d[i]=t0*x[i]+d[i];
```

The code shown below matches the code generated from the compiler except for the initial load from x and final store to d. Since our hand-written assembly code matches the code generated by the compiler, we may not be able to reduce the number of instructions required per flop, but we may be able to improve the number of cycles per instruction.

Before we try this, let us manually vectorize our implementation of the Horner code. To do this, we can use 128-bit quadword types from the `arm_neon.h` header file, which should be available in the default system include directory. Include this file:

```
#include <arm_neon.h>
```

Next, create a 128-bit version of the input and output arrays. This will group every four elements in each array, creating an array with one-fourth the number of elements but with four 32-bit values as each element:

```
float32x4_t *x4 = (float32x4_t *)x;

float32x4_t *d4 = (float32x4_t *)d;
```

Create temporary values of the same type:

```
float32x4_t t0,t1;
```

Now, create a parallel-for loop with one-fourth the number of iterations as before and using the unrolled code for the inner loop from above. The only change we must make is to use the intrinsic `vld1q_dup_f32()` to duplicate each coefficient value into the four-element temporary vectors. We can leave the fused multiply-accumulate operations in standard C code, since it is trivial for the compiler to map these statements to the `fmla` instruction. However, be sure to use our vectorized `x4` array instead of `x`.

```
#pragma omp parallel for

for (i=0;i<N/4/4;i++) { // the outer loop

        t0=vld1q_dup_f32(&coeff[0]);

        t1=vld1q_dup_f32(&coeff[1]);

        t1=t0*x4[i]+t1;

        t0=vld1q_dup_f32(&coeff[2]);

        t0=t1*x4[i]+t0;

        t1=vld1q_dup_f32(&coeff[3]);

        t1=t0*x4[i]+t1;

        t0=vld1q_dup_f32(&coeff[4]);

        t0=t1*x4[i]+t0;

        t1=vld1q_dup_f32(&coeff[5]);

        t1=t0*x4[i]+t1;

        t0=vld1q_dup_f32(&coeff[6]);

        t0=t1*x4[i]+t0;

        d4[i]=vld1q_dup_f32(&coeff[7]);

        d4[i]=t0*x4[i]+d4[i];

    }
```

Checking the output of the compiler for this loop, we see:

```
.L69:

    str q2, [x1, x0]

    mov v1.16b, v17.16b

    ldr q0, [x2, x0]
```

```
fmla  v1.4s, v0.4s, v2.4s
mov   v0.16b, v16.16b
str   q1, [x1, x0]
ldr   q3, [x2, x0]
fmla  v0.4s, v1.4s, v3.4s
mov   v1.16b, v8.16b
str   q0, [x1, x0]
ldr   q3, [x2, x0]
fmla  v1.4s, v0.4s, v3.4s
mov   v0.16b, v7.16b
str   q1, [x1, x0]
ldr   q3, [x2, x0]
fmla  v0.4s, v1.4s, v3.4s
mov   v1.16b, v6.16b
str   q0, [x1, x0]
ldr   q3, [x2, x0]
fmla  v1.4s, v0.4s, v3.4s
mov   v0.16b, v5.16b
str   q1, [x1, x0]
ldr   q3, [x2, x0]
fmla  v0.4s, v1.4s, v3.4s
mov   v1.16b, v4.16b
str   q0, [x1, x0]
ldr   q3, [x2, x0]
fmla  v1.4s, v0.4s, v3.4s
str   q1, [x1, x0]
add   x0, x0, 16
cmp   x0, x3
bne   .L69
```

This code resembles the compiler's optimized version of our naïve code, but it has additional store instructions to spill the t0 and t1 variables to the stack. Also notice additional load instructions used for repeated and redundant loadings from x array.

Despite these additional store and load instructions, running an instrumented version of this code achieves the same performance as our original naïve version with the two-level nested loop (about 2.5 Gflops/s, or about 1.4 flops/cycle assuming a 1.8 GHz clock rate for the Raspberry Pi 4).

To verify the correctness of any tuned implementation, your program should compare results of the optimized code with the original, simplified C implementation. When verifying floating-point code, you should not expect the results to match bit-for-bit due to differences in rounding error between different assembly implementations. Instead of checking for equivalence, make sure the results differ by no more than 1%.

```
For (i=0;i<N/4;i++) {

    // calculate element the simple way

    d_test[i]=coeff[0];

    for (j=1;j<8;j++) {

    d_test[i]*=x[i];

    d_test[i]+=coeff[j];

    }

    // compare to the corresponding element from the

    // optimized method

    error = fabs(d[i]-d_test[i])/d_test[i];

    if (error > 1.0e-2) {

      printf("verification error, d_test[%d]=%0.2e,\

      d[%d]=%0.2e, error=%0.2f%%\n",

      i,d_test[i],i,d[i],error*1.0e2);

      return 0;

    }

  }
```

2.8 ARM Cortex-A53/A72: minimizing cycles per instruction

On the ARM Cortex-A72, our current version of the Horner code requires about three cycles per instruction, on average. The ARM Cortex-A72 can issue up to three instructions in one cycle and supports speculative out-of-order execution, meaning that ideally our code would require only 0.33 cycles per instruction. However, only one NEON instruction can execute per cycle per core, so in the best case, we can only expect one cycle per instruction, assuming the NEON and move instructions can be executed in parallel. However, at three cycles per instruction, there must be an opportunity to reduce the cycles per instruction in our code.

One possible source of performance loss is the data dependency between the pairs of move and fmla instructions and between fmla instructions:

```
t0=vld1q_dup_f32(&coeff[2]);
t0=t1*x4[i]+t0;
t1=vld1q_dup_f32(&coeff[3]);
t1=t0*x4[i]+t1;
```

This corresponds to the assembly code:

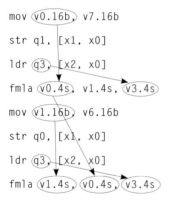

```
mov  v0.16b, v7.16b
str  q1, [x1, x0]
ldr  q3, [x2, x0]
fmla v0.4s, v1.4s, v3.4s
mov  v1.16b, v6.16b
str  q0, [x1, x0]
ldr  q3, [x2, x0]
fmla v1.4s, v0.4s, v3.4s
```

These dependencies exist within each loop iteration (they would have existed between iterations of the inner loop before we unrolled the inner loop) and will cause the processor to add stall cycles between the involved instructions to account for the latency of the move and fmla instructions. To reduce the impact of these dependencies, we must assign each dependent instruction the workload from a different iteration of the loop from that on which it depends. This approach is called software pipelining.

2.9 Software pipelining

Consider the following simple loop:

1: For i = 0 to n-1{
2:     r0 = load A[i]
3:     r0 = r0 + C
4:     A[i] = store r0}

In this case, there are RAW dependences between each pair of instructions in the loop body. Assume the latency of load and add is three cycles. This would give the following instruction schedule, assuming a single-issue, in-order processor:

Instruction	Cycle
Load A[0]	0
Add A[0]	3
Store A[0]	6
Load A[1]	7
Add A[1]	10
Store A[1]	13
Load A[2]	14
Add A[2]	17
Store A[2]	20
...	

In this case, the loop **iteration interval (II)**, or number of cycles per iteration, is seven cycles, giving a CPI of 7/3. This means that four out of every seven cycles is a stall.

Software pipelining is a method for interleaving loop iterations in order to separate the dependent instructions. To do this, unroll the loop three times and use different registers in each unrolled loop body:

1: For i = 0 to n−1 step 3{
2:     r0 = load A[i]
3:     r0 = r0 + C
4:     A[i] = store r0
5:     r1 = load A[i + 1]
6:     r1 = r1 + C
7:     A[i + 1] = store r1
8:     r2 = load A[i + 2]
9:     r2 = r2 + C
10:     A[i + 2] = store r2}

Now take the third instruction from iteration i (line 4), the second instruction from iteration $i + 1$ (line 6), and the first instruction from iteration $i + 2$ (line 8) and form a new loop:

1: For i = 0 to n-3{
2:   A[i] = store r0 (same as A[i + 1] in previous iteration)
3:   r1 = r1 + C (same as A[i + 2] in previous iteration)
4:   r2 = load A[i + 2]} (not from any previous iterations)

Now adjust the registers such that each instruction will write the register used in the next iteration:

1: For i = 0 to n-3{
2:   A[i] = store r0 (same as A[i + 1] in previous iteration)
3:   r0 = r1 + C (same as A[i + 2] in previous iteration)
4:   r1 = load A[i + 2]} (not from any previous iterations)

Now there are no RAW dependencies and the loop will still work, because when $i == 0$ instruction 4 will load A[2], when $i == 1$ instruction 3 will add A[2], and when $i == 2$ instruction 2 will store A[2].

The only problem is that the loop never loads A[0] and A[1], never adds A[0], never stores $A[n - 1]$ and $A[n - 2]$, and never adds $A[n - 1]$. To solve this, add a prolog and epilog to the loop:

Prolog:

1: r0 = load A[0]

2: r0 = r0 + C

3: r1 = load A[1]

Main loop:

4: For i = 0 to n-3{

5:   A[i] = store r0

6:   r0 = r1 + C

7:   r1 = load A[i + 2]}

Epilog:

8: A[n-2] = store r0

9: r0 = r1 + C

10: A[n-1] = store r0

The new loop will have the following schedule:

Instruction	Cycle
Store A[0]	6
Add A[1]	7
Load A[2]	8
Store A[1]	10
Add A[2]	11
Load A[3]	12
Store A[2]	14
...	

The processor will perform with the same CPI as the nonpipelined version of the code when executing the prolog and epilog, so the loop will begin in cycle 6, the same cycle A[0] was stored before. The loop's II is now only four cycles, since no stalls are required within the loop and only one stall is required between iterations to separate each store-add dependency and load-add dependency. The code has thus achieved a loop speedup of 7/4 and the only cost was one additional register.

One way to pipeline the Horner loop is to break it into "sections" along each of the dependencies between `fmla` instructions, under the assumption that this instruction has a longer latency than the move instruction (the other instruction in our loop that generates a data dependency).

We can conceptualize these "sections" as the loading of the coefficient(s) and the associated fused `fmla` instruction. We can then map the sequence of each of these seven sections in seven discrete time slots (shown in Figure 2.3 as table cells running vertically from top to bottom). We can further map the corresponding sequence for the next eight iterations of the loop, with each iteration initiation one slot after the previous. In the resulting table, none of the cells sharing the same row have a data dependency (aside from the move-fmla dependency within each cell). In the seventh through ninth slots there are seven iterations of the loop that can execute in parallel. Portions of the first and last six iterations must be executed outside of the loop in order to "fill" and "flush" the pipeline. All other iterations of the loop will execute in the pipelined loop body but with the interloop dependencies converted into loop-carried dependencies, which will insert additional instructions between dependent pairs of instructions. This will reduce the number of stalls and the number of cycles per instruction.

Before deploying this pipeline to code, change the single iteration of the loop to use different registers for each stage, as shown below:

```
t0=vld1q_dup_f32(&coeff[0]);

t1=vld1q_dup_f32(&coeff[1]);

t1=t0*x4[i]+t1;

t2=vld1q_dup_f32(&coeff[2]);
```

```
t2=t1*x4[i]+t2;

t3=vld1q_dup_f32(&coeff[3]);

t3=t2*x4[i]+t3;

t4=vld1q_dup_f32(&coeff[4]);

t4=t3*x4[i]+t4;

t5=vld1q_dup_f32(&coeff[5]);

t5=t4*x4[i]+t5;

t6=vld1q_dup_f32(&coeff[6]);

t6=t5*x4[i]+t6;
```

Phase	Iteration 0	Iteration 1	Iteration 2	Iteration 3	Iteration 4	Iteration 5	Iteration 7	Iteration 8	Iteration 9

prolog	t0=coeff[0];
	t1=coeff[1];
	t1=t0*x[i]+t1;								

prolog	t0=coeff[2];
	t0=t1*x[i]+t0;
		t0=coeff[0];
		t1=coeff[1];
		t1=t0*x[i]+t1;							

prolog	t1=coeff[3];
	t1=t0*x[i]+t1;
		t0=coeff[2];
		t0=t1*x[i]+t0;
			t0=coeff[0];
			t1=coeff[1];
			t1=t0*x[i]+t1;						

prolog	t0=coeff[4];
	t0=t1*x[i]+t0;
		t1=coeff[3];
		t1=t0*x[i]+t1;
			t0=coeff[2];
			t0=t1*x[i]+t0;
				t0=coeff[0];
				t1=coeff[1];
				t1=t0*x[i]+t1;					

prolog	t1=coeff[5];
	t1=t0*x[i]+t1;
		t0=coeff[4];
		t0=t1*x[i]+t0;
			t1=coeff[3];
			t1=t0*x[i]+t1;
				t0=coeff[2];
				t0=t1*x[i]+t0;
					t0=coeff[0];
					t1=coeff[1];
					t1=t0*x[i]+t1;				

prolog	t0=coeff[6];
	t0=t1*x[i]+t0;
		t1=coeff[5];
		t1=t0*x[i]+t1;
			t0=coeff[4];
			t0=t1*x[i]+t0;
				t1=coeff[3];
				t1=t0*x[i]+t1;
					t0=coeff[2];
					t0=t1*x[i]+t0;
						t0=coeff[0];
						t1=coeff[1];
						t1=t0*x[i]+t1;			

loop	t1=coeff[7];
	t1=t0*x[i]+t1;
		t0=coeff[6];
		t0=t1*x[i]+t0;
			t1=coeff[5];
			t1=t0*x[i]+t0;
				t0=coeff[4];
				t0=t1*x[i]+t0;
					t1=coeff[3];
					t1=t0*x[i]+t1;
						t0=coeff[2];
						t0=t1*x[i]+t0;
							t0=coeff[0];
							t1=coeff[1];
							t1=t0*x[i]+t1;		

loop		t1=coeff[7];
		t1=t0*x[i]+t1;
			t0=coeff[6];
			t0=t1*x[i]+t0;
				t1=coeff[5];
				t1=t0*x[i]+t0;
					t0=coeff[4];
					t0=t1*x[i]+t0;
						t1=coeff[3];
						t1=t0*x[i]+t1;
							t0=coeff[2];
							t0=t1*x[i]+t0;
								t0=coeff[0];
								t1=coeff[1];
								t1=t0*x[i]+t1;	

loop			t1=coeff[7];
			t1=t0*x[i]+t1;
				t0=coeff[6];
				t0=t1*x[i]+t0;
					t1=coeff[5];
					t1=t0*x[i]+t1;
						t0=coeff[4];
						t0=t1*x[i]+t0;
							t1=coeff[3];
							t1=t0*x[i]+t1;
								t0=coeff[2];
								t0=t1*x[i]+t0;
									t0=coeff[0];
									t1=coeff[1];
									t1=t0*x[i]+t1;

epilog				t1=coeff[7]; t1=t0*x[i]+t1;	t0=coeff[6]; t0=t1*x[i]+t0;	t1=coeff[5]; t1=t0*x[i]+t1;	t0=coeff[4]; t0=t1*x[i]+t0;	t1=coeff[3]; t1=t0*x[i]+t1;	t0=coeff[2]; t0=t1*x[i]+t0;
epilog					t1=coeff[7]; t1=t0*x[i]+t1;	t0=coeff[6]; t0=t1*x[i]+t0;	t1=coeff[5]; t1=t0*x[i]+t1;	t0=coeff[4]; t0=t1*x[i]+t0;	t1=coeff[3]; t1=t0*x[i]+t1;
epilog						t1=coeff[7]; t1=t0*x[i]+t1;	t0=coeff[6]; t0=t1*x[i]+t0;	t1=coeff[5]; t1=t0*x[i]+t1;	t0=coeff[4]; t0=t1*x[i]+t0;
epilog							t1=coeff[7]; t1=t0*x[i]+t1;	t0=coeff[6]; t0=t1*x[i]+t0;	t1=coeff[5]; t1=t0*x[i]+t1;
epilog								t1=coeff[7]; t1=t0*x[i]+t1;	t0=coeff[6]; t0=t1*x[i]+t0;
epilog									t1=coeff[7]; t1=t0*x[i]+t1;

Figure 2.3: Software pipeline of Horner's method.

```
d4[i]=vld1q_dup_f32(&coeff[7]);

d4[i]=t6*x4[i]+d4[i];
```

Before we deploy the software pipelined version of the Horner loop, we must change the OpenMP parallelism, since each core must execute a separate prolog and epilog. For this reason, we must use a **parallel pragma** instead of a **parallel-for pragma**. A consequence of this is that we must explicitly define the workload for each thread. We can use a static workload allocation scheme as opposed to dynamic scheme that would allocate workload to threads during processing. Note that this scheme is susceptible to workload imbalance.

Begin with parallel section and define parameters for the thread, such as the thread ID, the number of iterations for which the thread is responsible (the **workload**), and the starting iteration number. Also declare the needed local private variables to the thread.

```
#pragma omp parallel

    {

        // parameters

        uint32_t t = omp_get_thread_num();

        uint32_t workload = (N/4/4) / omp_get_num_threads();

        uint32_t start = t * workload;

        // locals

        float32x4_t t0,t1,t2,t3,t4,t5,t6,t7;

        float32x4_t *x4 = (float32x4_t *)x;

        float32x4_t *d4 = (float32x4_t *)d_improved2;
```

Begin your code with the prolog, which will contain a partial computation of the first six iterations (0 through 5). We will declare an iteration number variable i and increment it during the prolog to keep track of which iteration is being processed.

```
Uint32_t i=start;

                // prolog

                // iteration 0

                t0=vld1q_dup_f32(&coeff[0]);

                t1=vld1q_dup_f32(&coeff[1]);

                t1=t0*x4[i]+t1;

                t2=vld1q_dup_f32(&coeff[2]);
```

```
t2=t1*x4[i]+t2;

t3=vld1q_dup_f32(&coeff[3]);

t3=t2*x4[i]+t3;

t4=vld1q_dup_f32(&coeff[4]);

t4=t3*x4[i]+t4;

t5=vld1q_dup_f32(&coeff[5]);

t5=t4*x4[i]+t5;

t6=vld1q_dup_f32(&coeff[6]);

t6=t5*x4[i]+t6;

i++;


// iteration 1

t0=vld1q_dup_f32(&coeff[0]);

t1=vld1q_dup_f32(&coeff[1]);

t1=t0*x4[i]+t1;

t2=vld1q_dup_f32(&coeff[2]);

t2=t1*x4[i]+t2;

t3=vld1q_dup_f32(&coeff[3]);

t3=t2*x4[i]+t3;

t4=vld1q_dup_f32(&coeff[4]);

t4=t3*x4[i]+t4;

t5=vld1q_dup_f32(&coeff[5]);

t5=t4*x4[i]+t5;

i++;


// iteration 2

t0=vld1q_dup_f32(&coeff[0]);

t1=vld1q_dup_f32(&coeff[1]);

t1=t0*x4[i]+t1;

t2=vld1q_dup_f32(&coeff[2]);

t2=t1*x4[i]+t2;
```

```
t3=vld1q_dup_f32(&coeff[3]);

t3=t2*x4[i]+t3;

t4=vld1q_dup_f32(&coeff[4]);

t4=t3*x4[i]+t4;

i++;


// iteration 3

t0=vld1q_dup_f32(&coeff[0]);

t1=vld1q_dup_f32(&coeff[1]);

t1=t0*x4[i]+t1;

t2=vld1q_dup_f32(&coeff[2]);

t2=t1*x4[i]+t2;

t3=vld1q_dup_f32(&coeff[3]);

t3=t2*x4[i]+t3;

i++;


// iteration 4

t0=vld1q_dup_f32(&coeff[0]);

t1=vld1q_dup_f32(&coeff[1]);

t1=t0*x4[i]+t1;

t2=vld1q_dup_f32(&coeff[2]);

t2=t1*x4[i]+t2;

i++;


// iteration 5

t0=vld1q_dup_f32(&coeff[0]);

t1=vld1q_dup_f32(&coeff[1]);

t1=t0*x4[i]+t1;

i++;
```

The loop body will perform one step of each iteration in reverse order, so it performs the last step of iteration n, the second-to-last step of iteration $n+1$, etc. The loop will begin with the first iteration but end with iteration n-7.

```
For (i=start;i<(start+workload-6);i++) {

    d4[i]=vld1q_dup_f32(&coeff[7]);

    d4[i]=t6*x4[i]+d4[i];

    t6=vld1q_dup_f32(&coeff[6]);

    t6=t5*x4[i+1]+t6;

    t5=vld1q_dup_f32(&coeff[5]);

    t5=t4*x4[i+2]+t5;

    t4=vld1q_dup_f32(&coeff[4]);

    t4=t3*x4[i+3]+t4;

    t3=vld1q_dup_f32(&coeff[3]);

    t3=t2*x4[i+4]+t3;

    t2=vld1q_dup_f32(&coeff[2]);

    t2=t1*x4[i+5]+t2;

    t0=vld1q_dup_f32(&coeff[0]);

    t1=vld1q_dup_f32(&coeff[1]);

    t1=t0*x4[i+6]+t1;

}
```

The epilog will also contain partial computations of the last six iterations (n-6 to n-1).

```
// epilog

    // iteration n-6

    d4[i]=vld1q_dup_f32(&coeff[7]);

    d4[i]=t6*x4[i]+d4[i];


    // iteration n-5

    t6=vld1q_dup_f32(&coeff[6]);

    t6=t5*x4[i+1]+t6;

    d4[i+1]=vld1q_dup_f32(&coeff[7]);

    d4[i+1]=t6*x4[i+1]+d4[i+1];
```

```
// iteration n-4
t5=vld1q_dup_f32(&coeff[5]);
t5=t4*x4[i+2]+t5;
t6=vld1q_dup_f32(&coeff[6]);
t6=t5*x4[i+2]+t6;
d4[i+2]=vld1q_dup_f32(&coeff[7]);
d4[i+2]=t6*x4[i+2]+d4[i+2];


// iteration n-3
t4=vld1q_dup_f32(&coeff[4]);
t4=t3*x4[i+3]+t4;
t5=vld1q_dup_f32(&coeff[5]);
t5=t4*x4[i+3]+t5;
t6=vld1q_dup_f32(&coeff[6]);
t6=t5*x4[i+3]+t6;
d4[i+3]=vld1q_dup_f32(&coeff[7]);
d4[i+3]=t6*x4[i+3]+d4[i+3];


// iteration n-2
t3=vld1q_dup_f32(&coeff[3]);
t3=t2*x4[i+4]+t3;
t4=vld1q_dup_f32(&coeff[4]);
t4=t3*x4[i+4]+t4;
t5=vld1q_dup_f32(&coeff[5]);
t5=t4*x4[i+4]+t5;
t6=vld1q_dup_f32(&coeff[6]);
t6=t5*x4[i+4]+t6;
d4[i+4]=vld1q_dup_f32(&coeff[7]);
d4[i+4]=t6*x4[i+4]+d4[i+4];
```

```
// iteration n-1
t2=vld1q_dup_f32(&coeff[2]);
t2=t1*x4[i+5]+t2;
t3=vld1q_dup_f32(&coeff[3]);
t3=t2*x4[i+5]+t3;
t4=vld1q_dup_f32(&coeff[4]);
t4=t3*x4[i+5]+t4;
t5=vld1q_dup_f32(&coeff[5]);
t5=t4*x4[i+5]+t5;
t6=vld1q_dup_f32(&coeff[6]);
t6=t5*x4[i+5]+t6;
d4[i+5]=vld1q_dup_f32(&coeff[7]);
d4[i+5]=t6*x4[i+5]+d4[i+5];
}
```

The final performance values are shown in Table 2.1. The software pipelined version of Horner's method on the Cortex A72 requires about half the CPI as compared to the previous version, achieving nearly 5 Gflops/s or nearly 3 flops per cycle.

2.10 ARM11: using inline assembly language

GCC provides an interface that allows the programmer to embed inline assembly language into C/C++ code. Unlike writing an entire function in assembly, inline assembly allows the programmer to write only those components of the code that need to be written in assembly code.

Inline assembly allows the programmer to specify C/C++ variables and pointers as destinations and operands for instructions that normally take registers or register-based addresses. In this case, the compiler substitutes registers for the variables and automatically adds any additional load immediately or loads and stores instructions required to temporarily allocate the needed registers. The programmer may also directly use registers. In this case, the programmer must specify the affected registers in a **clobber list** so the compiler can ensure that the register state is not adversely affected by the inline instructions.

The syntax for inline assembly is shown below:

```
asm [volatile] (code : output operand list : input operand list : clobber list);
```

Table 2.1: Performance of horner code without programmer-supplied optimizations.

	Raspberry Pi 1	Raspberry Pi 3	Raspberry Pi 4
CPU	ARM11	Cortex A53	Cortex A72
Average B/W	233 MB/s	1.61 GB/s	3.35 GB/s
B/W bound	408 Mflops/s	2.81 Glops/s	5.86 Gflops/s
No optimization; single thread			
Observed throughput/ efficiency	12.13 Mflops/s	37.81 Mflops/s	135.2 Mflops/s
Efficiency	2.97%	1.35%	2.31%
Effective memory B/W	6.61 MB/s	20.6 MB/s	73.7 MB/s
CPI	2.78	1.52	0.65
Cache miss rate	23.61%	0.006%	0.05%
Instructions per flop	20.8	20.82	20.54
Maximum optimization (-O3); single thread			
Observed throughput/ efficiency	74.01 Mflops	601 Mflop/s	1.79 Gflops/s
Efficiency	18.1%	21.4%	30.5%
Effective memory B/W	40.33 MB/s	328 MB/s	973 MB/s
CPI	4.73	2.26	1.17
Cache miss rate	38.9%	1.74%	0.89%
Instructions per flop	2.00	0.88	0.86
Maximum optimization (-O3); four threads			
Observed throughput/ efficiency		710 Mflop/s	2.46 Gflops/s
Efficiency		25%	42%
Effective memory B/W		385 MB/s	1.34 GB/s
CPI		2.77	1.26
Cache miss rate		0.39%	0.51%
Instructions per flop		0.61	0.58
Manually unrolled loop (-O3); four threads			
Observed throughput/ efficiency		1.72 Gflops/s	3.19 Gflops/s
Efficiency		61%	54%
Effective memory B/W		938 MB/s	1.74 GB/s
CPI		3.02	2.29
Cache miss rate		1.85%	1.68%
Instructions per flop		0.23	0.25
Software pipelined (-O3); four threads			
Observed throughput/ efficiency		2.21 Gflops/s	4.80 Gflops/s
Efficiency		79%	82%
Effective memory B/W		1.20 GB/s	2.61 GB/s
CPI		1.65	1.18
Cache miss rate		1.22%	0.83%
Instructions per flop		0.33	0.32

If the volatile modifier is included, the compiler will exclude the statement(s) from being subject to compiler optimization. In other words, the compiler will generate the assembly code as written and not modify it for the purpose of optimization.

Code is one or multiple instructions enclosed in quotes. Each instruction should be followed by "\n\t" (newline then tab) to ensure proper formatting when the assembly code is generated from the compiler.

When writing short sequences of inline assembly code, the programmer can choose to enclose each instruction in an asm statement or combine multiple instructions within an asm statement. The advantage of enclosing individual instructions is that the input, output, and clobber lists are associated with only one instruction, making it easier to read. However, the programmer should be cautious when using registers to hold intermediate results between asm statements, since the compiler may generate instructions between asm statements that overwrite registers holding intermediate results. GCC's inline assembly syntax provides no way to specify which registers are used to transfer data between asm statements. As such, whenever a block of inline assembly instructions contains dependencies involving general purpose registers, the programmer should enclose the entire block of instructions within a single asm statement as opposed to using a separate asm statement for each instruction. This is not a concern when using floating-point registers, since GCC is unlikely to reuse these registers between asm statements.

The *output operand list* is a list of any C/C++ variables used as outputs for the assembly code.

The *input operand list* is a list of C/C++ variables that are used as inputs for the assembly code. It uses the same format as the output list.

The format of the input and output lists are

[*name*]"*MC*" (*expression*)[, ...]

- *name* is the name of symbol in the assembly code. The name is preceded by a percent sign (%) in the code.
- *M* is an optional *constraint modifier*, and is usually = for *write only* operand or + for read-write operand.
- *C* is a *constraint*, which is usually one of the following: **f** (floating-point register), **I** (immediate value), **r** (general purpose register), or **m** (memory address). For example, using "f" means that the corresponding operand will be placed by the compiler into a register prior to the instruction being fetched, and its value is specified in the inline assembly using a C/C++ expression.
- *expression* is the C/C++ expression, variable, or pointer representing the input or output.

The *clobber list* is a list of registers that will be modified by the instruction and is used when registers are specified directly.

For example, consider the following inline assembly statement:

```
asm("mov %[outval],%[inval], ror #2" : [outval]"=r"(b) :
   [inval]"r"(a));
```

If *a* and *b* are local variables stored on the stack, this line could be translated by the compiler into the following ARM assembly instructions:

`ldr r3, [sp, #0]` (allocate register r3 and load it with the value of a)

`mov r3, r3, ror #2` (perform the mov instruction, reused register r3 as output)

`str r3, [sp, #4]` (store the result into variable b on the stack)

Since Horner's method performs an equal number of multiply and add instructions, the programmer should use the floating-point multiply-accumulate instruction, since it performs two floating-point operations in a single instruction.

The ARMv6 Vector Floating Point (VFP) instruction set includes instructions for single- and double-precision add, subtract, multiply, multiply-accumulate (and variations), divide, and square root. Most floating-point instructions are fully pipelined, meaning that they can be initiated in consecutive clock cycles, except for divide, square root, and instructions that perform a double precision multiply. The VFP instruction set was replaced with the NEON instruction set in ARMv7, but programs containing scalar VFP instructions will still work on ARMv7 processors. Vector VFP instructions, covered later, are not supported by NEON.

2.11 ARM11: single instruction, multiple data

ARM11 processors do not offer NEON instructions but some, such as the one on the Raspberry Pi 1, provide vector instructions through its Vector Floating Point Unit (VFP) instructions. Unlike NEON instructions that operate on each SIMD element in parallel, vector VFP instructions require the same number of cycles to issue as the equivalent number of scalar instructions. In other words, it requires *n* cycles to issue an *n*-way vector instruction, while it would also take *n* cycles to issue *n* regular one-way instructions. While this may seem that using SIMD instructions is without benefit, these instructions can still deliver performance by providing for less code size and potentially reducing instruction cache misses, and more importantly they can hide the latency required by a dependent chain on SIMD instructions. For example, consider the following loop:

```
for (i=0;i<n;i++) {

    fmacs s0, s1, s2 // assume $s1 is loop-invariant

    fmacs s2, s1, s0 // $s0 depends on the result of

    // the previous instruction

    ...

}
```

The `fmacs` instruction is a fused-multiply accumulate instruction similar to the NEON `fmla` instruction described above.

Assume for the sake of this example that the latency of the `fmacs` instruction is four cycles, it will require five cycles to issue the first two instructions. Assuming it is not possible to move enough of the other instructions from the loop body to cover this latency, we can unroll the loop by a factor of 4 to find more instructions to hide the latency. In this way, instructions from other iterations are "borrowed" to cover the latency:

```
for (i=0;i<n;i+=4) {

   fmacs s0, s1, s2

   fmacs s2, s1, s0

   ...

   fmacs s4, s1, s2

   fmacs s6, s1, s4

   ...

   fmacs s8, s1, s2

   fmacs s10, s1, s8

   ...

   fmacs s12, s1, s2

   fmacs s14, s1, s12

   ...

}
```

This does not solve our problem since the instruction stream will have four cycles of uncovered latency between each pair of instructions. Now interleave the four pairs of instructions as follows:

```
for (i=0;i<n;i+=4) {

    fmacs s0, s1, $s2

    fmacs s4, s1, $s2

    fmacs s8, s1, $s2

    fmacs s12, s1, $s2

    fmacs s2, s1, $s0

    fmacs s6, s1, $s4
```

```
    fmacs s10, s1, $s8
    fmacs s14, s1, $s12

    …

}
```

Now there are three intervening instructions between each pair of dependent instructions. Note that a processor that is capable of dynamic out-of-order execution may have been able to automatically achieve this same reordering but depending on its capabilities, it may not be able to achieve the same performance as when it is done statically.

As a final step, replace the first four and second four instructions with a single SIMD instruction each.

The ARMv6 VFP instruction set offers SIMD instructions through a feature called *short vector instructions*, in which the programmer can specify a vector *width* and *stride* field through the *floating-point status and control register (FPSCR)*. Setting the FPSCR will cause all the thread's subsequently issued floating-point instructions to perform the number of operations and access the registers using a stride as defined in the FPSCR. Note that VFP short vector instructions are not supported by ARMv7 processors. Attempting to change the vector width or stride on a NEON-equipped processor will trigger an invalid instruction exception.

The 32 floating-point VFP registers are arranged in four banks of eight registers each (four registers each if using double precision). Each bank can be used as a short vector when performing short vector instructions. The first bank, registers **s0-s7** (or **d0-d3**), will be used as *scalars* in a short vector instruction when specified as the second input operand. For example, when the vector width is 8, the **fadds s16,s8,s0** instruction will add each element of the vector held in registers s8-15 with the scalar held in s0 and store the result vector in registers s16-s23.

The **fmrx** and **fmxr** instructions allow the programmer to read and write the FPSCR register. The latency of the **fmrx** instruction is two cycles and the latency of the **fmxr** instruction is four cycles. The vector width is stored in FPSCR bits 18:16 and is encoded such that values 0 through 7 specify lengths 1-8.

When writing to the FPSCR register, you must be careful to change only the bits you intend to change and leave the others alone. To do this, you must first read the existing value using the **fmrx** instruction, change bits 18:16, and then write the back using the **fmxr** instruction.

Be sure to change the length back to its default value of 1 after the kernel since the compiler would not do this automatically, and any compiler-generated floating-point code can potentially be adversely affected by the change to the FPSCR.

You can use the following function to change the length field in the FPSCR:

```
void set_fpscr_reg (unsigned char len) {

  uint32_t fpscr;

  asm("fmrx %[val], fpscr\n\t" : [val]"=r"(fpscr));

  len = len - 1;

  fpscr = fpscr & ~(0x7<<16);

  fpscr = fpscr | ((len&0x7)<<16);

  asm("fmxr fpscr, %[val]\n\t" : : [val]"r"(fpscr));

}
```

To use short vector instructions on the Horner code, you can set the maximum vector size of 8 by unrolling the outer loop by 8. To avoid the performance impact of data dependencies, you can fully cover the eight-cycle latency of the fmacs instructions by executing one instruction to multiply one coefficient for each group of 8 loop iterations.

In other words, unroll the outer loop to calculate eight polynomial values on each iteration and use short vector instructions of length 8 for each instruction. Since the fmacs instruction adds the value in its **Fd** register, the code requires the ability to load copies of each coefficient into each of the four **Fd** registers. To make this easier, re-write your coefficient array so each coefficient is replicated eight times:

```
float coeff[64] = {1.2,1.2,1.2,1.2,1.2,1.2,1.2,1.2,

1.4,1.4,1.4,1.4,1.4,1.4,1.4,1.4,…

2.6,2.6,2.6,2.6,2.6,2.6,2.6,2.6};
```

Change the short vector length to 8 and unroll the outer loop by 8, so change the iteration step in the outer loop to 4:

```
set_fpscr_reg (8);

for (i=0;i<N/4;i+=8) {
```

Now load the first coefficient into a scalar register and eight values of the **x** array into vector register **s15:s8**:

```
asm("flds s0, %[mem]\n\t" : : [mem]"m" (coeff[0]) : "s0");

asm("fldmias%[mem],{s8,s9,s10,s11,s12,s13,s14,s15}\n\t"::

[mem]"r"(&x[i]) : "s8", "s9", "s10", "s11", "s12", "s13", "s14", "s15");
```

Next load eight copies of the second coefficient into vector register **s23:s16** and perform our first `fmacs` by multiplying the **x** vector by the first coefficient and adding the result to the second coefficient, leaving the running sum in vector register **s23:s16**:

```
asm("fldmias %[mem],{s16,s17,s18,s19,s20,s21,s22,s23}\n\t": :

[mem]"r"(&coeff[8]) :

"s16", "s17", "s18", "s19", "s20", "s21", "s22", "s23");

asm("fmacs s16, s8, s0\n\t" : : :

"s16", "s17", "s18", "s19", "s20", "s21", "s22", "s23");
```

Now repeat this process but now swapping the vector registers s23:s16 with s31:s24:

```
asm("fldmias %[mem],{s24,s25,s26,s27,s28,s29,s30,s31}\n\t": :

[mem]"r"(&coeff[16]) :

"s24", "s25", "s26", "s27", "s28", "s29", "s30", "s31");

asm("fmacs s24, s8, s16\n\t" : : :

"s20", "s17", "s18", "s19", "s28", "s29", "s30", "s31");
```

Now repeat these last two steps two more times. End with the following code:

```
asm("fldmias %[mem],{s16,s17,s18,s19,s20,s21,s22,s23}\n\t": :

[mem]"r"(&coeff[56]) :

"s16", "s17", "s18", "s19", "s20", "s21", "s22", "s23");

asm("fmacs s16, s8, s24\n\t" : : :

"s16", "s17", "s18", "s19", "s20", "s21", "s22", "s23");

asm("fstmias %[mem],{s16,s17,s18,s19,s20,s21,s22,s23}\n\t" : :

[mem]"r" (&d[i]));
```

Be sure to reset the short vector length to 1 after the outer loop:

```
set_fpscr_reg (1);
```

Table 2.2 shows the resulting performance improvement on the Raspberry Pi 1 relative to a software pipelined implementation. The use of scheduled SIMD instructions provides a 37% performance improvement over software pipelining. This optimization increases CPI because each eight-way SIMD instruction requires eight cycles to issue but comes with a larger relative decrease in instructions per flop (the product of CPI slowdown and instructions per flop speedup gives a total speedup of 1.36).

Table 2.2: Performance improvement from short vector instructions versus software pipelining

Platform	Raspberry Pi 1
CPU	ARM11
Throughput/efficiency	1.37 speedup
	55.2% efficiency
CPI	0.43 speedup (slowdown)
Cache miss rate	1.89 speedup
Instructions per flop	3.17 speedup

Another benefit of this optimization is the reduction in cache miss rate due to the SIMD load and store instructions.

2.12 Chapter wrap-up

This chapter described programming techniques for optimizing code to increase kernel performance. The first optimization is the usage of OpenMP to take advantage of multiple cores. OpenMP is not specific to embedded systems or ARM processors but is nevertheless necessary for writing high-performance code on multicore embedded CPUs. The second optimization is the usage of vector datatypes to manually vectorize a loop for ensuring the use of SIMD instructions. The third optimization is software pipelining, which reduces the stall rate by transforming dependencies within the loop body into loop-carried dependencies. This increases the distance between dependent instructions, reducing the number of stalls and increasing CPI. This optimization is effective even for the Cortex-A15 that supports dynamic instruction scheduling. This chapter covered SIMD instructions on both ARM11 and ARM Cortex processors.

The examples in this chapter used code instrumentation with performance counters to evaluate each optimization using several metrics: instructions per flop, CPI, effective memory bandwidth, and floating-point throughout.

Each optimization technique is applied to a simple benchmark kernel that uses Horner's method to compute a polynomial over a 1D array. This kernel performs seven multiply-accumulates for every input and output word and is memory bandwidth bound. The next chapter covers new kernels for image transformation and new methodologies for tuning them.

Exercises

1. Consider the bit reverse example from Section 2.1. It may be possible to change the high-level code to improve performance without using hand-written assembly. Specifically, is it possible to reduce the number of instructions in the loop body by using a different termination condition for the loop? Why or why not?

2. Write a version of the Horner kernel that combines NEON instructions and software pipelining. Test it on an ARM-based development board and evaluate its efficiency with respect to its peak memory bandwidth.

3. Consider the following integer loop that calculates the derivative of an integer array:

4. Consider the problem of multiplying two single-precision matrices, A and B:

5. Matrix multiply is generally compute bound, since it performs $O(n^3)$ operations but only requires $O(n^2)$ data. Despite this, on modern processors, it still only achieves approximately 2/3 of the processor's peak floating-point performance. Achieving high performance for matrix multiply involves optimizing its mapping to the processor's hardware as well as optimizing the memory access pattern. In this exercise, we will evaluate methods for parallelizing it using OpenMP.

6. In the code above, any of the three loops could be parallelized with a "#pragma omp parallel for". Alternatively, in OpenMP 3.0, all three can be simultaneously parallelized by adding a "#pragma omp parallel for collapse(3)" in front of the outermost loop.

7. Try all four of these approaches when using A and B matrix sizes of 256 × 256, 512 × 512, and 1024 × 1024. Evaluate each in terms of floating-point operations per second.

8. For the Horner kernel, increase the number of coefficients to 16 and 32. What is the effect of this on the speedup of the SIMD approach as compared to the baseline implementation?

9. The OpenMP parallel for directive supports dynamic scheduling of loop iterations to threads. This approach also allows the "chunk size", or the number of iterations assigned at a time to each thread, to be specified by the programmer. Measure the performance of the baseline implementation of the Horner loop with dynamic scheduling and a chunk size of 8, 32, 64, and 128. What is the performance as compared to the static approach?

CHAPTER 3

Arithmetic optimization and the Linux framebuffer

The previous chapter examined a sample kernel that performed polynomial evaluation using Horner's method and applied several optimization techniques to improve its performance. These techniques provided a speedup over the compiler-generated code for each of the processors on which the code was evaluated.

This chapter will examine the effect of new optimization techniques on two new benchmark kernels. Each of these kernels can generate graphics using either the Linux framebuffer or using OpenCV, a third-party computer vision library that includes an interface to conveniently display graphics.

Graphical kernels are a common target for performance optimization because they operate on two-dimensional (2D) data and generally exhibit a computational and data complexity of at least $O(n^2)$. Additionally, video applications have real-time constraints, as the execution time for each frame cannot exceed one frame time. For example, a 30-frame-per-second (fps) video allows only 33 ms of execution time per frame, or 16 ns per pixel on average for high-definition (HD) resolution (1920 × 1080) frames. A processor with a 2 GHz clock, the processor must process each pixel within 29 clock cycles on average.

3.1 Graphics output libraries

This chapter examines two case study applications: interpolated affine image transformation and fractal rendering. These applications require the ability to "paint" pixels on an attached monitor. There are numerous Linux C/C++ libraries that facilitate graphics programming. Most of these are built on top of the X Windows environment. Examples of these include XLib, GTK, SDL, Motif, and Qt. These libraries, as well as the X Windows environment itself, provide advanced capabilities for building rich graphical and multimedia user interfaces and have facilities for creating basic user interface elements (sometimes called "widgets") as well as video and sound.

The chapter instead uses two methods for graphics display, the *Linux framebuffer*, which allows a program to write directly to the region of memory used to store the image currently being displayed on the monitor, and *OpenCV*, which is an easy-to-use computer vision library that requires the availability of an X Windows server.

The Linux framebuffer has minimal overhead but requires a monitor to be physically attached to the platform executing the code, i.e., a Raspberry Pi. Using an X Windows allows a user to view the graphical output when being connected remotely to the platform executing the code, such as a Linux, MacOS, or Windows desktop machine.

3.1.1 The Linux framebuffer

The framebuffer is represented by the device file `/dev/fb0` (or sometimes `/dev/fb1`) and can only be opened in write mode by the superuser (root account). Instead of `read()` and `write()` functions, the framebuffer is accessed using the system calls `ioctl()` and `mmap()`.

By default, the framebuffer will adopt the native resolution of the attached monitor, although both the resolution and the number of color bits per pixel can be changed using the Linux `fbset` command or using an `ioctl()` calls to the framebuffer device file.

The `ioctl()` system call accesses parameters for device files. The parameter set depends on each specific device. In the case of the framebuffer, it is used to get and set parameters such as resolution, bits per pixel, row length, and offsets. To illustrate this, open the framebuffer in read-write mode using the `open()` system call:

```
int fd;

fd = open("/dev/fb0", O_RDWR);

if (fd == -1) {

        perror("Error: cannot open framebuffer device");

        exit(0);

}
```

Notice that `open()` opens the file as opposed to `fopen()`. The difference is that `open()` returns an integer *file descriptor* while `fopen()` returns a pointer to a `FILE` data structure.

Next, call `ioctl()` once to retrieve information from the framebuffer:

```
struct fb_var_screeninfo vinfo;

if (ioctl(fd, FBIOGET_VSCREENINFO, &vinfo) == -1) {

        perror("Error reading variable information");

        exit(-1);

}
```

This will report the *x-resolution* (number of columns), *y-resolution* (number of rows), and the number of *bits per pixel*, which can be used to calculate the size of the screen in bytes and the size of each row:

```
screensize = vinfo.xres * vinfo.yres * vinfo.bits_per_pixel / 8;

row_size = vinfo.xres * vinfo.bits_per_pixel / 8;
```

Now map the framebuffer itself to a block of virtual memory within our program's process:

```
char *fbp;

fbp = (char *)mmap(0, screensize, PROT_READ | PROT_WRITE,

        MAP_SHARED, fd, 0);

if ((int)fbp == -1) err("Error: failed to map framebuffer \
            device to memory");
```

The program can now paint pixels by writing data to the region of memory pointed to by the *fbp* pointer. The code that draws pixels depends on the pixel size. For example, for 16-bit pixels (in which the most significant 5 bits are red intensity, the least significant 5 bits are blue intensity, and the middle 6 bits are green intensity):

```
*((unsigned short *)(fbp + i*(row_size) + j*2)) =
            (red << 11) | (green << 5) | blue;
```

The Linux framebuffer is a *zero-copy framebuffer*, meaning that a single write from the program updates the pixel on the monitor. As such, estimate the upper bound for our fps using the write memory bandwidth experiment from Chapter 1.

For example, the Raspberry Pi has a write bandwidth of 325 MB/s, and a $1920 \times 1080 \times 16$ frame is comprised of 4,147,200 bytes, so the program can achieve $1/(4{,}147{,}200/(325*2^{20})) = 82$ frames per second.

Once you are finished with the framebuffer you should unmap the memory and close the file:

```
munmap(fbp, screensize);

close(fd);
```

3.1.2 Using OpenCV to draw pixels

The Linux framebuffer works only on a physically connected monitor. However, single-board computers such as the Raspberry Pi are often used in **headless mode**: without a keyboard, mouse, and monitor. In this case, the user connects remotely using secure shell (SSH) and uses a local X Windows server to allow graphical output to be transmitted from the Raspberry Pi and displayed on the user's workstation.

Displaying graphics from a remote source is limited in its performance, as compared to displaying graphics directly to an attached monitor, but for the purposes of the applications described in this text, remote display is sufficient.

As mentioned earlier, there are a variety of libraries that can take advantage of the X Windows system's ability to display graphics over a network connection, including XLib, GTK, SDL, Motif, and Qt. In this section, we will describe what is perhaps the simplest way to display simple graphics in C/C++ code without the need to support graphical user interfaces: OpenCV.

OpenCV can be installed with the following command:

```
sudo apt-get install libopencv-dev
```

After this, you can deploy a framebuffer-like environment. First, include the relevant OpenCV header files:

```
#include <opencv2/opencv.hpp>

#include <opencv2/imgcodecs.hpp>

#include <opencv2/highgui.hpp>
```

Add the OpenCV namespace (note that OpenCV requires the use of C++):

```
using namespace cv;
```

Then, in a function, declare an object of type "Mat" whose height and width are set to the desired window size comprised of four-channel RGBA (red, green, blue, alpha/transparency) elements and initialized to zero:

```
Mat fb = Mat::zeros(480,640,CV_8UC4);
```

You can use the `.at()` method on the `Mat` class to write to specific pixel locations. Afterward, you can use the `imshow()` function to display the image on the screen. For the image to be updated, you must call `waitKey(1)` after `imshow()`, which causes a 1 ms wait to update the image.

The following example code will paint random pixels to the window:

```
while (1) {

    fb.at<uint32_t>(rand()%480,rand()%640)=rand();

    imshow("framebuffer",fb);

    waitKey(1);

}
```

3.2 Affine image transformations

Anyone who has played a video game or used image editing software is familiar with the idea of image transformations. An image transformation describes an operation that changes or distorts an image. A linear image transformation can be used to do things such as rotate, scale, shear, reflect, or project an image.

Assume that the location of pixel, represented as a row and column value, is stored as a two-element column vector **c**. A linear image transformation can be described as a 2×2 matrix *A* and can be applied to this pixel by multiplication:

$$c' = A \times c$$

c' is a column vector that represents the position of the pixel in the transformed image.

In an *affine transformation*, the matrix A is extended to become a 3×3 matrix and there is an additional element added to the pixel location vector c, although only the first two elements need to be used as the (x, y) pixel coordinate.

For example, the following three affine transformation matrices allow an image to be rotated clockwise by angle θ about the X, Y, and Z dimensions:

$$A_x = \begin{bmatrix} 1 & 0 & 0 \\ 0 & \cos\theta & -\sin\theta \\ 0 & \sin\theta & -\cos\theta \end{bmatrix}$$

$$A_y = \begin{bmatrix} \cos\theta & 0 & \sin\theta \\ 0 & 1 & 0 \\ -\sin\theta & 0 & \cos\theta \end{bmatrix}$$

$$A_z = \begin{bmatrix} \cos\theta & \sin\theta & 0 \\ -\sin\theta & \cos\theta & 0 \\ 0 & 0 & 1 \end{bmatrix}$$

The effect of affine transformations can be combined by multiplying multiple transformation matrices. For example, the program can rotate an image about the X, Y, and Z axes simultaneously by multiplying the three rotation matrices together, that is, $A_{xyz} = A_x \times A_y \times A_z$.

To transform an entire image, the code can iterate over all the pixels in the source image, calculate their new positions in the transformed image, and copy the pixel to its new location, but there is a problem with this approach. The transformed pixel locations will contain fractional values, making it unclear how to copy the pixels to their new positions in the transformed image. In other words, this method will generate a sequence of integral pixel locations for the **source** destination image and fractional pixel locations for the **destination (transformed)** image.

Alternatively, the program can iterate over all the pixel locations in the destination image and calculate the inverse transformation to determine each pixel's corresponding location in the source image, using the inverse transformations below. This will generate integral pixel locations for the destination image and fractional pixel locations for the source image. The program can use **interpolation** to calculate the estimated value of fractional source image pixel locations.

$$A'_x = \begin{bmatrix} 1 & 0 & 0 \\ 0 & 1/\cos\theta & \tan\theta \\ 0 & \tan\theta & -1/\cos\theta \end{bmatrix}$$

$$A'_y = \begin{bmatrix} 1/\cos\theta & 0 & -tan\theta \\ 0 & 1 & 0 \\ tan\theta & 0 & 1/\cos\theta \end{bmatrix}$$

$$A'_z = \begin{bmatrix} \cos\theta & -\sin\theta & 0 \\ \sin\theta & \cos\theta & 0 \\ 0 & 0 & 1 \end{bmatrix}$$

3.3 Bilinear interpolation

When performing the inverse transformation, many of the pixels in the transformed image will correspond to fractional locations in the source image. Since our source image is discretely "sampled" at integral pixel positions, the program must use a technique for calculating the pixel colors of locations between pixels. There are various methods for performing this type of *interpolation*. We will describe a simple method, *bilinear interpolation*.

When an inverse transformation maps one of the destination image pixels to fractional source pixel, the program must estimate the color of the resulting pixel location that exists between two rows and between two columns based on the pixels around it. In other words, this fractional coordinate is positioned somewhere inside of 2×2 pixel block. The interpolated pixel can be calculated using a weighted average of these four pixels, where the weights of each of the four pixels are calculated as a function of the fractional portion of the location in both dimensions.

Figure 3.1 depicts this situation, assuming the inverse transformation gives us pixel (i,j) and $i_{\text{int}} = i$, $i_{\text{frac}} = i - i$ and $j_{\text{int}} = j$, $j_{\text{frac}} = j - j$.

The weights would be calculated as:

$$\text{weight}\left(i_{\text{int}}, j_{\text{int}}\right) = \left(1 - i_{\text{frac}}\right) \cdot \left(1 - j_{\text{frac}}\right)$$
$$\text{weight}\left(i_{\text{int}}, j_{\text{int}} + 1\right) = \left(1 - i_{\text{frac}}\right) \cdot j_{\text{frac}}$$
$$\text{weight}\left(i_{\text{int}} + 1, j_{\text{int}}\right) = i_{\text{frac}} \cdot \left(1 - j_{\text{frac}}\right)$$
$$\text{weight}\left(i_{\text{int}} + 1, j_{\text{int}} + 1\right) = i_{\text{frac}} \cdot j_{\text{frac}}$$

3.4 Floating-point image transformation

The image transformation and interpolation calculations must be performed using fractional values, and floating point may seem like an obvious choice. One problem with using floating point is that each transformed pixel will begin and end with an associated pixel location and color value, both of which are integers. This will require typecasting between integers

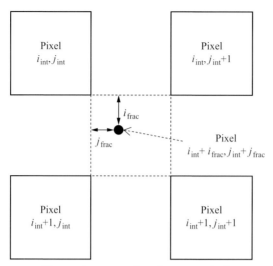

Figure 3.1: Fractional source pixel.

and floats for the intermediate calculations. Typecasting between integers and floating point requires the use of high-latency conversion instructions. We can measure the overhead added by these operations using the performance counters.

Our objective is to generate a video consisting of a sequence of frames depicting the image smoothly rotating around all three axes. Graphically, this will appear as a 2D image rotating in 3D space. To do this, gradually change the *X, Y,* and *Z* rotation of the image in each frame. For this the program needs to call a function before each frame that computes the transformation matrix for a given *X, Y,* and *Z* rotation angles. Since this function is called once per frame (as opposed to once per pixel), it is reasonable to expect it to have a negligible effect on performance.

The following function will calculate the transformation matrix as a function of *X, Y,* and *Z* angles and returns the first two rows and first two columns of the transformation matrix as arrays *c_row* and *c_col*:

```
void calc_coeffs(float c_row[2],
                 float c_col[2],
                 float scale,
                 float rot_x,
                 float rot_y,
                 float rot_z) {
    int i,j,k;
    float rotm_x[3][3]={{1.0f, 0, 0},
```

```
                    {0, 1.0f/cosf(rot_x),tanf(rot_x)},

                    {0, tanf(rot_x), -1.0f/cosf(rot_x)}},

        rotm_y[3][3]={{1.0/cosf(rot_y), 0, -tanf(rot_y)},

                    {0, 1.0f, 0},

                    {tan(rot_y), 0, 1.0f/cosf(rot_y)}},

        rotm_z[3][3]={{cosf(rot_z), -sin(rot_z), 0},

                    {sinf(rot_z), cosf(rot_z), 0},

                    {0, 0, 1.0f}},

        tempm0[3][3],tempm1[3][3],tempm2[3][3],sum;

    for (i=0;i<3;i++)                                          // (temp = A_x x A_y)

        for (j=0;j<3;j++) {

        sum=0.0;

        for (k=0;k<3;k++) sum += rotm_x[i][k] * rotm_y[k][j];

        tempm0[i][j] = sum;

        }

    for (i=0;i<3;i++)                                          // (temp = temp x A_z)

        for (j=0;j<3;j++) {

        sum=0.0;

        for (k=0;k<3;k++)sum += tempm0[i][k] * rotm_z[k][j];

        tempm1[i][j] = sum;

        }

    c_row[0] = tempm1[0][0];

    c_row[1] = tempm1[0][1];

    c_col[0] = tempm1[1][0];

    c_col[1] = tempm1[1][1];

    }
```

3.4.1 Loading the image

In this chapter we will examine the effects of optimizing image transformations, but we must first load a sample image into memory. In this section we will cover two approaches for loading an image: (1) using the OpenCV image codec library and (2) using native C/C++ code for loading PPM-formatted image.

3.4.1.1 Loading an image with OpenCV

OpenCV contains image codecs for most common image formats. The `imread(<filename>)` function loads an image and returns the raw image data in an OpenCV `Mat` object.

For example, the following code will load an image and display it.

```
Mat img = imread("image_name.jpg");

imshow("image",img);

waitKey(); // wait for the user to press a key
```

Once an image is loaded into a `Mat` object named `img`, the raw pixels can be accessed in row-major order using the `img.data` member. In row-major order, each row is stored in consecutive memory addresses in order from the top row.

The number of rows, columns, pixel size in bytes, and number of color channels can be retrieved from `img.rows`, `img.cols`, `img.elemSize()`, and `img.channels()`, respectively. `img.type()` will return the element type as an enumerated type whose format is

```
CV_<bits><[USF]>C<channels>
```

where `<bits>` is the number of bits per pixel channel;`U` is for unsigned, `S` for signed, and `F` for float; and `channels` is the number of channels. For example, `CV_8UC3` is for unsigned 8-bit with three channels.

Likewise, `img.depth()` returns the depth of a matrix element as an enumerated type that follows the same convention as above but without the `C<channels>` suffix. As an example, `img.depth()` may return `CV_8U`.

Alternatively, a `Mat` object can be created with an existing C/C++ array, assuming it is stored in row-major order, using the following code:

```
CMat img(rows,cols,CV_8UC3,buffer);
```

where `rows` and `cols` are set to the desired image size, `CV_8UC3` defines the element (pixel) type to be 8-bit unsigned 3-channel (24-bit red, green, and blue [RGB] pixels), and the buffer points to an existing image buffer stored in row-major order.

You can load a source image, specify its size for the transformation cod, and create a buffer pointer using the code below:

```
Mat img = imread("image_attachment.jpg");

int rows = img.rows;

int cols = img.cols;

unsigned char *src_image = img.data;
```

You can create a destination image and buffer pointer using the code below:

```
Mat img2 = Mat::zeros(rows,cols,CV_8UC3);

unsigned char *dst_image = img2.data;
```

3.4.1.2 Loading a PPM image with native C/C++

In cases where OpenCV codec support is not available, an existing image can be converted into an uncompressed file format that can trivially be read in raw form using a native `read()` call. One such format is PPM, and it is supported by most common image editors.

A PPM contains both ASCII text and binary data. A header comprised of ASCII text appears at the beginning of the file. The header is followed by binary data representing each row of the image in row-major row. Each row is comprised of pixels ordered in ascending column order (left to right). Each pixel is usually stored as three consecutive bytes corresponding to the RGB color channels.

The PPM header consists of the following four values in ASCII separated by whitespace (spaces, tabs, newlines, line feeds):

1. the format's "magic number" P6,
2. the number of columns,
3. the number of rows, and
4. the maximum color value (usually 255).

PPM files may also contain comment lines that begin with #.

To read a PPM file and convert it into a 16-bit format in memory, begin with the following declarations:

```
FILE *myFile;                                     // file pointer

int rows=0, cols=0, maxcolorvalue=0;              // header information

int i,j;                                          // loop vars

static unsigned short *src_image;                 // pointer to image in memory
```

Next, open the file and read the header information. The tool that converted the image to a PPM file may have inserted one or more lines of comments before the header. To skip these, repeatedly execute the `fscanf()` function to search for integers, looking for the first integer that is large enough to represent each value in the header:

```
myFile = fopen("lena.ppm","r+");                  // open the file

if (!myFile) {perror("image file");exit(0);}      // check for error

for (int field=0;field<3;field++) {
```

```
        int buffer = field == 0 ? &cols :
            field == 1 : &rows :
            &maxcolorvalue;
        fscanf (myFile,"%d",buffer);                          // try to read value
    while (*buffer<160) {                              // search file for legitimate value
            fseek(myFile,1,SEEK_CUR);                        // advance file one byte
            fscanf (myFile,"%d",buffer);                          // try again
        }
    }
```

In a PPM file, each pixel is stored as three bytes representing RGB intensity. Use this same 24-bit format to store the image in memory.

Now that the program has the row and column count it can allocate *rows* × *columns* × 3 bytes. *src_image* is declared as an unsigned character pointer (unsigned char *).

```
    src_image=(unsigned char *)malloc(rows*cols*3);           // allocate memory for image
    if (!src_image) {                                       // check return value of malloc
        perror("Allocating memory for source image");
        exit(0);
    }
```

Advance the file pointer by one byte to move beyond the newline character after the header. Then read the contents of the image directly into the image array.

```
    fseek(myFile,1,SEEK_CUR);                              (advance file pointer by one byte)
    fread(src_image,1,rows*cols*3,myFile);                      (read image contents)
```

3.4.2 Rendering frames

Initialize the X, Y, and Z angles to 0. Inside of an infinite while-loop, increment each by 1, 0.5, and 0.25 degrees per frame, respectively (0.0175, 0.0087, and 0.0044 rad), and calculate the corresponding transformation matrix.

```
    float rot_x=0,rot_y=0,rot_z=0,scale=1.0f;
    float c_row[2],c_col[2];
    while (1) {
```

```
rot_x += 0.0175f; // 1 degree per frame

rot_y += 0.0087f; // 0.5 degree per frame

rot_z += 0.0044f; // 0.25 degree per frame

calc_coeffs(c_row, c_col, scale, rot_x, rot_y, rot_z);
```

The transformation will rotate the image relative to the origin point row 0 column 0, which is the *upper left* pixel. To perform the transformation around the center point of the image, one must change the location of each pixel before applying the transformation. To do this, subtract one-half the image width from the column value and one-half the image depth from the row value before applying the transformation, and read these values after the transformation (note that the compiler will convert the divide-by-2 operations with a shift right by 1 bit). For each destination pixel at row i and column j, calculate the source image pixel location *src_pixel*.

In this case, *src_pixel* is declared as a two-element array of type float. The program must also have an integer version of these indices, since it needs them to index the image array. This array is named *src_pixel_int* in the code below.

```
// source pixel coordinates from reverse transform
float src_pixel[2];
// source pixel coordinates from reverse transform (truncated)
int src_pixel_int[4];
float frac[2],weights[4]; // interpolation weights
int r[4],g[4],b[4]; // source color channels
int red,green,blue; // calculated color channels
for (int i=0;i<rows;i++)
  for (int j=0;j<cols;j++) {

    src_pixel[0] = c_row[0] * (float)(i-(rows/2)) +
      c_row[1] * (float)(j-(cols/2));
    src_pixel[1] = c_col[0] * (float)(i-(rows/2)) +
      c_col[1] * (float)(j-(cols/2));
    src_pixel_int[0] = (int)floorf(src_pixel[0]) + (rows/2);
    src_pixel_int[1] = (int)floorf(src_pixel[1]) + (cols/2);
```

Check if the calculated source pixel, along with its neighbors to the right, below, and diagonally right and down, falls within the boundary of the source image. If so, calculate the distance of the fractional source pixel to its neighbors in a 2-element float array named *frac*, calculate the interpolation weights in a 4-element float array named *weights*, and load the 4 neighbor source pixels into integer variables.

Depending on the rotation angles, some frames will have more source pixels outside the image area than others. As a result, this if-statement will cause some frames to render faster than others.

```
// set default color to black for pixels whose corresponding
// source pixels are outside the boundary of the image
red=0; green=0; blue=0;
if ((src_pixel_int[0] >= 0) &&
    (src_pixel_int[0] < (rows-1)) &&
    (src_pixel_int[1] >= 0) &&
    (src_pixel_int[1] < (cols-1))) { // calculate
                                        fraction
                                        (row)
    frac[0] = src_pixel[0] - floorf(src_pixel[0]); // calculate
                                                      fraction
                                                      (column)
    frac[1] = src_pixel[1] - floorf(src_pixel[1]); // (calculate
                                                      interpolation weights)
    weights[0] = (1.0f-frac[0]) * (1.0f-frac[1]);
    weights[1] = (1.0f-frac[0]) * (frac[1]);
    weights[2] = (frac[0]) * (1.0-frac[1]);
    weights[3] = (frac[0]) * (frac[1]);
```

In order to calculate each transformed pixel the program must have access to each of the three-color channels from each of the four pixels surrounding each of the source pixels identified with the transformation.

Figure 3.2 shows an image of size *rows* rows and *cols* columns where each pixel is 24 bits. Each row of the image (the *x*-dimension) is stored consecutively. To access a pixel, calculate its offset relative to the beginning of the *src_pixel* array but remember that each pixel is comprised of three bytes. For example, the pixel at location (*x,y*) is stored at pixel location

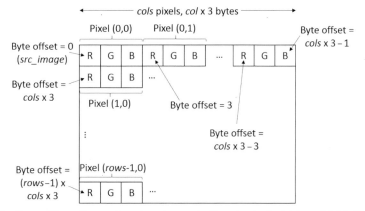

Figure 3.2: Byte offsets for each color channel of each pixel within a 24-bit RGB frame.

$(y \times cols + x)$ since getting to row y requires that the program skip down y rows each of size *cols*, but this value must be multiplied by 3 to reach the byte offset. This gives us:

$$(y \times cols + x) \times 3 \text{ for the red channel}$$

$$(y \times cols + x) \times 3 + 1 \text{ for the green channel}$$

$$(y \times cols + x) \times 3 + 2 \text{ for the blue channel}$$

Declare three 4-element integer arrays for each color channel, that is, int r[4], g[4], b[4]. The three-color channels from each of the four pixels around the source pixel can be extracted using the following code:

```
r[0] = src_image[(src_pixel_int[0]*cols+src_pixel_int[1])*3];

g[0] = src_image[(src_pixel_int[0]*cols+src_pixel_int[1])*3+1];

b[0] = src_image[(src_pixel_int[0]*cols+src_pixel_int[1])*3+2];

r[1] = src_image[(src_pixel_int[0]*cols+src_pixel_int[1]+1)*3];

g[1] = src_image[(src_pixel_int[0]*cols+src_pixel_int[1]+1)*3+1];

b[1] = src_image[(src_pixel_int[0]*cols+src_pixel_int[1]+1)*3+2];

r[2] = src_image[((src_pixel_int[0]+1)*cols+src_pixel_int[1])*3];

g[2] = src_image[((src_pixel_int[0]+1)*cols+
          src_pixel_int[1])*3+1];

b[2] = src_image[((src_pixel_int[0]+1)*cols+
          src_pixel_int[1])*3+2];
```

```
  r[3] = src_image[((src_pixel_int[0]+1)*cols+
          src_pixel_int[1]+1)*3];

  g[3] = src_image[((src_pixel_int[0]+1)*cols+
          src_pixel_int[1]+1)*3+1];

  b[3] = src_image[((src_pixel_int[0]+1)*cols+
          src_pixel_int[1]+1)*3+2];
```

With the four pixels the program can calculate the interpolated value.

```
  red = (int)((float)(r[0]) * (weights[0]) +
            (float)(r[1]) * (weights[1]) +
            (float)(r[2]) * (weights[2]) +
            (float)(r[3]) * (weights[3]));
  green = (int)((float)(g[0]) * (weights[0]) +
              (float)(g[1]) * (weights[1]) +
              (float)(g[2]) * (weights[2]) +
              (float)(g[3]) * (weights[3]));
  blue = (int)((float)(b[0]) * (weights[0]) +
              (float)(b[1]) * (weights[1]) +
              (float)(b[2]) * (weights[2]) +
              (float)(b[3]) * (weights[3]));
}
```

3.4.2.1 Rendering frames in OpenCV

When using OpenCV to display the output image, you can maintain two representations of the output image, the CMat object named "img2" and a pointer to its buffer named "dst_image". The code will write output pixels directly into the buffer pointed to by dst_image outside of the if-statement that checks the bounds of src_pixel_int, as shown below:

```
dst_image[(i*cols+j)*3+0] = red;

dst_image[(i*cols+j)*3+1] = green;

dst_image[(i*cols+j)*3+2] = blue;
```

After the for-loop nest that iterates over all destination pixels, the code will call imshow("img2",img2); followed by waitKey(1); to display the next frame.

3.4.2.2 Rendering frames on framebuffer

The framebuffer is physically organized in row-major order but it will likely be larger than our image. Additionally, the pixels may not consist of 24 bits. To check, you can use the "fbset" tool at the command line, which will show an output similar to the following:

```
mode "1920x1200"
  geometry 1920 1200 1920 1200 16
  timings 0 0 0 0 0 0 0
  rgba 5/11,6/5,5/0,0/16
endmode
```

The last value on the second line of output indicates the color depth. In our case it is 16 bits. The fourth line displays the format of each pixel, in which the red value is 5 bits starting at bit offset 11 (spanning bits 15 down to 11), the green value is 6 bits starting at bit offset 5 (spanning bits 10 down to 5), the blue value is 5 bits starting at bit offset 0 (spanning bits 4 down to 0), and the alpha (transparency) value is 0 bits (not used). If your framebuffer uses 24- or 32-bit color you can change it to 16 bits using the fbset command with superuser credentials (see the main page for details).

To paint the interpolated pixel value to the framebuffer, calculate the pixel offset in the framebuffer while simultaneously converting the 24-bit pixel to a 16-bit pixel. Each 8-bit color channel can be converted into a 5- or 6-bit value by shifting to the right. The resulting value must be shifted to the left according to the bit offsets defined by the framebuffer:

```
*((unsigned short *)(fbp + i*row_size + j*2)) =
    (red >> 3 << 11) | (green >> 2 << 5) | (blue >> 3);
```

3.5 Analysis of floating-point performance

Graphical rendering applications are often concerned with maximizing the number of frames (or pixels) per second. This metric is affected by the number of executed instructions per pixel, average cycles per instruction (CPI), the number of floating point operations per second (flops), and the cache miss rate.

To measure each of these metrics you can use the performance monitoring code from Chapter 1 and customize the cnts_dump() function. Note that using perf_event requires that the code be executed with the root user, which may cause problems generating graphics with OpenCV. To solve this, enter the following commands to grant the root user access to send graphical data to your X Windows server:

```
sudo touch ~/.Xauthority
sudo xauth add $(xauth -f ~jbakos/.Xauthority list | tail -1)
```

With respect to floating-point operations, each pixel requires 35 flops:

- · 4 floating point multiplies and 2 floating point adds when transforming each pixel,
- 2 floating point subtracts and 2 floating point floor operations when calculating the fractions,
- 4 floating point multiplies when calculating the weights, and
- 12 floating point multiplies and 9 floating point adds when interpolating each color channel.

When compiled with maximum compiler optimization and executed on the Raspberry Pi 1, the slowest frame achieves roughly:

- 1.3 million pixels per second,
- 5 fps,
- 225 instructions per pixel,
- 50 Mflops/s, and
- ~ 6.5 instructions per flop,
- CPI 2.6 and the cache miss rate ranges from 4 to 11%,

And when executed on the Raspberry Pi 4 with one thread, the slowest frame achieves roughly:

- 7.6 million pixels per second,
- 28 fps,
- 496 instructions per pixel,
- ~14 instructions per flop,
- 267 Mflops/s,
- CPI 0.48, and
- the cache miss rate is 0.06%.

Note that spawning four threads on the Raspberry Pi Gen 4 (by adding `#omp omp parallel for` to the outer loop) did not improve performance beyond the single-threaded implementation, indicating that the graphical I/O might be acting as the bottleneck.

Many of the instructions needed per flop are needed to convert between floating point and integer types and the next section will address how to eliminate this aspect of the code.

3.6 Fixed-point arithmetic

As described in Chapter 2, floating-point instructions have a longer latency than integer instructions, meaning that several clock cycles must elapse between when a floating-point instruction begins execution and when its result is available. By itself this is not a problem, but floating-point code is often comprised of a series of instructions that depend on the intermediate result calculated by a previous instruction. Without a sufficient number of nondependent, ancillary instructions to schedule in between the dependent floating-point instructions, this situation will cause stalls to be inserted between the dependent instructions, reducing the utilization of the hardware.

Some programmers will always use floating-point instructions (by declaring variables as floating point) whenever the program requires a fractional number or large whole number that has a magnitude outside the range of an integer. However, in some cases this is unnecessary, since integers—when used as *fixed-point* values—can represent both fractional and very large values. The shorter latency of integer instructions will often translate into increased throughput for code containing chains of dependent instructions.

Graphics code, which contains type conversions between floating point and integers, will receive the added benefit of less type-conversion instructions (instructions that transfer and convert values between integer and floating-point registers).

In a fixed-point value, the program treats an integer as having an implicit decimal point, or *radix point*, placed at some location other than after bit 0. A **signed** n-bit value having m bits to the right of the radix point has a fixed range of

$$-2^{n-m-1} \text{ to } 2^{n-m-1} - 2^{-m}$$

and an equivalent **unsigned** value has a range of

$$0 \text{ to } 2^n - {}^m - 2^{-m}$$

both in increments of 2^{-m}.

Since fixed-point values usually place the implied radix point within the middle of the value, they are usually defined as an (n,m) value, in which there are n total bits of which m bits fall to the right of the radix point. This means that there are m fractional bits.

For example, a signed (7,4) fixed-point value would cover the range -4 to 3.9375 in increments of 0.0625. A binary value of 010.1101 represents $2^1 + 2^{-1} + 2^{-2} + 2^{-4} = 2.8125$.

The increment, or the significance of the rightmost bit, or *unit in the last place (ulp)*, determines the representation's *accuracy*.

When using the (n,m) notation, a regular integer that does not contain any fractional bits is considered a (32,0) fixed-point value. In this way, if the program multiplies a (32,8) value by a regular integer such as a loop counter, it is multiplying a (32,8) value by a (32,0) value and producing either a (64,8) product or a (32,8) product, depending on if it uses a multiply instruction that produces a 32- or 64-bit product, respectively.

3.6.1 Fixed point versus floating point: Accuracy

In fixed-point representation there is a tradeoff between range and accuracy. Accuracy captures the approximation error, or the average difference between a desired real number and the closest representable value in the format.

In fixed-point representation, the accuracy depends on how many bits are allocated to the right of the radix point. This is an (n,m) fixed-point value, and the accuracy is 2^{-m}.

The accuracy of floating-point values, on the other hand, depends on the value of the exponent. Calculated in the same way, the accuracy of a floating-point number is $2^{exponent-23}$.

3.6.2 Fixed point versus floating point: Range

There are some cases when fixed point cannot substitute for floating point. Floating point's advantage over fixed point is its range. Range can be defined in two ways. When defined in terms of the number line, the range of an (n,m) fixed-point value is $2^{n-m}-1$, which for our signed (7,4) example is only 7.

The range of an IEEE 754 floating-point value is 2^{2^e}, where e = the width of the exponent field. For example, a single-precision floating-point value has a range of 2^{256} and can represent a value from approximately -2^{-128} to 2^{128}.

Range can also be defined in terms of the ratio between the largest and smallest representable magnitude, often called *dynamic range*. The dynamic range of an (n,m) fixed-point value is $(2^{n-m-1} - 2^m)/2^{-m} = 2^{n-1} - 1$, the same as for any other integer. For our signed (7,4) example it is 63.

The dynamic range of a floating-point number is $2^{\left(2^{e-1}-1\right)}/2^{-2^{e-1}} = 2^{2^e-1}$. For single precision floating point this is $(2^{127}/2^{-128}) = 2^{255}$.

Floating-point instructions are thus necessary when a program requires a larger range than can be provided by fixed point. Graphics, audio, and signal processing code often require a determined range, determined by the number of pixels or available colors, or have a predetermined signal range. For example, digital audio data is usually confined to the range of $[-2,2)$, so digital audio uses a (16,14) fixed-point data type.

3.6.3 Fixed point versus floating point: Precision

The *precision*, or maximum number of significant bits that can be stored in a fixed-point value, depends on its value. Because the radix point is fixed, values that contain leading 0 bits will prevent the use of all the available bits in the format. For example, a (7,4) value 011.1101 has 6 significant bits, but 000.0010 has only 2 significant bits.

A signed (n,m) value has a precision of $n - 1$ bits when its value falls within the ranges:

- $[2^{n-m-2}, 2^{n-m-1} - 2^{-m}]$ and $[-2^{n-m-1}, -2^{n-m-2} - 2^{-m}]$

For example, for our (7,4) example there are 64 values in the range [2, 3.9375] and [−4 to −2.0625]

The precision drops to $n - 2$ bits when its value falls within the ranges:

- $[2^{n-m-3}, 2^{n-m-2} - 2^{-m}]$ and $[-2^{n-m-2}, -2^{n-m-3} - 2^{-m}]$

For example, for our (7,4) example there are 32 values in the range [1, 1.9375] and [− 2 to −1.0625]

The precision drops to $n - 3$ bits when its value falls within the ranges:

- $[2^{n-m-4}, 2^{n-m-3} - 2^{-m}]$ and $[-2^{n-m-3}, -2^{n-m-4} - 2^{-m}]$

For example, for our (7,4) example there are 16 values in the range [0, 0.9375] and [− 1 to −0.0625]

…and so on. As stated earlier, the precision depends on the number of leading 0-bits for a positive number or the number of leading 1-bits for a negative number. In other words, lower-magnitude values have lower precision. This is why digital photographs show more noise in darker areas.

Assuming every value is equally likely, an n-bit signed number offers $n - 1$ bits of precision (all bits except its sign bit) for half of its representable values, $n - 2$ bits of precision for half of the remaining values, $n - 2$ bits for half of the remaining values, and so on.

On average this is $\sum_{i=1}^{n}(n-i)\cdot 2^{-i}$ bits, so our (7,4) value offers approximately 5 bits of precision.

On the other hand, a floating-point value offers $s + 1$ bits of precision, where s is the number of bits in the significand (mantissa) field. Since the exponent field occupies some of bits in a floating-point value, a fixed-point value will generally offer more precision than a floating-point value of the same bit width.

Calculated this way, a 32-bit fixed-point value has approximately 30 bits of precision, while a 32-bit single precision floating-point value has 24 bits of precision.

3.6.4 Using fixed point

C and C++ lack built-in support for fixed point. A programmer wishing to use fixed-point types must either explicitly incorporate considerations for fixed-point arithmetic into the code or use a prewritten library.

A challenge when using fixed point is keeping track of the position of the radix point before and after each fixed-point operation.

When adding or subtracting, the radix points must be aligned for both operands. For example, a (32,16) operand can be added or subtracted with another (32,16) operand, but a (32,16) operand cannot be added to a (32,32) operand without first arithmetically shifting the operand having the radix point furthest to the left (the 32,32 operand) by the difference in *m*-values (by 16 bit positions).

3.6.5 Efficient fixed-point addition

Consider the following preprocessor macro, which adds a (32,*rp1*) value with a (32,*rp2*) value and returns a (32,min(*dp1*,*dp2*)) sum.

To do this, create a #define that expects the usage:

```
ADDFP(<result>, <operand 1>, <operand 2>,

  <radix point location in operand 1>,

  <radix point location in operand 2>)
```

In order to align the radix point before adding, the code must first identify which operand's radix point is further to the left and shift this value to the right by the difference in radix point positions. Afterward, the values are added and sum will have a radix point at the same position as the operand having the rightmost radix point.

For example, assume the following two values:

$$op1 = 0110.011(rp = 3)(= 6.375_{10})$$

$$op2 = 01.01111(rp = 5)(= 1.46875_{10})$$

To align the radix points, shift op0 one bit to the right:

$$op1 = 0110.011(rp = 3)(= 6.375_{10})$$

$$op2 = 0001.011(rp = 3)(= 1.375_{10}, 2\text{ bits shifted off} = 11)$$

$$\text{sum with } inf. \text{ precision} = 0111.11011(= 7.84375_{10})$$

$$\text{computed sum}(\text{round down}) = 0111.110_2 = (7.750_{10})\text{error} = 0.09375$$

$$\text{computed sum}(\text{round up}) = 0111.111(= 7.875_{10})\text{error} = 0.03125$$

With infinite precision the sum is 7.84375_{10}, but assuming no explicit rounding, the computed sum is 7.750_{10}, a difference of the value having been dropped as a result of shifting off ($0.00011_2 = 0.09375_{10}$).

When the most significant (left-most) bit shifted out is 1, the result should be rounded up by adding one into the rightmost bit position once the radix point has been repositioned.

The following preprocessor macro performs this behavior. The macro assumes that the sum and both operands are allocated as 32-bit variables. Note also that the macro definition in enclosed in an outer level of parentheses, which is needed for cases where the macro is invoked within statements containing other operators whose precedence relative to the operators in the macro may interfere with the behavior of the macro. In other words, we must ensure that the macro is evaluated independently from operations that occur within the same statement in which the macro is invoked.

```
#define ADDFP(op1,op2,rp1,rp2)                                        \
        ((rp1 > rp2) ?                                                \
        ((op1>>(rp1-rp2)) + op2) + (op1>>(rp1-rp2-1)&1) :             \
        (op1 + (op2>>(rp2-rp1))) + (op2>>(rp2-rp1-1)&1))
```

Shifting one of the operands right prior to adding is a natural usage of ARM's flexible second operand feature. As shown in the compiler-generated code below, the compiler takes advantage of this feature.

The compiler-generated code will vary depending on the values specified for op1, op2, rp1, and rp2. If all are given as constants, then the compiler will fold the macro expansion into a constant. For example, consider the line below:

```
res = ADDFP(5,6,5,6);
```

The compiler will replace this code by a single instruction setting res to the value 8, the result of adding 5 to 6>>1 and rounding down (adding 0), as shown below:

```
mov w1, 8
```

It is more likely to be the case that op1 and op2 will be specified as variables and rp1 and rp2 constants, since most fixed-point code will use a hard-coded number of fractional bits in each fixed-point variable. In this case, the compiler will eliminate both the conditional behavior and the subtraction of the rp1 and rp2 values, since the outcome of the comparison between rp1 and rp2 and their numerical difference is constant.

For example, consider the following code:

```
res = ADDFP(a,b,5,6);
```

The compiler will generate the following corresponding code:

```
and w1, w2, 1
add w2, w23, w2, asr 1
```

Note that in the example above, determining the round-up flag, which is the most significant bit of the sequence of bits to be shifted out in the operand having more fractional bits, requires only a single bitwise-AND instruction because the difference in radix point position is only 1. Consider an example where this is not the case:

```
res = ADDFP(res,a,b,5,7);
```

In this case, the compiler generates an additional instruction to extract bit 1 from the operand having the greater number of fractional bits:

```
add w1, w20, w2, asr 2

ubfx w2, w2, 1, 1

add w1, w1, w2
```

The `ubfx` instruction performs "Unsigned Bit Field Extract", where the second operation and is the source register, the third operand is an immediate indicating the least significant bit of the bit field to extract, and the fourth operand is an immediate indicating the width of the bit field to extract.

If all operands are variables, then the compiler must generate code to perform the comparison of the `fp1` and `fp2` and must use shift and bitwise-and instructions to extract the most significant bit of shifted-out bits, since the `ubfx` instruction requires that the bit field be known at compile-time.

Consider the example below:

```
res = ADDFP(a,b,c,d);
```

The efficiency of the generated assembly code depends on if the target is an ARMv7 or ARMv8 architecture. In this case, ARMv7 can take advantage of conditional instructions while ARMv8 cannot.

3.6.5.1 ARMv8 implementation

The compiler generates the corresponding assembly code, in which the code in block 1 corresponds to the computation needed if rp1 < rp2 and the code in block 2 corresponds to the computation needed otherwise.

The compiler's code begins with *rp1* and *rp2* loaded into registers w20 and w0. It compares these values to reach either block of code, which subtracts rp1 and rp2, isolates the most significant of the bits to be shifted out of the operand with more fractional bits, performs a preliminary add of the operands, and then rounds up if needed.

Block 1 (entry point):

```
cmp w20, w0

ble .L56
```

```
sub w2, w20, w0

sub w1, w2, #1

asr w2, w21, w2

add w19, w2, w19

asr w1, w21, w1

and w1, w1, 1

add w1, w1, w19

.L57:
```

(code after macro expansion)

Block 2:

```
.L56:

sub w2, w0, w20

sub w1, w2, #1

asr w2, w19, w2

add w0, w2, w21

asr w1, w19, w1

and w1, w1, 1

add w1, w1, w0

b .L57
```

3.6.5.2 ARMv7 implementation

The compiler's code begins with *rp1* and *rp2* loaded into registers r0 and r5. It compares these values and uses the resulting status bits to calculate the difference as rp1 − rp2 or rp2 − rp1. After this it shifts the operand with the greatest radix point twice—once to align the radix point and once to align the round bit—and then calculates the final sum.

Notice the redundant subtract instructions on lines 5 and 6.

```
1    cmp     r5, r0
2    mov     r6, r0
3    rsbgt   r4, r0, r5
4    rsble   r4, r5, r0
5    subgt   r3, r4, #1
6    suble   r3, r4, #1
```

```
 7    movgt   r3, r8, asr r3
 8    movle   r3, r7, asr r3
 9    addgt   r4, r7, r8, asr r4
10    addle   r4, r8, r7, asr r4
11    and     r3, r3, #1
12    mov     r0, #1
13    add     r4, r4, r3
14    mov     r2, r4
```

3.6.5.3 More efficient implementation for ARMv7

Using inline assembly language, the programmer can implement this operation with fewer instructions and with fewer data dependencies.

There are a few things to keep in mind when using inline assembly language to make sure your inline assembly code does not interfere with the compiler-generated code and vice versa.

When explicitly writing to specific registers directly (as opposed to substitutions), make sure you add the registers to the clobber list to avoid overwriting live registers being maintained by the compiler.

Also, when doing this make sure the instruction that writes to the register and the instruction that subsequently reads from that register are both encapsulated into a single asm() block to avoid the register being overwritten by the compiler in between the inline assembly statements. To avoid this, all the instructions will be included in a single asm() block.

When using condition instructions, keep in mind that any auxiliary instructions generated to support substitutions will not be conditional.

Finally, when compiling be sure to use the "-marm" option to prevent THUMB mode, which treats conditional instructions differently than ARM mode.

First, define a slightly modified version of the macro with the result included in the parameter list:

```
1    #define ADDFP2(res,op1,op2,rp1,rp2) \
```

To avoid data dependencies, this implementation will maintain two versions of each operand: the original value and the shifted and rounded version. To support this, the code begins by copying the operand values to registers r1 and r2.

```
2    asm("mov r1,%[op1val]\n\t\
```

```
3    mov r2,%[op2val]\n\t\
```

Subtract the radix point positions and store the difference in register r0.

```
4       sub r0,%[rp1val],%[rp2val]\n\t\
```

Right-shift operand 1 by the difference in radix points. From this point on, r1 will serve as the shifted version of operand 1.

Refer to `%[op1val]` as the original value of operand 1, which substitutes to another register still holding the original value.

Instead of using the flexible second operand, use the stand-alone shift instruction to shift operand 1, but also use the s-suffix. This way, the last bit shifted out will be stored in the carry-out (c) flag, used for rounding later. Note that this flag is not written when the shift amount is zero, so the code must account for this possibility.

```
5       asrs r1,r1,r0\n\t\
```

Add 1 to the shifted value if the c-flag is set.

```
6       addhs r1,r1,#1\n\t\
```

Subtract the radix point positions in reverse order and store the result in register r0.

```
7       sub r0,%[rp2val],%[rp1val]\n\t\
```

Shift the original value of operand 2 and round if necessary. This version of operand 2 will now reside in register r2.

```
8       asrs r2,r2,r0\n\t\
```

```
9       addhs r2,r2,#1\n\t\
```

Now subtract the radix points again to reset the flags.

```
10      subs r0,%[rp1val],%[rp2val]\n\t\
```

If rp1 ≥ rp2, add the shifted/rounded operand 1 to the original operand 2.

```
11      addpl r1,r1,%[op2val]\n\t\
```

If rp1 < rp2, add the original operand 1 to the shifted/rounded operand 2.

```
12      addmi r1,%[op1val],r2\n\t\
```

If equal, the rounding operation would have produced unpredictable results, so deal with equal radix point positions separately.

```
13      addeq r1,%[op1val],%[op2val]\n\t\
```

Move the calculated sum back to register associated with the result.

```
14      mov %[resval],r1\n\t" :\
```

The only output is the result value.

```
15      [resval]"=r"(res) :\
```

The input values:

```
15      [rp1val]"r"(rp1), [rp2val]"r"(rp2),\
```

```
16      [op1val]"r"(op1), [op2val]"r"(op2) :\
```

Add the clobber list, which ensures the compiler is aware of which of the general-purpose registers that it did not allocate are written in the inline assembly.

```
17      "r0", "r1","r2");
```

When executing the code on a Cortex A15 processor core, the inline assembly version of the fixed point is seven times faster than the compiler-generated code.

3.6.6 Efficient fixed-point multiplication

Unlike addition and subtraction, any two fixed-point values (n_1,m_1) and (n_2,m_2) can be multiplied without first aligning the radix point, but the multiplication will position the product's radix point to bit $m_1 + m_2$. In order to reposition the product's radix point at bit m_1 or m_2, the program must perform adjustments to the product. Thus, in fixed-point addition and subtraction one of the operands must be adjusted *prior* to performing the operation, while in multiplication the product must be adjusted *after* performing the operation.

For example, the product of a (64,32) value and a (64,32) value is a (128,64) value. To avoid the growth of product width, the product is usually shifted to the right and converted back to a 64-bit value to prepare for subsequent operations.

Any integer multiply where the product is allocated the same number of bits as the operands has the potential to overflow. To cope with this, C compilers can allocate a $2n$-bit product of n-bit operands, but only when the operands are cast as datatypes having $2n$ bits. This allows the product to be shifted as a $2n$-bit value and optionally converted back to an n-bit value.

When using gcc/g++ on ARMv7 and ARMv8, the "int" datatype is 32 bits, the "long" datatype is 32 bits on ARMv7 and 64 bits on ARMv8, and the "long long" datatype is 64 bits on ARMv7 and also 64 bits on ARMv8. On ARMv8 "__int128" and "unsigned __int128" provides a 128-bit integer type.

3.6.6.1 Multiplying fixed-point on ARMv8

For example, when multiplying two (64,32)-bit integers of type `long`, the following code will guarantee that the nonfractional bits in the product are not lost when storing to a (64,32) product:

```
long a=1<<32; // a is 1.0 in (64,32) format

long b=1<<32; // b is 1.0 in (64,32) format

long c;

// c will also be 1.0 in (64,32) format

c = ((__int128)a * (__int128)b) >> 32;
```

To add rounding to the nearest unit in the last place, the programmer may add:

```
c += (((__int128)a * (__int128)b) >> 31) & 1;
```

This code generates the following assembly code for ARMv8. First, use the `mul` and `smulh` instructions to produce the 128-bit signed product in the pair of 64-bit registers {`x19,x2`}, which hold the variables `a` and `b`:

```
1       mul   x2, x19, x25
2       smulh x19, x19, x25
```

Next, use the `extr` instruction to extract a 64-bit register from the register pair. The `extr Xd, Xn, Xm, #lsb` instruction performs the operation `R[xd] = {Xn,Xm} >> #lsb`, which matches our high-level code exactly. This produces the unrounded (64,32) product in register `x19`.

```
3       extr  x19, x19, x2, 32
```

To perform rounding, logical-shift the lower 64 bits of the product as a 32-bit value by 31 bits to the right. This will zero the upper 32 bits and shift out the lower 31 bits, leaving bit 31 of the product.

```
4       lsr   w1, w2, 31
```

Add bit 31 of the product to the final product to round up if needed.

```
5       add   x1, x1, x19
```

3.6.6.2 Multiplying fixed-point on ARMv7

For example, when multiplying two (32,16)-bit integers of type `long`, the following code will guarantee that the nonfractional bits in the product are not lost when storing to a (32,16) product:

```
long a=1<<16; // a is 1.0 in (32,16) format
```

```
long b=1<<16; // b is 1.0 in (32,16) format

long c;

// c will also be 1.0 in (32,16) format

c = ((long long)a * (long long)b) >> 16;
```

This code generates the following assembly code. First, perform signed multiply of two 32-bit registers and store least significant word of product in r4 and most significant word of product in r5.

```
1      smull r4, r5, r4, r0
```

Right-shift lower 32 bits of product by 16 bits. It is not clear why the compiler used the s-suffix without generating any subsequent conditional instructions.

```
2      lsrs r2, r4, #16
```

Combine previous result by lower 32 bits of product left-shifted by 16 bits.

```
3      orr r2, r2, r5, lsl #16
```

The result of these instructions is shown graphically in Figure 3.3.

Notice that there are two shift operations. The first shifts the least significant 32 bits of the product in r4 RIGHT by 16 bits, which moves the radix point to the right to compensate for the new fractional bits generated by the multiply.

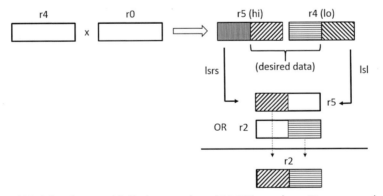

Figure 3.3: Two (32,16) values multiplied to produce (64,32) product. To convert the product to a (32,16) value, the lower 16 bits of r5 and the upper 16 bits of r4 need to be combined into a single register. To do this, the compiler uses shift operations to isolate the bits and uses an OR instruction to combine them into a single register.

The second shifts the most significant 32 bits of the product in r5 LEFT by 16 bits. The purpose is to position the bits—that when shifted RIGHT—cross the boundary between the upper and lower half of the product. These are lower-order bits in the left product that will form the higher-order bits of the final 32-bit product.

To add rounding capability to this code, the programmer can again take advantage of how shifting operations leave the last shifted-out bit in the *c* flag.

```
4       addhs r2, r2, #1
```

3.6.6.3 Fixed-point multiply macro on ARMv8

To implement a general macro for fixed-point multiply of operands each having an arbitrary radix point position, the code must decide where to place the radix point of the product.

A common method is to set the radix point of the product to match the operand having the rightmost position. To do this, the code will shift the product to the right by the position of the left-most radix point.

The macro has arguments for two operands and the corresponding radix point positions of each operand:

```
#define MULTFP(op1,op2,rp1,rp2)\
    (rp1 < rp2 ? ((__int128)op1 * (__int128)op2 >> rp2) +\
    (((__int128)op1 * (__int128)op2 >> (rp2-1)) & 1) :\
    ((__int128)op1 * (__int128)op2 >> rp1) +\
    (((__int128)op1 * (__int128)op2 >> (rp1-1)) & 1))
```

Recent versions of gcc/g++ are able to generate efficient implementations of this code, partly due to the (mostly) lack of conditional instructions and the addition of the `extr` instruction.

3.6.6.4 Fixed-point multiply macro on ARMv7

It is possible to define an efficient fixed-point multiply macro for ARMv7 by leveraging conditional instructions. First, define the macro and include a parameter for specifying the result location:

```
1       #define MULTFP(res,op1,op2,rp1,rp2)\
```

Next, compare the radix point positions. The `cmp` instruction sets the flag bits as a subtract instruction: if the first compared value is greater or equal to the second value, then the carry flag will be set to one and zero otherwise. This is because all subtracts produce a carryout except when resulting in a difference that would result in an unsigned underflow.

```
2       asm("cmp %[rp1val], %[rp2val]\n\t\
```

Compute the *left-shift value*, which is the difference between 32 and the position of the left-most radix point position. Since calculation depends on which radix position is further left, use conditional instructions.

```
3       rsbgt r0,%[rp1val],#32\n\t\
4       rsble r0,%[rp2val],#32\n\t\
```

Perform the multiply, storing the upper portion of the product in r5 and the lower portion of the product in r4.

```
5       smull r4, r5, %[op1val], %[op2val]\n\t\
```

Right-shift the lower half of the product using conditional shift instructions, shifting by the greater of the radix point positions. Use the s-suffix to retain the last bit shifted out—the round bit—in the carry flag. This behavior is supported when using shift instructions or when using the flexible second operand with the movs, mvns, ands, orrs, eors, bics, teq, or tst instructions.

```
6       lsrgts r2, r4, %[rp1val]\n\t\
7       lsrles r2, r4, %[rp2val]\n\t\
```

Using the flexible second operand, left-shift the upper half of the product by the distance previously calculated in r0, and using a bitwise OR to merge with the previously shifted value.

```
8       orr r2, r2, r5, lsl r0\n\t\
```

Round up using the last shifted-off bit from the lower half of the product. The carry flag is not changed if the shift amount is zero, in which case the carry flag would remain in the state that resulted from the cmp instruction. As a result this macro will not produce correct results if both radix point positions are zero.

```
9       addhs r2, r2, #1\n\t\
```

Line 6 sets the value of r1 to −1 when the radix point positions are equal in order to cancel the round-up operation. Apply this correction now.

```
10      mov %[resval],r2\n\t" :\
11      [resval]"=r"(res) :\
12      [op1val]"r"(op1),[op2val]"r"(op2),\
13      [rp1val]"r"(rp1),[rp2val]"r"(rp2) :\
14      "r0", "r1", "r2", "r4", "r5");
```

3.6.7 Determining radix point position

The radix point should be placed to accommodate the range and the accuracy requirements of the application. The range is determined by the number of bits to the left of the radix point. The accuracy is determined by the number of bits to the right of the radix point.

In general, the programmer should select the minimal number of fractional bits to satisfy the accuracy requirement. Leaving as many bits as possible to the left of the radix point will minimize the likelihood of arithmetic overflow when performing multiplies.

For example, consider an application whose minimal range requirement is 2^n and minimal accuracy requirement is 2^{-m}. Assuming $n + m \leq 32$, the requirements are met using a $(32 - m, m)$ format.

Figure 3.4 shows a case where $32 - 2m \geq n$. In this case, after multiplying two values of this type, there are enough bits remaining left of the radix point in the lower 32 bits of the product value that there is no risk of overflow if only 32 bits are allocated to the product.

3.6.8 Range and accuracy requirements for image transformation

In the image transformation example, the variables must be converted from floating to fixed point.

If all fractional intermediate variables use a consistent fixed-point format, the program has the following range and accuracy requirements.

Range: Transformed row and column values must be able to address a pixel within the frame's resolution (1920×1200, in our example implementation). This requires at least 11 (unsigned) bits to the left of the radix point. Color channel values need only 8 bits.

Accuracy: Weight calculations should have sufficient accuracy to discriminate between individual color channel values when multiplied against color channels from the source image. In other words, the accuracy of the weights must match the precision of the color data, meaning that there must be at least 8 fractional bits when multiplying against color values. Using a $(32,8)$ format provides 24 bits of range and 8 bits of accuracy, fulfilling both requires for the image transformation.

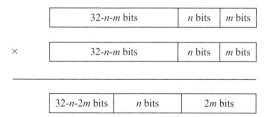

Figure 3.4: Multiplying two $(32,m)$ values when $n + 2m < 32$.

3.6.9 Converting from floating-point to fixed-point arithmetic

This section describes a method for converting the image transformation code described earlier in the chapter to fixed point. The code uses high-level language to perform the fixed-point arithmetic.

Begin by changing the type of the arrays *src_pixel, frac*, and *weights* to **int**. Then, define two parameters that can be used to adjust the position of the radix point (*m*) and its corresponding numerical significance (2^m).

```
#define FRACBITS 8

#define FRAC_SIG 256
```

The rotation transformation requires the use of sine and cosine functions, and there are no fixed-point versions of these in the POSIX standard math library. Although it is possible to implement them or use a third-party library, doing so will have negligible impact on performance since the program calls these functions once per frame when computing the transformation matrices. As such, the program can calculate these values using floating point and convert the floating-point values to fixed point.

To do this, define a fixed-point version of the transformation matrix by declaring new variables `c_row_fp` and `c_col_fp` as 2-element arrays of type int.

After the call to `calc_coeffs()`, add the following code to convert the floating-point transformation matrix to fixed point. To convert, multiply the floating-point values by the 2^f, where *f* = the number to bits to the right of the radix point, then converting the result to an integer as shown below:

```
c_row_fp[0] = (int)(c_row[0] * (float)FRAC_SIG);

c_row_fp[1] = (int)(c_row[1] * (float)FRAC_SIG);

c_col_fp[0] = (int)(c_col[0] * (float)FRAC_SIG);

c_col_fp[1] = (int)(c_col[1] * (float)FRAC_SIG);
```

The inner loop body begins by multiplying the destination pixel location at row *i* column *j* (or *x* = *j*, *y* = *i*) by the transformation matrix. This time no int-to-float typecasting is necessary.

The following lines map each pixel location in the transformed image to a (fractional) pixel location in the source image. Each line adds two products of a (32,8) transformation matrix value (*c_row_fp*) and a (32,0) loop counter value. When added, the two (32,8) products produce a (32,8) sum, which is stored in the *src_pixel* array.

```
src_pixel[0] = c_row_fp[0] * (i-(rows/2)) +
        c_row_fp[1] * (j-(cols/2)); // (32,FRACBITS)
```

```
src_pixel[1] = c_col_fp[0] * (i-(rows/2)) +

    c_col_fp[1] * (j-(cols/2));
```

After this convert `src_pixel` to a (32,0) type and round down by shifting right by the number of fractional bits.

```
src_pixel_int[0] = (src_pixel[0] >> FRACBITS) + (rows/2); // (32,0)

src_pixel_int[1] = (src_pixel[1] >> FRACBITS) + (cols/2);
```

Use a bitwise-AND operation to extract the fractional portion of `src_pixel`. To extract the lower m bits from any value, perform a bitwise-AND with $2^m - 1$:

```
frac[0] = src_pixel[0] & (FRAC_SIG-1); // (32, FRACBITS)

frac[1] = src_pixel[1] & (FRAC_SIG-1);
```

When calculating the weights, subtract the fractional point of each source pixel location from 1. Since 1 must be expressed in the same fixed-point format as the fractional values computed above, use the defined value for 2^m. Multiplying two (32,m) values produces a (32,2m) product.

```
weights[0] = (FRAC_SIG-frac[0]) * (FRAC_SIG-frac[1]); // (32,2x

                                                      // FRACBITS)

weights[1] = (FRAC_SIG-frac[0]) * (frac[1]);

weights[2] = (frac[0]) * (FRAC_SIG-frac[1]);

weights[3] = (frac[0]) * (frac[1]);
```

Extract the RGB values of the four source pixels as before. When calculating the interpolated color values, you must remember to shift the final value, which is in (32,2m) format, 2m bits to the right to compute the final (32,0) color value.

```
red = ((r[0]) * (weights[0]) +

    (r[1]) * (weights[1]) +

    (r[2]) * (weights[2]) +

    (r[3]) * (weights[3])) >> FRACBITS*2;

green = ((g[0]) * (weights[0]) +

    (g[1]) * (weights[1]) +

    (g[2]) * (weights[2]) +

    (g[3]) * (weights[3])) >> FRACBITS*2;
```

```
blue = ((b[0]) * (weights[0]) +

    (b[1]) * (weights[1]) +

    (b[2]) * (weights[2]) +

    (b[3]) * (weights[3])) >> FRACBITS*2;
```

3.7 Fixed-point performance

As compared to floating point, using fixed point reduces the latency after each arithmetic instruction at the cost of additional instructions required for rounding and radix point management, although if the overhead code contains sufficient instruction level parallelism the impact of these additional instructions on throughput may not be substantial.

On the other hand, for graphics applications like image transformation that require frequent conversions between floating point and integer, using fixed point may result in a reduction of executed instructions.

In fact, when compared to the floating-point implementation on the Raspberry Pi 1, the fixed-point implementation achieves approximately the same CPI and cache miss rate but decreases the number of instructions per pixel from 225 to 160. This resulted in a speedup of throughput of approximately 40%.

3.8 Real-time fractal generation

A **fractal** is a mathematical set that exhibits infinitely repeating self-similar patterns at increasingly finer scales.

Perhaps the most well-known fractal is the **Mandelbrot set** shown in Figure 3.5. The Mandelbrot set is a set of complex numbers, all of which have a Euclidean norm that is less than 2. In other words, when the complex numbers in the Mandelbrot set are plotted on a 2D space where the real part is plotted on the X-axis and the imaginary part is plotted on the Y-axis, every point would be contained within a radius 2 circle of the origin.

Plotting member points with a single color and all nonmember points using a spectrum of colors according to how "close" they are to being the set creates a rendered image can be quite beautiful, especially when viewed with high magnification in certain areas.

A complex value is defined as being a member of the Mandelbrot set if the series produced by an infinite recursive evaluation of the polynomial $P_c(z) = z^2 + c$ is bounded within a radius 2 circle of the origin (a complex absolute value), where c is the point being tested for membership and z begins at 0.

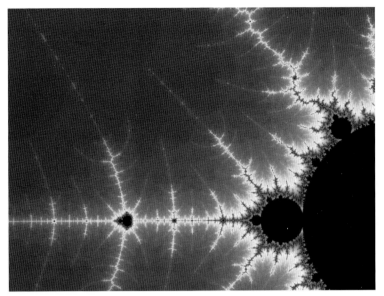

Figure 3.5: Mandelbrot set.

The program can test an arbitrary point c by computing the series of values $P_c(0)$, $P_c(P_c(0))$, $P_c(P_c(P_c(0)))$, $P_c(P_c(P_c(P_c(0))))$, $P_c(P_c(P_c(P_c(P_c(0)))))$, ... For any value of c in the Mandelbrot set, no value in this series will have a complex absolute value greater than 2. Some values of c will eventually produce a value whose absolute value does exceed this bound. Some of these points require a very high number of evaluations before this happens. Points that exhibit this behavior appear near the boundary between member and nonmember points and can also be considered points of interest because these points are usually surrounded by interesting visual features.

In practice, an arbitrary *cutoff* is used to test if a value falls within the Mandelbrot set. An example of this is when the number is marked as being in the set if the polynomial is not disqualified (evaluate to a complex absolute value > 2) after 500 polynomial evaluations. This criterion can lead to false positives, but when the fractal is used only for visual display the effect of false positives is only a subjective degradation of image quality. A higher cutoff will reduce the number of points that are falsely judged to be members but will increase the execution time for member pixels.

The number of evaluations before disqualification determines the point's color. Usually, lighter colors are used for points that require a higher number of evaluations.

For example, to test the membership of the value $0.50 + 0.75i$:

Set $c = 0.50 + 0.75i$

Set initial $z = 0$

$$P_c(0) = 0^2 + (0.50 + 0.75i) = 0.50 + 0.75i \text{ (distance from origin} = 0.90)$$
$$P_c(0.50 + 0.75i) = (0.50 + 0.75i)^2 + (0.50 + 0.75i)$$
$$= 0.19 + 1.50i \text{ (distance from origin} = 1.51)$$
$$P_c(0.19 + 1.50i) = (0.19 + 1.50i)^2 + (0.50 + 0.75i)$$
$$= -1.71 + 1.31i \text{ (distance from origin} = \textbf{2.15})$$

In this case, the third evaluation of the polynomial gave a value outside the radius 2 circle, so the original value, $0.50 + 0.75i$, is not a member of the Mandelbrot set.

Testing another value, $0.25 + 0.50i$:

Set $c = 0.25 + 0.50i$

Set initial $z = 0$

$$P_c(0) = 0^2 + (0.25 + 0.50i) = 0.25 + 0.50i \text{ (distance from origin} = 0.56)$$
$$P_c(0.25 + 0.50i) = (0.25 + 0.50i)^2 + (0.25 + 0.50i)$$
$$= 0.063 + 0.75i \text{ (distance from origin} = 0.75)$$
$$P_c(0.063 + 0.75i) = (0.063 + 0.75i)^2 + (0.25 + 0.50i)$$
$$= -0.31 + 0.59i \text{ (distance from origin} = 0.67)$$
$$P_c(-0.31 + 0.59i) = (-0.31 + 0.59i)^2 + (0.25 + 0.50i)$$
$$= -0.0073 + 0.13i \text{ (distance from origin} = 0.13)$$
$$P_c(-0.0073 + 0.13i) = (-0.0073 + 0.13i)^2 + (0.25 + 0.50i)$$
$$= 0.23 + 0.50i \text{ (distance from origin} = 0.55)$$

Even after 1000 evaluations, the polynomial never evaluates to any value having a complex absolute value greater than 2. This is not a guarantee that it will *never* occur. In fact, there are some c-values that will generate a series that remains within the circle for an extremely high number of iterations before finally evaluating to the point outside the circle.

The following pseudocode shows the main loop for generating each frame:

for i = 0 to rows-1 begin

for j = 0 to cols-1 begin

Initialize c: transform j,i into x0,y0 based on pre-established x- and y-ranges

Initialize z: x = 0, y = 0

Set iteration = 0

while ((x*x + y*y) < = 4) and (iteration < cutoff) begin

    xtemp = x*x − y*y + x0

    y = 2*x*y + y0

    x = xtemp

    iteration++

end // while

if iteration == cutoff then

  color = black,

else

  color = f(iteration)

end // for j

end // for i

3.8.1 Pixel coloring

Pixels that correspond to c-values that the program determines to be members of the Mandelbrot set are usually colored black. Pixels that correspond to c-values whose sequence of polynomial evaluations quickly escape the radius $= 2$ boundary around the origin are usually also darkly colored.

Pixels that correspond to c-values that require a high number of evaluations before being disqualified are usually colored a bright color. You can write your own function that determines the RGB components of each pixel that corresponds to each nonmember point as a function of the number of polynomial evaluations required before the point exits the radius 2 circle.

The function can be a simple linear function, such as

$$\text{pixel}_{\text{red}} = \frac{\text{coeff}_{\text{red}} \cdot \text{evaluations}}{\text{zoom}}$$

$$\text{pixel}_{\text{green}} = \frac{\text{coeff}_{\text{green}} \cdot \text{evaluations}}{\text{zoom}}$$

$$\text{pixel}_{\text{blue}} = \frac{\text{coeff}_{\text{blue}} \cdot \text{evaluations}}{\text{zoom}}$$

Attenuating the color intensity by the zoom factor avoids oversaturation of colors for extreme zoom levels.

Since the number of evaluations may be large, the calculated value may exceed the maximum value of the corresponding color channel. To avoid a potential overflow, you must use *saturating arithmetic* when calculating each pixel value. This way, if the calculated value exceeds the maximum allowed value, set it to the maximum value.

3.8.2 Zooming in

When rendering each frame of the Mandelbrot set, the program should maintain the *c*-value of the nonmember point, requiring the greatest number of evaluations before disqualification. This point can serve as the central point when zooming, referred to as the target point, $(target_x, target_y)$.

The program will begin by plotting the entire Mandelbrot set (often initially in the range $-2.5 \leq x < 1.0, -1 \leq y < 1$) and then zoom in to get a closer look at a target point within each frame. This produces a visually appealing video sequence.

Our first challenge is to develop a method to determine the *c*-value for each pixel given a specified zoom level.

Establish variables to keep track of the minimum and maximum values for the X- and Y-axes. This way, the frame area is *discretized* at regular intervals.

This way, for a given frame (x_{min}, x_{max}), (y_{min}, y_{max}), the x and y values for any (row,col) are computed as

$$c_{real} = x = \frac{col}{pixels_{width}} \cdot (x_{max} - x_{min}) + x_{min}$$

$$c_{imag} = y = \frac{pixels_{height} - 1 - row}{pixels_{height}} \cdot (y_{max} - y_{min}) + y_{min}$$

The range of values in each dimension is determined by the center point $(target_x, target_y)$, the aspect ratio, the zoom level, and the room rate.

If the initial range of the Y-axis is $[-1.25, 1.25)$, the corresponding range for the X-axis is *aspect ratio* $\times$ 2.5, or $[-2.0, 2.0)$ for a 16×10 framebuffer (aspect ratio = 1.6). To implement zooming, update the boundaries of the plotted area using the point of interest to center the frame while narrowing the range. To reveal the repeating patterns in the Mandelbrot set, the program must zoom in at an exponential rate:

$$min_x = target_x - \frac{aspect\ ratio}{rate^{frame}}$$

$$max_x = target_x + \frac{aspect\ ratio}{rate^{frame}}$$

$$min_y = target_y - \frac{1}{rate^{frame}}$$

As you zoom in, the difference in c-value between adjacent pixels will decrease. Since the target point is associated with one pixel on the frame, you should recalculate a new target point on each frame.

3.8.3 Range and accuracy requirements

As the zoom level increases, the difference between the values of adjacent pixels shrinks at an exponential rate. Eventually the processor runs out of precision for whatever data type the program is using to represent each c-value. When this occurs the difference in values between adjacent pixels will shrink to a value that can no longer be represented, assigning the same X- or Y-value for multiple pixels, thus reducing the effective resolution.

Since the conversion between pixel locations and c-values requires the mixing of integers and fractional values (often represented as floating point) and the ranges of representable fractional values are fixed to predetermined values, this is another application that calls for the use of fixed-point arithmetic.

Recall that:

$$|c| \le 2$$

And thus:

$$-2 \le \text{real}(c) \le 2$$
$$-2 \le \text{imag}(c) \le 2$$

On each evaluation of $P(z)$:

$$-2 \le \text{real}(z) \le 2$$
$$-2 \le \text{imag}(z) \le 2$$

Recall that:

$$P(z) = z^2 + c$$
$$\text{real}(P(z)) = \text{real}(z)^2 - \text{imag}(z)^2 + \text{real}(c)$$
$$\text{imag}(P(z)) = 2 \cdot \text{real}(z) \cdot \text{imag}(z) + \text{imag}(c)$$

Thus:

$$-6 \le \text{real}(z) \le 6$$
$$-10 \le \text{imag}(z) \le 10$$

and:

$$0 \le \mathrm{real}\big(P(z)\big)^2 \le 36$$
$$0 \le \mathrm{real}\big(P(z)\big)^2 \le 100$$

To use a consistent format for all fractional values, allocate 8 bits to the left of the radix point, that is, 7 bits plus a sign bit. For 32-bit values, this gives an accuracy of 2^{-24}.

Setting the zoom *rate* = 1.5 gives approximately

$$24 \times log(2)/log(1.5) = 41 \text{ frames}$$

before pixels begin to alias and lose effective resolution. Using 64-bit values will give us

$$56 \times log(2)/log(1.5) = 95 \text{ frames}$$

3.9 Chapter wrap-up

This chapter described two methods for displaying graphical output, the Linux framebuffer and OpenCV, which allows programs to produce graphical output without needing heavy-weight libraries or graphical desktop servers.

Using the framebuffer, the chapter described a floating-point implementation of affine image transformation and characterized its performance on the Raspberry Pi 1 and Raspberry Pi 4. While the latency of the floating-point instructions can be hidden using independent operations on other pixels, the overhead required to convert pixel indices from integers to floating-point values and back to integers resulted in many instructions required per pixel.

To overcome this problem, the chapter introduced fixed-point representation and arithmetic. Fixed-point arithmetic gives the programmer access to fractional number arithmetic using integer instructions and without using floating point. Fixed point is available to applications that have a narrow, predefined numerical range.

The chapter described the accuracy, range, and precision of fixed-point values as compared to floating point. To explore the practical aspects of fixed point, the chapter showed example macros for fixed-point addition and multiplication, written in both high-level language and inline assembly code.

Using these macros as examples, the chapter demonstrated how using inline assembly language allows the programmer to exploit architectural features useful in fixed-point arithmetic that are not available to the C-language code. An example of this is taking advantage of the status register to capture the last shifted-out bit to implement rounding.

After this, the chapter described how to convert the image transformation example from floating point to fixed point. This provided a 40% improvement to performance by reducing the number of instructions per pixel.

As another example of a computationally expensive graphical application, the chapter introduced Mandelbrot set generation. Although the Mandelbrot set has few practical applications, it serves as a benchmark for a compute-intensive and arithmetically intensive program and has the advantage that speeding up the application produces a visible improvement in frames per second as the images as rendered in real time on an attached monitor.

The Mandelbrot set is also amenable to fixed-point arithmetic but requires careful selection of radix point location to maintain sufficient range and maximize precision. The behavior of the Mandelbrot set, in terms of the number of zoom levels, is determined by the amount of precision in the intermediate data types. This makes fixed-point arithmetic, being amenable to multiprecise integer arithmetic, even more attractive for this application.

The next chapter covers methods for capturing frames from a USB-based camera for processing with computer vision algorithms. This chapter's optimization strategy is memory optimization through loop transformation.

Exercises

1. Write a fixed-point implementation of the Mandelbrot generator.
    a. You will notice that the performance is inconsistent between different pixels and different frames. Why is this?
    b. What is the arithmetic intensity of the innermost loop body, in operations per byte accessed from memory? What is the corresponding performance bound for your ARM CPU? How does it compare to your observed performance?
    c. Measure the following performance metrics for the innermost loop body:
    d. Use inline assembly to implement the innermost loop body and measure the performance impact with respect to the metrics from part c. What is the speedup as compared to the compiler-generated code?
        • instructions per iteration
        • instructions per operation
        • CPI
        • cache miss rate

2. Parallelize the Mandelbrot set generator using OpenMP. Apply the parallel-for directive to the outer-most (row) loop.
    a. Measure the average number of cycles required for each iteration of the innermost loop (to evaluate the polynomial) for one thread and two threads for the initial

frame. Use these measurements to calculate the speedup, in terms of pixels per second, of two threads over one thread.

b. Measure the time to compute all the pixels in the first frame when using the dynamic schedule as compared to the static schedule.

3. What makes it difficult to apply SIMD operation for the Mandelbrot set generator? What is the most efficient method for applying SIMD operation for the Mandelbrot set generator?

4. Measure the effective write throughput for the Linux Framebuffer. Is it equivalent to the write throughput for a memory array allocated from the heap?

5. Calculate the arithmetic intensity of the image transformation program in operations per pixel. What is its performance bound given the effective memory throughput of your ARM CPU? How does it compare to your observed performance?

6. Use OpenMP to add multicore support to the fixed-point image transformation program. To do this, apply the parallel for pragma to the outer-most (row) loop.

7. Measure its performance on a four-core ARM CPU. How does its performance scale when executed with one, two, three, and four threads?

8. Use intrinsics to add NEON SIMD support to the fixed-point version of the image transformation program. Use four-way operations to compute the following calculations for a group of four pixels: source pixel location, fraction extraction, and weight calculation. To what degree does this improve performance?

9. We cannot easily optimize the Mandelbrot generator program using SIMD instructions, since neighboring pixels may require a different number of polynomial evaluations and each iteration of the polynomial is dependent on the previous evaluation. An alternative approach is to implement the loop in inline assembly, unroll by at least four, and then use software pipelining to improve loop CPI. In this case, we should avoid conditional branches inside the unrolled loop. Since diverging c-values will continue to diverge with subsequent evaluations, we can wait to check the loop exit condition after each group of four iterations. However, performing additional polynomial evaluations after a $P_c()$ potentially diverges outside the radius 2 circle will require us to account for the additional range requirements for our fixed-point format. Recalculate the fixed-point range requirements for this optimization and determine to what degree this will reduce the maximum zoom level.

10. The principal advantages of fixed point are the reduction in operation latency and the ability to avoid type conversions in certain types of graphics codes. Chapter 2 highlights an example program whose performance is sensitive to operation latency, Horner's method. Assuming that we can tolerate the range limitations of fixed point in our Horner's method code, would converting it to fixed-point improve performance? Explain your answer.

11. Section 3.6.5 showed two different implementations of a generalized fixed-point addition preprocessor macro. The first was generated by gcc under maximum optimization,

and the second was hand-coded using inline assembly language. Both implementations required approximately the same number of instructions.

12. In this question we examine the inline assembly implementation of generalized fixed-point multiply described in Section 3.6.6.

    a. Show the read-after-write data dependencies in both implementations. Assuming the processor uses single instruction, in order issue, and assuming the latency of all integer arithmetic operations is four cycles, how many compare the number of data stall cycles needed for both implementations?

    b. Rewrite the inline assembly version of the fixed-point addition macro to schedule the instructions such that dependent instructions are separated as much as possible. To what degree are the stalls reduced, assuming the latency given in part a?

    c. Write code that demonstrates how all three implementations (compiler generated, inline assembly, and scheduled inline assembly) can be characterized for performance.

    d. How does it compare, in terms of number of instructions and runtime performance, as compared to the equivalent compiler-generated code for:

    ```
    res = (((long long)op1 * (long long)op2) >> (rp1>rp2?

            rp1:rp2)) +(rp1>rp2 ? ((((long long)op1 * (long long)op2) >> (rp1-1))&1) :

            ((((long long)op1 * (long long)op2) >> (rp2-1))&1));
    ```

    e. Make sure you use the "-O3" and "-marm" switches when compiling with gcc.

    f. Schedule the instructions of the inline assembly version of the multiply macro to minimize data dependency stalls. Measure its performance relative to the version given in Section 3.6.6.

    g. For the inline assembly implementation, how much more throughout is achieved if changed such that the radix point positions are fixed instead of variable as in the code? For this question, use both the number of instructions and actual runtime behavior.

13. Calculating the pixel values for a Mandelbrot set requires a function for converting the iteration count to the R, G, and B color channels. Setting all three channels to the same value will generate a gray image, so the slope of each color channel function should be unique, and whichever slope is greatest will determine the hue of the image.

14. As described in Section 3.8.1, the number of polynomial evaluations may exceed the value that exceeds the range of a color channel. To avoid a potential overflow, you must use *saturating arithmetic* when calculating each pixel value. This way, if the calculated value exceeds the maximum allowed value, set it to the maximum value.

15. Write a C macro that performs an 8-bit unsigned saturating multiply. The function will take two 8-bit operands and produce an 8-bit product set to 255 if the product

exceeds 255. The macro must not include branch instructions and be scheduled for data dependencies.

16. This exercise will explore increasing the precision of the fixed-point types for the Mandelbrot generator to 64-bit.

    a. Using a zoom rate of 1.5^{zoom}, to what level can the frame be zoomed before exceeding this precision?

    b. Define a macro in C for adding two (64,56) fixed-point values. The macro can perform the 128-bit add using four 32-bit adds and use the carry flag to implement carries from each 32-bit group to the next most significant 32-bit group.

    c. Define a macro in C for multiplying two (64,56) fixed-point values. Build this macro on top of the 64-bit add macro from part b.

    d. As shown in Figure 3.6, a simple way to perform a 64-bit multiply is to perform a series of four 32-bit multiply/shift/accumulate operations that each produce a 64-bit result.

    e. In the figure, two 4-bit values, A and B, holding values 11_{10} and 14_{10}, respectively, are each separated into two 2-bit upper and lower portions, named A1, A0 and B1 and B0. Assuming the products are 4 bits, the 8-bit product is computed as $(A1*B1) \ll 4 + (A1*B0) \ll 2 + (A0*B1) \ll 2 + (A0*B0)$.

    f. To apply this to a 64-bit multiply, each of the two 64-bit values must be held in two 32-bit registers. Each multiply generates a 64-bit result, allowing for a 128-bit final product.

    g. Using these macros, implement a 64-bit Mandelbrot set generator and measure the resultant performance difference.

    h. Implement both macros in inline assembly language and measure the result speedup of the Mandelbrot generator as compared to that of part d.

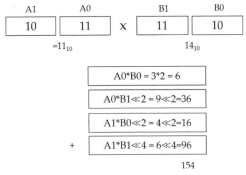

Figure 3.6: An 8-bit multiplier implemented with 4-bit multipliers.

CHAPTER 4

Memory optimization and video processing

Chapter Outline

The optimization objective in the previous chapter was to reduce the average number of cycles per instruction (CPI) by replacing higher latency instructions with lower latency instructions, specifically by replacing floating-point operations with fixed-point operations. Chapter 3 also covered the Linux framebuffer and the OpenCV image codecs and image display functionality to permit exploration of practical applications for this type of optimization.

For some applications, stalls caused by the processor having to wait for memory access have a greater impact on performance than stalls resulting from instruction latency. This is an effect of the phenomenon called the *memory wall*.

There are many programming and compiler techniques for improving memory system performance. One approach is to reduce memory references using techniques such as loop merging, which allows intermediate results that are conveyed through memory between adjacent loops to instead be conveyed through registers within a single loop body. Another approach is based on transforming loop nests or adding additional nested loops to reorder memory references without changing the kernel's functionality but reducing the address distance between consecutive memory references. This can improve cache performance by reducing cache line replacements caused by conflict misses.

This chapter introduces an example of the latter type of memory optimization. Loop transformations can improve cache performance by increasing temporal locality by reducing the time between memory address reuses. This type of optimization is useful for loops that access memory according to a regular pattern. A common type is *stencil loops*, used often in scientific applications and image processing.

To continue with the theme of graphical applications, this chapter's case studies focus on image processing using stencil loops. These will include the Gaussian blur and the Sobel derivative filter. To make these more interesting, this chapter will introduce a method for accessing real-time video data from an attached USB camera using both OpenCV and the Video4Linux subsystem. This, together with optimized image processing kernels and the Linux framebuffer, will allow us to use real-time computer vision as an application and performance objective.

4.1 Stencil loops

Most compute-intensive kernels take one or more arrays as input and produce one or more arrays as output. For example, linear algebra kernels such as matrix-matrix multiply perform pairwise multiply-accumulates between elements of the input arrays for each operand and produce an output array for the product matrix.

Stencils, on the other hand, compute each output array element as a function of input array elements whose locations are defined relative to the coordinate of the output element. The input and output arrays are often two-dimensional (2D) or three-dimensional (3D). For example, the kernel may compute output element (x,y) as a function of the input elements *above*, *below*, *to the left*, and *to the right*, that is, $(x,y-1)$, $(x,y+1)$, $(x-1,y)$, and $(x+1,y)$, respectively, although any pattern is possible.

Stencil loops are common in scientific and image-processing code. They are often embedded deeply in nested loops, such as when a stencil loop is applied iteratively (multiple times) to each frame of a video stream. As such, the stencil loop is generally the most expensive component of any application that requires it, so stencil loops are often a target for optimization.

Luckily, stencil loops have two properties that allow for optimization. The first is their *data-level parallelism*. In cases where the input and output array are separate, each output element may be computed independently of the other output elements. This makes these types of stencil loops "embarrassingly parallel", meaning that concurrent processors and/or functional units can compute output elements in parallel with little synchronization overhead. In other cases, the input and output arrays reside in the same memory pool, which creates dependencies between output elements. In this case, the stencil loop is still parallelizable, but the code must constrain the order in which output elements are computed.

The second property is their *data reuse*. Input elements referenced by one output often overlap with elements referenced by other outputs. This way, stencils may reuse input data through the processor's cache. However, stencil patterns are often complex in the sense that they span multiple dimensions, and this can lead to conflict misses in the cache. This is especially problematic when there is a long delay between the first and second time the loop references a particular input element, which is especially challenging for larger input spaces and/or stencil points.

4.2 The 2D filter

Figure 4.1 depicts the relationship between the input and output arrays for a 3 × 3 filter in which the input array is shown on the left and the output array is shown on the right. The elements of the first four rows and first four columns of each array are labeled with letters A through P.

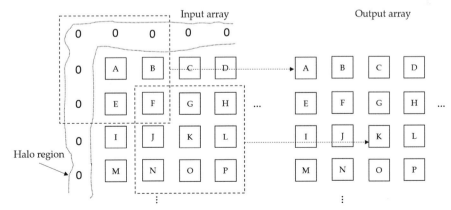

Figure 4.1: 3 × 3 mean filter.

In the 3×3 filter, each location of the output array is computed as the arithmetic mean of the 3×3 neighborhood of input elements centered on the corresponding location in the input array. For example, output element K will reference input elements F, G, H, J, K, L, N, O, and P.

Locations close to the boundary of the output array would reference locations outside the bounds of the input array. For example, output element A references only input elements A, B, E, and F.

Stencil loops often exhibit a high level of data reuse, where the same input element can be used multiple times when computing different output elements. As such, stencil loops have a high arithmetic intensity, but their performance depends on the ability of the memory system to take advantage of the locality of data access, since otherwise, the stencil may access off-chip memory through cache misses more than necessary.

Stencil loops are often used to implement *convolution filters*, which are comprised of a set of coefficients—or weights—with one weight for each of the corresponding input elements in the stencil. The filtering operation multiplies each coefficient against the corresponding input elements and sums the products. In the 2D case, if the coefficients are stored in an $(n \times n)$ matrix $\boldsymbol{G}$ and the input array is stored in matrix $\boldsymbol{I}$, then the output value $\boldsymbol{O}_{r,c}$ is computed as

$$O_{r,c} = \sum_{i=1}^{n} \sum_{j=1}^{n} G_{i,j} I_{r+i-\left\lfloor\frac{n}{2}\right\rfloor-1, c+j-\left\lfloor\frac{n}{2}\right\rfloor-1}$$

$$\sum_{j=1}^{n} G_{i,j} I_{r+i-\left\lfloor\frac{n}{2}\right\rfloor-1, c+j-\left\lfloor\frac{n}{2}\right\rfloor-1}$$

This requires n^2 multiplies and n^2 adds per output ($2n^2$ operations).

4.2.1 Computing the 2D filter as a matrix-vector or vector-matrix multiplication

Stencils can be applied using matrix-vector multiplication. One method is to load the coefficients as a flattened (1D array) into the vector and load the input elements into the matrix. The input elements corresponding to each stencil are loaded into the rows of the matrix. The resulting matrix-vector product will contain one output of the filter per row of the matrix.

Another approach is to use a vector-matrix multiplication, in which the input elements are loaded into the vector and the coefficients are loaded into the columns of the matrix. In this case, each the mapping between the coefficients and the matrix rows must be adjusted to reproduce the pattern of input-coefficient pairs matching the movement of the stencil across the input array.

In the second case, the matrix can be held constant while the vector is updated to process the entire input array, reducing the memory overhead needed to complete the computation.

The main limitation of the above approach is that the number of matrix rows is limited to the size of the stencil.

The convolutional layers of a convolutional neural network (CNN) perform one stencil per input channel and sum the outputs associated with each input channel, limiting the number of matrix rows to the stencil size multiplied by the number of input channels. Additionally, the convolutional layer computes multiple output arrays, allowing the maximum number of matrix columns to become the number of input elements multiplied by the number of output channels.

Conceptualizing the convolution as a vector-matrix or matrix-matrix multiplication is useful when the target platform includes hardware acceleration for matrix multiplication, that is, hardware support for 2D SIMD. Some ARM-based processors do have this capability, such as the Apple M1 chip designed for desktop computers, but most embedded ARM processors only offer 1D SIMD support. As such, in this text we will focus on traditional convolution methods since the focus is on the memory access pattern of the input data.

4.3 Separable filters

Any 2D filter whose coefficient matrix can be calculated as the product of a column vector and row vector is **separable**, meaning that it is equivalent to performing a 1D row filter on I to compute intermediate matrix $I2$, followed by a column filter on $I2$ to compute output O. In other words, any 2D filter with coefficient matrix $G = CR$ can be performed as a series of two 1D filters using coefficient vectors C and R.

A row filter is performed using

$$O_{r,c} = \sum_{i=1}^{n} G_i I_{r,c-i-\left|\frac{n}{2}\right|-1}$$

and a column filter is performed using

$$O_{r,c} = \sum_{i=1}^{n} G_i I_{r-i-\left|\frac{n}{2}\right|-1,c}$$

Figure 4.2 shows these two passes. The dashed rectangle shows which input elements are used to compute each output element. The shaded coloration shows which output elements have already been computed. The outputs from the row pass are used as inputs for the column pass, but one pass must complete before the next pass may begin. As such, the output elements need not be computed in any order.

This approach requires n multiplies and n adds per output per pass, or $4n$ ops per output in total. This reduces the computational load from $2n^2$ to $4n$.

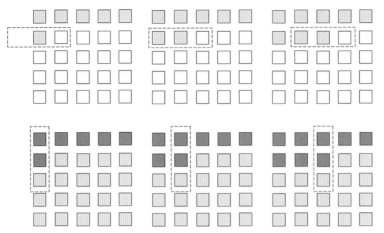

Figure 4.2: Row pass (top) and column pass (bottom) of a separable 3 × 3 2D filter.

Figure 4.3: 2D Gaussian blur using 7 × 7 coefficient array sampled from normal distribution applied to the "Lena" image. Note the black line that borders the bottom and right edges, which is produced from the filter coefficients being multiplied against implicit zeros that exist beyond the boundaries of the image.

4.3.1 Gaussian blur

Gaussian blur is a weighted mean filter in which the coefficients are normalized samples from a Gaussian probability density function (PDF).

As shown in Figure 4.3, applying the Gaussian blur makes images appear out of focus, producing an effect that softens the edges. The amount of blurring depends on the number of coefficients.

In other words, the Gaussian blur is a *low pass filter* that attenuates high-frequency signals from the image, where the high-frequency signals comprise the sharply defined edges in the image. The Gaussian blur is a common operation in image editing and many computer vision algorithms.

Image formats usually store pixel values as integers, whereas the Gaussian PDF is defined over real numbers. Because of this, the image data is typically converted into floating- or fixed-point format when applying the Gaussian blur.

A 2D Gaussian blur is separable because the 2D Gaussian PDF is equivalent to the product of two 1D Gaussian PDFs:

$$G_{x,y} = \frac{1}{\sqrt{2\pi\delta^2}}\, e^{-\frac{x^2}{2\delta^2}} \frac{1}{\sqrt{2\pi\delta^2}}\, e^{-\frac{x^2}{2\delta^2}} = \frac{1}{2\pi\delta^2}\, e^{-\frac{x^2+y^2}{2\delta^2}}$$

The Gaussian blur is implemented using the following algorithm.

Row pass:

for i=1 to rows

  for j=1 to columns

   sum = 0;

   for k=1 to n

    image_j = j+k-floor(n/2);

    if (image_j > 0) && (image_j <= columns)

     *sum = sum + image(i,image_j) * G(k)*

    end

   end

    blurred(i,j)=sum

  end

end

Column pass:

for i=1 to rows

  for j=1 to columns

   sum = 0;

  for k=1 to n

    image_i = i+k-floor(n/2);

    if (image_i > 0) && (image_i <= rows)

> $sum = sum + blurred(image\_i,j) * G(k);$
>
> > end
>
> end
>
> $blurred2(i,j)=sum$
>
> end
>
> end

You can compute the coefficients using the Linux Octave commands

```
g_1D = normpdf (-floor(N/2):floor(N/2),0,1);

g_1D = g_1D./sum(g_1D);
```

4.3.2 The Sobel filter

A grayscale image can be represented as a function $I(x,y)$, which evaluates to the pixel intensity at pixel location (x,y). Many computer vision tasks require, as input, the partial derivatives of the image, that is, $\delta I(x, y)/\delta x$, $\delta I(x, y)/\delta y$ in the X and Y direction. These partial derivatives are often abbreviated as $I_x(x,y)$ and $I_y(x,y)$. The *Sobel filter* is a popular method to calculate these partial derivatives.

Figure 4.4 shows the effect of applying the Sobel filter to calculate the X and Y partial derivatives on the original Lena image. In these images, white pixels represent edges.

As shown in Figure 4.5, the Sobel filter also can distill an image to its edges, the boundaries between the objects in the image. To do this, one can calculate the norm of each pixel's X and Y derivative, that is,

$$\sqrt{\left(\frac{\delta I(x,y)}{\delta x}\right)^2 + \left(\frac{\delta I(x,y)}{\delta y}\right)^2}$$

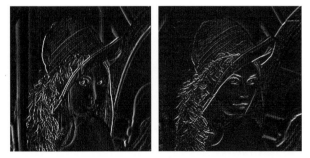

Figure 4.4: I_x (left), I_y (right) of Lena image using Sobel filter.

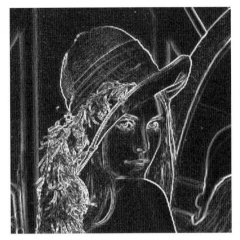

Figure 4.5: Norm of (I_x, I_y) of Lena image.

To use this "edge detection" method, the program must fully compute the X and Y derivatives from the source image, resulting in two intermediate images. It must then combine these intermediate images using the norm operation to compute a final image.

The coefficient matrices for the Sobel filter are

$$G_x = \begin{bmatrix} -1 & 0 & 1 \\ -2 & 0 & 2 \\ -1 & 0 & 1 \end{bmatrix}$$

and

$$G_y = \begin{bmatrix} 1 & 2 & 1 \\ 0 & 0 & 0 \\ -1 & -2 & -1 \end{bmatrix}$$

which are separable into row pass and column pass filters:

$$G_x = \begin{bmatrix} -1 & 0 & 1 \\ -2 & 0 & 2 \\ -1 & 0 & 1 \end{bmatrix} = \begin{bmatrix} 1 \\ 2 \\ 1 \end{bmatrix} \begin{bmatrix} -1 & 0 & 1 \end{bmatrix}$$

$$G_y = \begin{bmatrix} 1 & 2 & 1 \\ 0 & 0 & 0 \\ -1 & -2 & -1 \end{bmatrix} = \begin{bmatrix} 1 \\ 0 \\ -1 \end{bmatrix} \begin{bmatrix} 1 & 2 & 1 \end{bmatrix}$$

As seen in the images above, high-frequency noise creates false edges in the filtered image, so often the image is filtered with a Gaussian filter prior to applying the Sobel filter.

Figure 4.6: Sobel filter output (I_x, I_y, and edges) when image is prefiltered with Gaussian.

Figure 4.6 shows the effect of the Gaussian when applied as a preprocessing step before applying the Sobel filter. Notice that many of the white dots have been removed.

4.3.3 The Harris corner detector

Some computer vision applications require a method for identifying anchor points in an image for the purpose of establishing a correspondence between multiple images taken of the same scene from different perspectives. This is useful for video tracking, image stitching, and 3D modeling.

One way to identify anchor points is to find *corners*, an intersection of at least two edges. More generally, a corner is any point on the image whose surrounding *patch*, or square sub-region centered on the point, would change significantly if the patch area were shifted in any direction.

This is depicted in Figure 4.7.

There are many methods for detecting corners in an image. One of the most common is the *Harris detector*. The Harris detector looks for a pixel that has a large "shift difference" when patch W is shifted by (u,v) pixels, shown below as $E(u,v)$:

$$E(u,v) = \sum_{x,y \in W} w(x,y) \left[I(x+u, y+v) - I(x,y) \right]^2$$

$I()$ represents the image, and $w()$ represents the weights of the pixels in the patch.

This section examines a simple case where the weights are set to all ones. As such this term is dropped from the equation.

To simplify the computation and avoid boundary checking, the Harris detector is normally approximated using the first-order Taylor expansion of the above expression, as shown below:

$$E(u,v) = \sum_{x,y} \left[I(x+u, y+v) - I(x,y) \right]^2$$

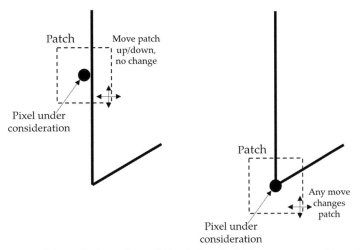

Figure 4.7: Two candidate pixels evaluated for their suitability as corners. The pixel on the left is near an edge and its corresponding patch would only change with a horizontal or diagonal movement. The pixel on the right is located on a corner, and its corresponding patch would change the patch significantly for any movement.

$$\approx \sum_{x,y} \left[\left(I(x,y) + uI_x(x,y) + vI_y(x,y) - I(x,y) \right) \right]^2$$

where I_x and I_y are the partial derivatives of I with respect to x and y.

$$= \sum_{x,y} u^2 I_x(x,y)^2 + 2uv I_x(x,y) I_y(x,y) + v^2 I_y(x,y)^2$$

$$= \begin{bmatrix} u & v \end{bmatrix} \left(\sum_{x,y} \begin{bmatrix} I_x(x,y)^2 & I_x(x,y)I_y(x,y) \\ I_x(x,y)I_y(x,y) & I_y(x,y)^2 \end{bmatrix} \right) \begin{bmatrix} u \\ v \end{bmatrix}$$

The matrix $M = \sum_{x,y} \begin{bmatrix} I_x(x,y)^2 & I_x(x,y)I_y(x,y) \\ I_x(x,y)I_y(x,y) & I_y(x,y)^2 \end{bmatrix}$ measures the patch's center pixel's "corner response" R, as

$$R = det(M) - k \left(trace(M) \right)^2$$

where

$$det\left(\begin{bmatrix} a & b \\ c & d \end{bmatrix} \right) = ad - bc$$

and

$$trace\left(\begin{bmatrix} a & b \\ c & d \end{bmatrix} \right) = a + d$$

and k is parameter, typically set to $k = 0.04$.

R is subjected to a threshold, where any value over a threshold is considered a corner.

Figure 4.8 shows the corners (shown in white) for the Lena image for different threshold values for a patch size of 5×5. These images are generated using the following steps:

1. Apply 7×7 separated Gaussian filter
2. Compute I_x and I_y using Sobel filter
3. Apply 5×5 Harris corner detector, which performs:
   a. Compute products of derivatives at each pixel $(I_x^2, I_y^2, I_x I_y)$
   b. Compute the response at each pixel

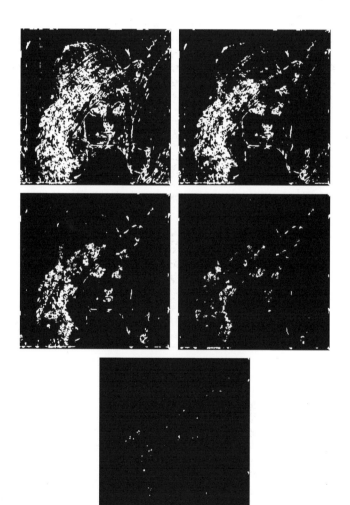

Figure 4.8: Corners in Lena image using threshold values $= [1e6 \ 1e7 \ 1e8 \ 1e9 \ 1e10]$.

4.3.4 Lucas-Kanade optical flow

Like corner detection, optical flow is a common calculation in computer vision. Optical flow is an approximation of the movement of pixels between consecutive frames. Like corner detection, there are many different algorithms for computing it. This section describes a version case of Lucas-Kanade optical flow. The full version of Lucas-Kanade also includes a hierarchical method for evaluating the optical over subsampled versions of the image, which is not included in this description.

The movement of each pixel from one video frame to the next is represented as a *flow field*, a 2D array of two-element vectors that indicates the X and Y movement of each pixel. Optical flow attempts to solve the following equation for the Δx and Δy terms (Δt is an independent variable representing the time between frames).

$$I(x,y,t) = I\left(x + \Delta x, y + \Delta y, t + \Delta t\right)$$

As before, the expression is approximated using the first-order Taylor expansion:

$$I(x,y,t) = I(x,y,t) + I_x(x,y)\Delta x + I_y(x,y)\Delta y + I_t(x,y)\Delta t$$

Also as before, $I_x()$ and $I_y()$ are the X and Y partial derivatives and are computed using the Sobel filter. $I_t()$ is the T partial derivative, which is estimated as the average difference in pixel intensities between the current and next frame within a patch, shown below as having size 2×2 pixels:

$$I_t(x,y) = \frac{\left(I^n(x,y) - I^{n+1}(x,y)\right) + \left(I^n(x+1,y) - I^{n+1}(x+1,y)\right) + \left(I^n(x,y+1) - I^{n+1}(x,y+1)\right) + \left(I^n(x+1,y+1) - I^{n+1}(x+1,y+1)\right)}{4}$$

The first-order Taylor expansion can be reduced as shown, in which the objective of optical flow is to solve for v_x and v_y, which are estimations for Δx and Δy:

$$I_x(x,y)v_x + I_y(x,y)v_y = -I_t(x,y)$$

This gives an underdetermined system of equations, having only one equation and two unknowns. A way to work around this problem is to assume that all pixels within a patch of n pixels exhibit the same movement. For example, a 3×3 patch would give the following system of equations:

$$I_x\left(x-1,y-1\right)v_x + I_y\left(x-1,y-1\right)v_y = -I_t\left(x-1,y-1\right)$$

$$I_x\left(x,y-1\right)v_x + I_y\left(x,y-1\right)v_y = -I_t\left(x,y-1\right)$$

$$I_x\left(x+1,y-1\right)v_x + I_y\left(x+1,y-1\right)v_y = -I_t\left(x+1,y-1\right)$$

$$I_x\left(x-1,y\right)v_x + I_y\left(x-1,y\right)v_y = -I_t\left(x-1,y\right)$$

$$I_x\left(x,y\right)v_x + I_y\left(x,y\right)v_y = -I_t\left(x,y\right)$$

$$I_x(x+1,y)v_x + I_y(x+1,y)v_y = -I_t(x+1,y)$$

$$I_x(x-1,y+1)v_x + I_y(x-1,y+1)v_y = -I_t(x-1,y+1)$$

$$I_x(x,y+1)v_x + I_y(x,y+1)v_y = -I_t(x,y+1)$$

$$I_x(x+1,y+1)v_x + I_y(x+1,y+1)v_y = -I_t(x+1,y+1)$$

This system of equations is now an overdetermined system, having nine equations and two unknowns. Overdetermined systems are solvable under certain conditions. The problem is described using linear algebra as shown below:

Let

$$A = \begin{bmatrix} I_x(x-1,y-1) & I_y(x-1,y-1) \\ I_x(x,y-1) & I_y(x,y-1) \\ \dots & \dots \end{bmatrix}$$

and

$$b = \begin{bmatrix} -I_t(x-1,y-1) \\ -I_t(x,y-1) \\ \dots \end{bmatrix}$$

Then

$$A\begin{bmatrix} v_x \\ v_y \end{bmatrix} = b$$

$$\begin{bmatrix} v_x \\ v_y \end{bmatrix} = A^{-1}b$$

$$\begin{bmatrix} v_x \\ v_y \end{bmatrix} = \left(A^T A\right)^{-1} A^T b$$

$$\begin{bmatrix} v_x \\ v_y \end{bmatrix} = \left(\sum_{x,y} \begin{bmatrix} I_x(x,y)^2 & I_x(x,y)I_y(x,y) \\ I_x(x,y)I_y(x,y) & I_y(x,y)^2 \end{bmatrix}\right)^{-1} A^T b$$

The inverse of a 2×2 matrix is computable quickly. A^T is a $2 \times n$ matrix and b is an $n \times 1$ vector, so $A^T b$ evaluates to a 2×1 vector.

This simple version of optical flow is an example of a memory-bounded stencil loop.

4.4 Memory access behavior of 2D filters

The memory access behavior of stencil loops such as 2D filters involves reading overlapping sets of inputs. This type of access pattern exhibits temporal and spatial locality, allowing a cache to potentially achieve a high rate of data reuse. However, certain code optimizations may be needed to achieve maximum cache performance.

Cache misses are categorized according to their cause: *compulsory*, *capacity*, and *conflict*.

Compulsory misses occur on the first access to a cache block. The primary method to reduce compulsory misses is the use of cache prefetching technology. The effectiveness of prefetching depends on the regularity and predictability of the access pattern. Luckily, image filtering (and stencil loops in general) is both regular and predictable.

Capacity misses occur because of the cache not having sufficient capacity to exploit the available locality. The primary method to reduce capacity misses is to increase the size of the cache.

Conflict misses occur when multiple memory addresses compete for a single cache line.

In the case of image filtering, images are usually stored in row-major order, and conflict misses can occur when reading columns. For example, when the image's row size is such that pixels from column c in row r map to the same cache line as pixels from column c in row $r + n$, a conflict miss may cause cache lines to be discarded and subsequently reread from memory the next time the program revisits row r.

In the case of a separatable filter that processes pixels in a separate row filter pass and column filter pass, the output pixels computed in the row pass are subsequently read in the column pass. Since the entire image must be processed with the row pass before the column pass may begin, it is reasonable to assume that none of the output pixels from the row pass will remain in the cache long enough to be reused in the column pass.

There are many hardware approaches for reducing conflict misses, such as increasing cache associativity, improving the replacement policy, and using victim caches, but there are also software methods for reducing conflict misses. The programmer can potentially reduce conflict misses using memory allocation and loop transformation techniques to optimize the access pattern. Memory allocation techniques include interleaving multiple arrays into one array or changing the dimensionality of an array (e.g., transposing a matrix).

Loop transformations include such techniques as loop interchange (swapping the inner and outer loop), loop fusion (combining two loops into one), loop fission (splitting one loop into two), and loop tiling (or blocking). Unfortunately, compilers are not generally able to apply these types of optimization automatically, so it is up to the programmer. This chapter focuses on loop tiling due to its effectiveness for stencil loops.

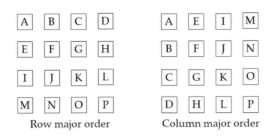

Figure 4.9: 4 × 4 Arrays collapsed using row-major and column-major order. Row-major order stores the elements across each row in consecutive memory locations, while column-major order stores the elements across each column in consecutive memory locations. In this figure, consecutive letters represent consecutive memory addresses.

4.4.1 2D data representation

2D data structures such as images and matrices must be superimposed onto organized into a 1D array of elements when stored in memory or transmitted across of communication channel. For memory this is an important consideration because both cache and DRAM achieve higher performance when consecutive accesses have consecutive addresses.

Figure 4.9 shows two different methods for projecting an image onto a 1D memory space: *row-major* and *column-major*. Row-major is perhaps the most common. In this case, pixels across each row are stored in consecutive memory locations, while pixels across each column are stored in locations separated by the row size. For example, traversing the third column would require pixel addresses C, G, K, O.

4.4.2 Filtering along the row

Assume the image is stored in row-major order and consider a 1D horizontal (along the row) filter having three coefficients. When filtering the image, the processor will load three input values from consecutive memory locations for each filter evaluation. Since the filter uses a sliding window, the processor will reload two of these same elements in the next iteration. Because of the overlap, the processor will read each pixel three times.

If written as a standard averaging filter, the code will perform five arithmetic operations per output: three multiplies and two adds. For each output pixel, the filter will write one pixel and read at least one pixel, since one new pixel is revealed as the filtering window advances by one element.

With an arithmetic intensity of only five operations per two pixels, this filter will most likely be memory bound and its performance will depend on its cache miss rate. The miss rate depends on what portion of memory accesses is reused from the cache through a cache hit.

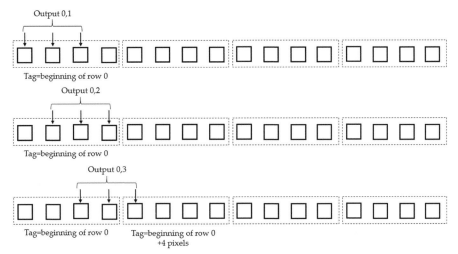

Figure 4.10: Runtime behavior of a 3-tap 1D row filter.

The programmer can roughly estimate cache performance using a simplistic cache and execution model by making the following assumptions:

- the cache is fully associative,
- consider only the load instructions,
- cache lines hold four pixels each (equivalent to 16-byte cache lines), and
- do not consider outputs whose inputs would reside outside the image boundaries.

This simple model is depicted in Figure 4.10, assuming the outputs are processed in row-major order. As the filter operates there is a **cache line replacement after every two outputs** for this 3-input horizontal filter, but no cache line will ever need to be loaded again after being replaced.

4.4.3 Filtering along the column

For the column filter, on every filter evaluation the processor will load a pixel from a different row. To fully utilize the cache, the column filter should process each output element in row-major order. This way, for each consecutive filter evaluation, the processor will read consecutive inputs along the row.

This is depicted in Figure 4.11. In this case there is a **cache line replacement on every fourth input element** for this 3-input vertical filter. At first glance this seems better than the horizontal filter, but only one element is read from each cache line, meaning that the vertical filter has less temporal locality.

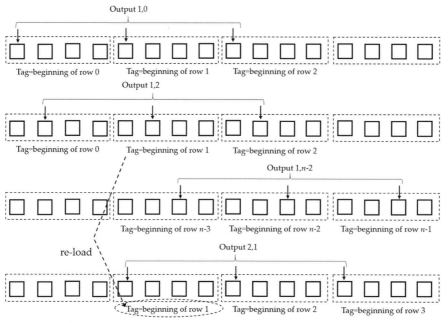

Figure 4.11: Runtime behavior of a 3-tap 1D column filter.

This is a problem because by the time all the outputs from row 1 are processed, the cache lines containing the lower-numbered columns for rows 1 and 2 would likely have been replaced and need to be loaded again into the cache.

In other words, like the row filter, the column filter reads each input element n times (where n = the filter size), but the time between reuses is equivalent to the time needed to process a row of output elements. Between reuses, the input elements to be reused will be replaced unless the cache is able to retain at least $n \times c$ pixels, where c is the number of columns.

4.5 Loop tiling

As shown in Figure 4.12, by changing the order in which the output elements are evaluated, the image can effectively be subdivided into a series of smaller vertical strips. This will reduce the effective number of columns from c to c_t, which will reduce the number of repeated cache line fills.

The drawback of this type of subdividing is that it prevents reuse of pixels in cache lines that straddle the divisions between vertical strips. Also, for 2D stencils such as the Harris corner detector that cannot be separated into a row and column pass, using this partitioning approach will prevent the horizontal component of the stencil from reusing input pixels in the strips to the left and the right.

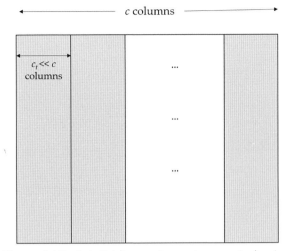

Figure 4.12: Subdividing an image into vertical strips.

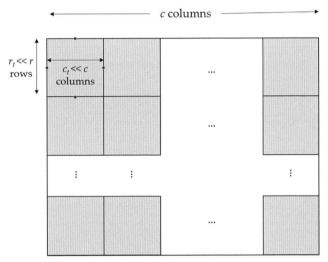

Figure 4.13: Subdividing the image into rectangular subimages.

As shown in Figure 4.13, partitioning the image into rectangular subimages that are processed in row-major order solves this problem. This partitioning is achieved using loop tiling. Loop tiling changes the order in which input and output elements are accessed. Instead of accessing all indices in each dimension before incrementing the index of the next dimension (i.e., processing all the columns in each row before proceeding to the next row), the iteration space is decomposed into a series of smaller blocks where all the indices within each block are processed before moving to the next block. To do this, the programmer must add additional levels of loops, where the outer loops process each block—or tile—of the image space and the inner loops process individual elements within each tile.

For example, consider the following loop:

```
for (i=0;i<SIZE_Y;i++)

  for (j=0;j<SIZE_X;j++)

    do_something(i,j)
```

This loop can be tiled by adding two additional levels of nesting:

```
for (i=0;i<ceiling(SIZE_Y/TILESIZE_Y);i++)

  for (j=0;j<ceiling(SIZE_X/TILESIZE_X);j++)

    for (ii=i*TILESIZE_Y;ii<(i+1)*TILESIZE_Y;ii++)

      if (ii<SIZE_Y)

        for (jj=j*TILESIZE_X;jj<(j+1)*TILESIZE_X;jj++)

          if (ii<SIZE_X)

            do_something(ii,jj)
```

Tiling is depicted in Figure 4.14. The left side shows the nontiled access pattern for a row-wise traversal. To the right is a tiled version, which processes each 2 × 2 pixel tile in the image.

4.6 Tiling and the stencil halo region

As shown in Figure 4.15, a 2D stencil comprising *n* rows and *m* columns will access *n*-1 rows above and below the tile boundaries, and *m*-1 columns to the left and right of the tile boundaries. These pixels form the *halo region* around each tile. When tiling a stencil loop, the

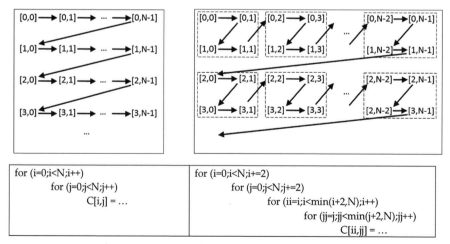

Figure 4.14: Nontiled and tiled access pattern.

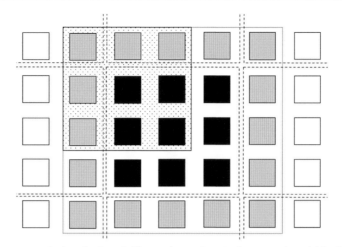

Figure 4.15: The output pixels of a 3 × 3 filter using a 3 × 3 tile are colored black. The dashed lines show the tile boundaries with respect to the output pixels for each tile. The gray pixels represent the halo region of the center tile. The patterned box covers the input pixels for tile output location (0,0).

programmer may wish to buffer each tile in a smaller array whose row size matches the tile width. In this case, the programmer must also copy the halo region.

4.7 Example 2D filter implementation

This section describes how to build a tiled image filter to explore the performance impact of tile optimization.

Begin by defining a structure to store a 2D value:

```
struct size {
    int x;
    int y;
};
```

Define a structure to hold the tile size, its location in an image, and the image size:

```
struct tile {
    struct size tile_size, tile_loc, image_size;
};
```

Before filtering each tile, the program must determine how to handle tiles on the image boundary, specifically those where part of the tile extends beyond the image boundary, as shown in Figure 4.16.

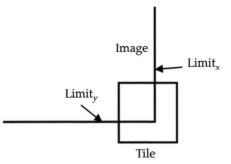

Figure 4.16: Boundary tile.

To do this, determine if the program is processing a boundary tile. If so, determine if the *right* or *bottom edge* of the tile is outside the limits of the original image. Use a function to pre-compute the limitations for the *X* and *Y* dimension:

```
void find_limit(struct tile *mytile,struct size *limit)

{

limit->x = ((mytile->tile_loc.x + 1) * mytile->tile_ size.x - 1 >

        mytile->image_size.x) ?

        mytile->image_size.x % mytile->tile_size.x :

        mytile->tile_size.x;

 limit->y = ((mytile->tile_loc.y + 1) * mytile->tile_size.y - 1 >

        mytile->image_size.y) ?

        mytile->image_size.y % mytile->tile_size.y :

        mytile->tile_size.y;

}
```

Next, write functions that apply a 2D filter to a tile. The function will take as input:

(1) a tile object, which defines the size of the tile and its location within the image,
(2) a pointer to a grayscale, floating-point representation of the input image,
(3) a pointer to the output image,
(4) a pointer to the coefficient array,
(5) the size of each filter dimension,
(6) the usable portion of the tile, to avoid writing beyond the edge of image when processing boundary tiles, and
(7) a flag that specifies when the output image already contains one of the components of a direction vector, useful when calculating the Sobel filter.

```
void filter_tile2d (struct tile *mytile,

                 float *in,

                 float *out,

                 float *coeffs_2d,

                 int fsize,

                 struct size *limit,

                 int vec) {
```

The filter must iterate over each value in the tile, requiring a two-level nested loop. Each dimension of the loop must be constrained by **limit** input, which can be precomputed using the **find_limit**() function prior to calling this function.

```
int i,j,k,l,offset,coeff_radius,img_x,img_y;

float sum;

coeff_radius = fsize >> 1; // divide by 2

for (i=0;i<limit->y;i++) {

        img_y = mytile->tile_loc.y * mytile->tile_size.y + i;

    for (j=0;j<limit->x;j++) {

        img_x = mytile->tile_loc.x * mytile->tile_size.x + j;

        sum = 0.0;
```

The filter itself is a pairwise multiple-accumulate between pixels and their corresponding coefficients. Use if-statements to avoid accessing halo pixels that are outside the boundaries of the image.

Assuming we process the filter as a 2D filter as opposed to two passes of a 1D filter as is possible for a separable filter, the actual filtering requires another two-level nested loop to process each coefficient. Note the loop variables *k* and *l*.

```
for (k=-coeff_radius;k<(coeff_radius+1);k++) {

    if (((img_y + k) >= 0) && ((img_y + k) < mytile-> image_size.y))

        for (l=-coeff_radius;l<(coeff_radius+1);l++)

            if (((img_x + l) >= 0) && ((img_x + l) < mytile->image_size.x)) {
```

This loop calculates the offset of each input pixel. In this case assume the pixels are contained within a tile buffer whose dimensions match the size of the tile and its enclosing halo region.

```
offset = (i + coeff_radius + k) *

        (mytile->image_size.x + coeff_radius) + j + coeff_radius + 1;

sum+= in[offset] *coeffs_2d[(k + coeff_radius) *

        fsize + (1 + coeff_radius)];

   }

}
```

Lastly, calculate the address of the output pixel and store it. If the **vec** flag is set, the output is calculated as the norm for the current output value and the newly calculated value.

```
offset = (i+coeff_radius) *(mytile->image_size.x +

            coeff_radius) + j + coeff_radius;

if (vec) {

        out[offset] = sqrtf(out[offset] *out[offset] + sum *sum);

} else {

    out[offset] = sum;

}

   }

  }

 }
```

4.8 Capturing and converting video frames

The chapter's examples require test images to verify functionality. One way to acquire an image is to read an image file as described in Chapter 3. However, we will also describe how to integrate your code with an attached USB camera. This requires a function to capture images from a camera and a function to convert each tile from a captured image into the floating-point format expected by the filtering functions. Depending on how you capture the images, your USB camera may provide different image formats.

After the program processes each tile it can convert each pixel to the framebuffer pixel format (16-bit *RGB*, in this case) and write it directly to the framebuffer.

This requires a new function:

```
void export_tile (struct tile *mytile,
          unsigned char *fbp,
          float *in,
          int fsize,
          struct size *limit) {
    int i,j,offset,location,coeff_radius,scaled_5bit,scaled_ 6bit;
    float lum;
    coeff_radius = fsize>>1;
    for (i=0;i<limit->y;i++) {
      for (j=0;j<limit->x;j++) {
        offset = (i+coeff_radius) *
              (mytile->image_size.x+coeff_radius)+j+coeff_radius;
        lum = in[offset];
```

When converting from a single grayscale value to *RGB*, the program can assign the grayscale value to all three-color components.

Each pixel value is stored as a normalized value in the range [0,1], so the program can separately compute the red, green, and blue values by multiplying against their maximum value and converting back to integer. In 16-bit *RGB*, the maximum value for red and blue is 31 and for green it is 63.

```
scaled_5bit = (int)(lum * 31.0);
scaled_5bit = scaled_5bit > 31 ? 31 : scaled_5bit & 0x1F;
scaled_6bit = (int)(lum * 63.0);
scaled_6bit = scaled_6bit > 63 ? 63 : scaled_6bit & 0x3F;
```

Next the program must calculate the framebuffer and write the pixel into the framebuffer:

```
location = ((mytile->tile_loc.y * mytile->tile_size.y +
          i)+vinfo.yoffset) * finfo.line_length +
          (mytile->tile_loc.x * mytile->tile_size.y +
          j+vinfo.xoffset) * (vinfo.bits_per_pixel/8);
```

```
        *((unsigned short *)(fbp + location)) = (scaled_5bit << 11) |
            (scaled_6bit << 5) | scaled_5bit;

    }

  }

}
```

4.9 Capturing frames from a webcam

Many ARM-based platforms include a USB interface and USB-based webcams are relatively inexpensive, which allows for relatively easy development and performance optimization of real-time video processing. In this section we describe two methods for capturing video frames as images from an attached camera. The first method uses OpenCV, which is simple to implement (at least when using the native image size supported by the camera and the RGB colorspace, the default colorspace used by OpenCV) and does not require superuser permissions. However, capturing frames with OpenCV adds significant execution time overhead. The second method uses Video4Linux, a Linux driver, that offers more flexibility in setting the size and colorspace of the captured images while also being faster.

4.9.1 Using OpenCV to capture video

As compared to the OpenCV configuration used in Chapter 3, an additional module is required, "VideoIO". Thus you will need the following header files:

```
#include <opencv2/opencv.hpp>

#include <opencv2/imgcodecs.hpp>

#include <opencv2/highgui.hpp>

#include <opencv2/videoio.hpp>
```

When compiling your code, you will also need to specify the include directory:

```
"/usr/include/opencv4"
```

and the linker options:

```
"-lopencv_videoio -lopencv_core -lopencv_imgcodecs -lopencv_highgui"
```

In addition to providing access to image capture, these options will also retain the ability to decode image files and display images on the screen to an X Windows server.

The following code will capture an image and display it on the screen at the highest possible frame rate:

```
namedWindow("Display window");

VideoCapture cap(0); // assuming use of "cv" namespace

if (!cap.isOpened()) { // check for errors

    fprintf(stderr,"ERROR: cannot open camera");

    exit(1);

}

Mat image; // allocate image to which to capture

while (1) {

    cap >> image; // capture image

    imshow("Display window",image); // display image

    waitKey(1); // move ahead with minimum delay

}
```

The captured format can be queried by accessing the following fields:

- `image.rows, image.cols`: height and width
- `image.elemSize()`: bytes per pixel
- `image.channels()`: number of color channels

The captured data can be queried by accessing the `image.datastart` pointer.

OpenCV will decode the image captured by the camera and generally store it as 24-bit RGB data.

4.9.2 Using Video4Linux to capture video

Video4Linux is an alternative approach for capturing video. Video4Linux is a driver framework built into most Linux distributions that provides a standard interface for video capture. The following example code uses the webcam to capture 640×480 resolution images using the *YUYV* colorspace. The reader is encouraged to attempt to process even larger image sizes. However, the bandwidth of a typical USB2 interface will limit the maximum resolution to approximately 1024×768 at 30 frames per second for uncompressed video. Some USB cameras support higher-resolution video using compression, in which case your software will need to use an addition library to decompress the video. Note that this decompression is included in OpenCV but not in Video4Linux.

To get started with Video4Linux, add the following includes:

```
#include <stdio.h>

#include <stdlib.h>

#include <sys/ioctl.h>

#include <sys/select.h>

#include <sys/mman.h>

#include <linux/videodev2.h>

#include <string.h>
```

Since the program is using the Linux framebuffer, the following includes will also be necessary:

```
#include <unistd.h>

#include <fcntl.h>

#include <linux/fb.h>
```

The program must initialize the Video4Linux camera interface before it can capture frames from camera. The initializing function will return two values that will allow us to maintain the state of the capture system: a variable of the "struct v4l2_buffer" type and a pointer to the capture buffer. Use a global variable for the file handle.

```
int open_cam (struct v4l2_buffer *buf,void **buffer) {

        struct v4l2_format fmt;

        struct v4l2_requestbuffers req;
```

The Video4Linux driver creates a device file at **/dev/video0** whenever a webcam is attached. If this file does not exist then you may need to install support for Video4Linux into your Linux distribution.

Like most Linux kernel modules, your program communicates with the Video4Linux module by opening its corresponding device file and issuing system calls using the file descriptor.

In this case you must use the **ioctl()** function to set capture parameters and the **mmap()** function to retrieve captured images.

Begin by setting the resolution to 640 columns by 480 rows and setting the pixel format to *YUYV*. Since each pixel is represented by two bytes, this means that each frame requires 614,400 bytes, or 147.5 Mbit/s, to transmit 30 frames per second.

Begin by opening the capture device:

```
fd1 = open("/dev/video0",O_RDWR);

    if (fd1==-1) { // fd1 is global

        perror("opening video device");

        return 0;

}
```

Next, clear the format structure and set it up for video capture mode and set its resolution to 480 rows by 640 columns.

```
memset (&fmt,0,sizeof(fmt));

fmt.type = V4L2_BUF_TYPE_VIDEO_CAPTURE;

fmt.fmt.pix.width = 640;

fmt.fmt.pix.height = 480;
```

Use the following code to select *YUYV* mode:

```
fmt.fmt.pix.pixelformat = V4L2_PIX_FMT_YUYV;

fmt.fmt.pix.field = V4L2_FIELD_NONE;

if (ioctl(fd1,VIDIOC_S_FMT,&fmt)==-1) {

        perror("setting pixel format");

        return 0;

}
```

After calling `ioctl()`, the format structure will be updated. The program must also check it to ensure that the driver applied the expected settings:

```
if (fmt.fmt.pix.pixelformat != V4L2_PIX_FMT_YUYV) {

fprintf(stderr,"capture device did not accept YUYV format\n");

        return 0;

}

if ((fmt.fmt.pix.width != 640) || (fmt.fmt.pix.height != 480)) {

        fprintf(stderr,"driver is sending image at %d x %d\n",

fmt.fmt.pix.width, fmt.fmt.pix.height);

        return 0;

}
```

Now that the resolution and color depth are set, the program can instruct the driver to capture frames using memory-mapped I/O:

```
memset (&req,0,sizeof(req));

req.count = 1;

req.type = V4L2_BUF_TYPE_VIDEO_CAPTURE;

req.memory = V4L2_MEMORY_MMAP;

if (ioctl(fd1,VIDIOC_REQBUFS,&req)==-1) {

        perror("requesting buffer");

        return 0;

}
```

The next step is to query the driver to determine the size of the buffer used to send frames back to user space, and then create the memory mapping:

```
memset(buf,0,sizeof(buf));

buf->type = V4L2_BUF_TYPE_VIDEO_CAPTURE;

buf->memory = V4L2_MEMORY_MMAP;

buf->index = 0;

if (ioctl(fd1,VIDIOC_QUERYBUF,buf)==-1) {

        perror("querying buffer");

        return 0;

}

*buffer = mmap(0,buf->length,PROT_READ |

        PROT_WRITE,MAP_SHARED,fd1,buf->m.offset);

if (ioctl(fd1, VIDIOC_QBUF, buf)==-1) {

        perror("queuing buffer");

        return 0;

}
```

The last step before capturing is to turn on the streaming function of the camera:

```
if (ioctl(fd1,VIDIOC_STREAMON,&buf->type)==-1) {

        perror("start capture");

        return 0;
```

```
    }

    return 1;

    }
```

Once the initialization returns successfully the program is ready to begin receiving frames from the camera.

The next function will capture a frame from the camera. This is a synchronous function, meaning that it would not return until the frame has been successfully captured.

```
int capture_frame (struct v4l2_buffer *buf) {

        fd_set fds;

        int ret;

        struct timeval tv;
```

The Linux `select()` system can synchronize the software with the frame capture rate of the camera. `select()` is used to block a program's execution until new data is ready to be read. It is often used when using the Sockets API to wait for incoming network data.

Make sure you open the framebuffer after opening the capture device to ensure that the capture device's file descriptor has a value greater than the framebuffer. Otherwise, the `select()` call will fail.

```
    tv.tv_sec=0;

    tv.tv_usec=0;

    FD_ZERO(&fds);

    FD_SET(fd1, &fds);

    ret = select(fd1+1, &fds, NULL, NULL, &tv);

    if(ret == -1) {

        perror("waiting for frame");

        return 1;

    }
```

The next two IO control calls will dequeue a framebuffer from Video4Linux and then enqueue another request for a buffer.

```
    if(ioctl(fd1, VIDIOC_DQBUF, buf) == -1) {

        perror("retrieving frame");

        return 1;
```

```
    }

    if (ioctl(fd1, VIDIOC_QBUF, buf) == -1) {

        perror("queuing buffer");

        return 0;

    }

}
```

4.9.3 YUV and chroma subsampling

OpenCV represents all captured frames using RGB pixel values, but when using Video4Linux some webcams will only provide other colorspaces, such as the *YUV colorspace*. *YUV* stores each pixel as three values: *luminance* (*Y*), representing the brightness of the pixel, and two *chrominance* (*U*, *V*)—or color—values.

The luminance values that comprise the image by themselves represent a grayscale version of the image. This is convenient because many computer vision and image processing algorithms require only the grayscale version of the image. If, for example, the camera used the *RGB* colorspace, calculating the grayscale value of each pixel would require an additional calculation such as:

$$\text{gray} = 0.299 \times \text{red} + 0.587 \times \text{green} + 0.114 \times \text{blue}$$

The chrominance values provide the color values that allow *YUV* values to be converted into *RGB* values when needed. *U* represents the difference between the red color intensity and luminance, and *V* represents the difference between the blue intensity and luminance. Combined, the luminance and chrominance values can be translated into red, green, and blue color channels.

YUV values can be translated into *RGB* values by combining the luminance with the chrominance values using the following conversion expressions:

$$R = Y + 1.13983 \times (V - 128)$$

$$G = Y \quad 0.39465 \times (U - 128) \quad 0.58060 \times (V - 128)$$

$$B = Y + 2.03211 \times (U - 128)$$

As shown in the expressions, the red channel is a combination of luminance and the *V*-chrominance values, the green channel is a combination of luminance and both chrominance values, and the blue channel is a combination of the luminance and *U*-chrominance value.

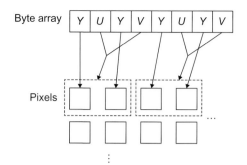

Figure 4.17: In *YUYV* format, a *Y* value is stored for each pixel and a (*U*,*V*) value is stored for each pair of pixel values horizontally.

Webcams may also use a technique called *chroma subsampling* to reduce the number of bits required for each pixel. Of these techniques, *YUYV* is a variation on *YUV* that stores the chroma information at half the resolution of the luminance information. This reduces the average number of bits per pixel from 24 bits per pixel (assuming 8-bit values for *Y*, *U*, and *V*) to 16 bits per pixel.

As shown in Figure 4.17, in this format there is a luminance for each pixel, but there is only one chrominance value for every two horizontally adjacent pixels.

The following function will convert each tile and halo region of pixels from *YUYV* to gray-scale floating point and store the resulting values in an array large enough to hold only the tile and the halo region.

The function will have a similar interface to the filter function:

```
void extract_tile (unsigned short *in_image,
            struct tile *mytile,
            float *out,
            int fsize,
            struct size *limit) {
  int i,j,offset,img_x,img_y,coeff_radius;
  float lum;
  coeff_radius = fsize>>1;
  for (i=-coeff_radius;i<limit->y+coeff_radius;i++) {
    img_y = mytile->tile_loc.y * mytile->tile_size.y + i;
    if ((img_y >= 0) && (img_y < mytile->image_size.y)) {
      for (j=-coeff_radius;j<limit->x+coeff_radius;j++) {
```

```
        img_x = mytile->tile_loc.x * mytile->tile_size.x + j;

    if ((img_x >= 0) && (img_x < mytile->image_size.x)) {
```

At this point the program must calculate separate offsets to find the luminance value in the YUYV image (every second byte) as well as the offset within the target image:

```
offset_cam = (img_y) * mytile->image_size.x * 2 +
        img_x * 2;
offset = (i+coeff_radius) * (mytile->image_size.x +
        coeff_radius) + j+coeff_radius;
```

The program can convert each luminance value to floating point by normalizing against its maximum value:

```
        lum = (float)(*((unsigned char *)in_image+offset_cam)) / 255.0;
        out[offset] = lum;
        }
      }
    }
  }
}
```

4.10 Applying the 2D tiled filter

Now that we can receive video frames from the camera, let us test if we can write a loop that applies a filter to each tile of each input image. The loop will iterate for each tile so that it can be structured as a two-level nested loop.

This function should accept the image size and tile size as arguments, so before the loop, initialize a "struct tile" variable (named mytile in the code below) such that it contains these sizes.

The program can use OpenMP to distribute the outer loop's workload across the thread pool. This way, each thread will process a set of tile rows.

The last tile in each dimension may straddle the image boundary, so the loop bound must "round up" partial tiles. To do this, use a trinary expression that adds one to the image size-tile size quotient when the corresponding modulo is nonzero.

```
#pragma omp parallel for firstprivate(mytile)

for (i=0;i<(mytile.image_size.y % mytile.tile_size.y ?

                mytile.image_size.y / mytile.tile_size.y + 1 :

                mytile.image_size.y / mytile.tile_size.y);i++) {

  mytile.tile_loc.y = i;

  for (j=0;j<(mytile.image_size.x % mytile.tile_size.x ?

                mytile.image_size.x / mytile.tile_size.x + 1 :

                mytile.image_size.x / mytile.tile_size.x);j++) {

      mytile.tile_loc.x = j;
```

For each tile the program must compute its internal limits to prevent the filter loop from exceeding the image boundaries in either dimension for any tile whose right or bottom edge extends beyond the image boundary.

Next, the grayscale version of the image tile is extracted from the *YUYV* frame. Note that you must adapt the `extract_tile()` function to perform the RGB-to-grayscale conversion if the captured data is in RGB format.

From this data, perform the 2D version of both the *X* and *Y* Sobel operator. After computing the *X* and *Y* partial derivatives for each pixel, calculate the resultant norm. Lastly convert the tile to 16-bit *RGB* and write it into the framebuffer.

```
      find_limit(&mytile,&limit);
      extract_tile(in_image,&mytile,frame,3,&limit);
      filter_tile2d(&mytile,frame,filtered_x, xsobel_2d,3,&limit,0);
      filter_tile2d(&mytile,frame,filtered_xy, ysobel_2d,3,&limit,1);
      export_tile(&mytile,fbp,filtered_xy,&limit);
  }

}
```

Use perf_event to instrument the code at this level to measure the performance counters before and after the OpenMP parallel section. This way you can measure the performance metrics for processing each frame.

4.11 Applying the separated 2D tiled filter

When processing a separated 2D filter using a 1D row filter pass followed by a 1D column filter pass, you must make sure the halo region pixels passed to the second pass reflect the updates generated by the first pass in the tiles above, below, to the left, and to the right of the current tile.

The easiest way to guarantee this is to process the entire image using the row filter before applying the column filter. However, since all tiles must be processed by one pass before beginning the second pass, this will cause a long delay between when the row pass writes its pixels and when the column reads the same pixels. We leave the details of this implementation as an exercise.

4.12 Top-level loop

In order to measure the performance impact of different tile sizes, the code will vary the tile size while capturing frames from the camera. To do this, assume the tiles are square and store the widths of each size in a zero-terminated array:

```
int dims[15] = {8,16,32,48,64,96,128,160,192,224,256,288, 320,352, 0};
```

Use an infinite loop to capture each frame and apply the Sobel filter. After exhausting all tile sizes, set the tile size to match the image size, which will provide a baseline performance resulting from no tiling.

```
k = 0;
while (1) {
   t_size.x = t_size.y = dims[k];
   if (t_size.x == 0) { // now filter without tiling
        k=0;
   // assume image is 640x480 here, change if needed
        t_size.x = 640;
        t_size.y = 480;
   } else k++;
capture_frame (&buf);
filter_16bit_cam (buffer, t_size, 480, 640, fbp);
   }
```

Figure 4.18: Cache miss rate and CPI for 2D Sobel edge detection filter for a range of square tile sizes, from 8 × 8 pixels to 352 × 352 pixels, and without tiling. This performance includes the function that converts and buffers each frame and the function that writes the framebuffer. Cache miss rate roughly correlates with average CPI. The highest-performing tile was 8 × 8, which provided a speedup of 1.7 in miss rate as compared to the nontiled version.

4.13 Performance results

Figure 4.18 shows the cache miss rate and CPI for the filter function on the Raspberry Pi. The filter function includes the tile conversion code and framebuffer output code. Note that some tile sizes are unreasonably large as compared to the frame size of 640 × 480.

The worst cache miss rate occurs when there is no tiling, but the worst CPI occurs with tile size 288 × 288. CPI improves slightly when tiling is discontinued. This is likely due to lower instruction CPI that results from the reduction of executed branch instructions from needing fewer iterations of the tile loops.

4.14 Chapter wrap-up

This chapter described tile-based loop optimization, whose objective is to reduce the cache miss rate by reordering memory references to improve memory access locality. To demonstrate this optimization, the chapter examined image filtering using stencil loops and described a complete computer vision pipeline that applied Sobel edge detection to frames captured from a video stream using a USB camera and displaying the output to a monitor via the Linux framebuffer. The performance counters revealed an unexpected trade-off, revealing that the tiling approach introduces overhead in the form of additional branch penalties, but overall performance was still highest when using small tile sizes due to the tiling allowing for a lower cache miss rate.

The next chapter introduces OpenCL, a general-purpose programming model for coprocessors such as graphical processing units.

Exercises

1. Section 4.7 describes how to design a generalized 2D filter, both as a true 2D filter and as a separated filter comprised of a 1D horizontal filter and 1D vertical filter pass. In this exercise we will measure the impact of exploiting data-level parallelism for both the 1×3 1D horizontal filter and the 1×3 1D vertical filter.

2. Unroll the innermost loop by four and use NEON SIMD intrinsics or inline assembly instructions to perform the loads, multiplications, additions, and stores from the unrolled iterations in parallel. Make sure you include code to use a scalar version of the code when the number of elements remaining is less than four.

3. Measure the resulting performance of both filters relative to the original implementation with respect to Gflops and cache miss rate.

4. Using the OpenMP directive num_threads clause, measure the speedup in floating-point throughput when the filter function is performed using two, three, and four threads relative to the single-thread performance.

5. Convert the filter function from floating point to fixed point using signed (32,29) format. Measure the performance impact relative to the original implementation with regard to CPI.

6. Implement a 7×7, 9×9, and 11×11 tiled Gaussian filter and measure the improvement of the best tile size as compared to no tiling.

7. As described in Section 4.3.3, the Harris corner detector is a feature extraction algorithm used to identify intersections of edges in an image for use as interest points. The input to this algorithm is the X and Y partial derivatives computed by the Sobel filter.

8. Calculate the number of flops per byte for this stencil (assuming the partial derivatives are available as inputs) as compared to that of the 2D Sobel filter. Which has the higher arithmetic intensity?

9. As described in Section 4.3.4, Lucas-Kanade optical flow is an optical flow algorithm used to determine the movement of pixels between frames. The input to this algorithm is the X and Y partial derivatives computed by the Sobel filter.

10. Calculate the number of flops per byte for this stencil (assuming the partial derivatives are available as inputs) as compared to that of the 2D Sobel filter. Which has the higher arithmetic intensity?

11. Instrument your code to measure the time required to extract and filter a tile and the time required to write a tile to the framebuffer. Use OpenMP to implement a double buffering scheme, in which these steps are performed in parallel. In other words, while a tile is being extracted, write the most recently filtered tile to the framebuffer. Each of these steps should be independently multithreaded as well. Measure the speedup achieved by this approach.

12. The Smith-Waterman sequence alignment algorithm, which aligns two sequences against each other, can be implemented using a stencil loop that reads and writes to the

same matrix. Given two strings A and B, the Smith-Waterman algorithm can be implemented as generating the matrix H:

$$H_{i,j} = min \begin{cases} H_{i-1,j-1} + S(A_i, B_j) \\ H_{i-1,j} - d \\ H_{i,j-1} - d \end{cases}$$

13. In this case, the stencil reads the input element diagonally to the upper left, above, and below the output element. This creates a set of dependencies that requires that the output elements can be generated in parallel only along the diagonal, and there must be barrier after each diagonal is processed.

14. Write a tiled implementation of this kernel using OpenMP using the coding style described in the Sobel example given in this chapter.

15. Separable filters reduce the algorithmic complexity of the filter but complicate tiling, since each pass of the separable kernel must be performed over the entire image to guarantee that the halo region pixels reflect the updates from the previous pass. This potentially reduces the locality of the tiled filter.

16. Write a tiled version of the separable Gaussian blur and compare its throughput and cache miss rate to that of the equivalent tiled nonseparated filter. Do this for filter sizes of 7×7, 9×9, and 11×11.

CHAPTER 5

Embedded heterogeneous programming with OpenCL

Chapter Outline

Most smartphone and tablet users take for granted their ability to encode and decode high definition video and render three-dimensional (3D) graphics in real time. These tasks would not be possible without the help of specialized coprocessors such as graphical processing units (GPUs).

Even the high-performance quad-core ARM Cortex A72—with its single instruction, multiple data (SIMD) units, out-of-order speculative superscalar architecture, and advanced caches—is not capable of performing these tasks on its own. For this reason, all modern embedded system-on-chip (SoC) processors contain a diverse set of specialized coprocessor technologies. The most advanced of these support general-purpose programming using *Open Computing Language* (*OpenCL*).

For example, the Xilinx Zynq Ultrascale+ device supplements its quad ARM Cortex-A53 processors with an integrated *Field Programmable Gate Array* (*FPGA*) fabric which can be used to implement customized digital logic circuits to perform specific kernels at high throughput and low latency.

Another example is the Texas Instruments Jacinto™ processor, which supplements its dual ARM Cortex A72 processors with the C7x *Digital Signal Processor* (*DSP*) with its Very Long Instruction Word microarchitecture offering 80 GFlops/s peak floating-point or 256 Gops peak integer throughput and a matrix multiply accelerator (MMA) that offers 8 TOPs peak integer throughput.

Smartphone and tablet SoCs include mobile GPUs, but unlike desktop and server GPUs, whose market is dominated by NVIDIA, AMD, and Intel, the market for low-power, mobile-embedded GPUs is still competitive, diverse, and vibrant. They include such microarchitectures as the

- **ARM Mali GPU**,
- **Imagination Technologies PowerVR GPU**,
- **Broadcom VideoCore GPU**,
- **Qualcomm Adreno GPU, and**
- **NVIDIA Embedded GPU**.

Desktop and server GPUs are connected to their own high-speed memory system and typically offer 10× the memory bandwidth as compared to their host CPU. The drawback of this approach is that all input and output data must be exchanged between the host memory and device memory, which adds overhead as compared to using the CPU only.

Embedded GPUs generally share the same memory system as their host CPU, so they do not have an advantage in memory bandwidth, but they are not subject to CPU-GPU communication overhead.

General-purpose programming for embedded GPUs is still relatively new and the associated runtime libraries and compilers are immature. This chapter uses the ARM Mali-T628 GPU as found on the $179 ODROID-XU3 platform as a case study.

Like other embedded GPUs, the ARM Mali supports general-purpose programming using *OpenCL*, which is an open, technology-independent framework for writing performance-oriented, explicitly data parallel code for a wide variety of microarchitectures.

There are several challenges when programming embedded GPUs. First, as with any *heterogeneous platform*—a platform comprised of a set of different processor technologies—the programmer must manually identify which components of the application to map to the coprocessors. Even after carefully implementing these components on the coprocessor, the programmer must adjust parameters that affect coprocessor performance in ways that are specific to the coprocessor used. Luckily, OpenCL provides mechanisms to allow the programmer to query the runtime environment to get hints on how to set these parameters for the specific coprocessor technology used.

5.1 GPU microarchitecture

This chapter revisits Horner's method kernel from Chapter 2 to illustrate the concepts and performance factors involved in OpenCL programming.

Recall that our Horner's method kernel performs the following loop:

```
1   for i = 0 to n-1
2     sum = coeff[0]
3     for j = 1 to 7
4       sum = sum * input_val[i]
5       sum = sum + coeff[j]
6     endfor
7   endfor
```

The performance bottleneck in this code is the data dependency between lines 4 and 5. In Chapter 1 we addressed this using two different approaches: *software pipelining*, which focused on the inner loop, and explicit *SIMD parallelism*, which focused on the outer loop.

GPUs can use both these approaches simultaneously without assembly language or intrinsics by combining SIMD datapaths with dynamically interleaving instructions from different iterations of the outermost loop in the same execution pipeline. This allows GPUs to use instructions from other threads to hide the latency required by data dependencies and load instructions, providing *pipeline parallelism*. On the other hand, each instruction executed can perform one operation from multiple iterations of the outermost loop, providing data-level or *SIMD parallelism*.

Returning to our example, assume the GPU is executing the inner loop. Also, assume the multiply from line 4 requires a four-cycle latency. Normally this requires three stalls after each time that line 4 is executed. Instead of issuing stalls, the GPU will issue three instructions, one from each of three *other* iterations of the outer loop. This way, the GPU can keep the pipeline flowing without needing to insert any stalls. Also, the GPU may have four lanes, meaning that it can issue one instruction from each of four iterations of the outer loop *in each cycle*.

Figure 5.1 shows how a four-SIMD lane GPU would execute this loop assuming it was processing 16 iterations of the outer loop. Notice that the latency required by the dependency between lines 4 and 5 can be covered by instructions from the other iterations. To support the resulting instruction throughput, GPUs contain many parallel functional units and extremely large register files.

5.2 OpenCL

Like OpenMP, OpenCL presents the programmer with a multithreaded programming model. In OpenCL, threads are called *work-items*. As with OpenMP, a thread, or work-item, is a serial instruction stream that works cooperatively with others to advance the objective of the program. Also, as with OpenMP, work-items can share a common memory space and use shared memory locations to communicate and can have variables explicitly allocated as private. *Read-modify-write* and *producer-consumer*-type accesses to shared memory are usually synchronized among work-items using locks and barriers. However, this is where the similarity between OpenMP threads and OpenCL work-items ends.

With OpenMP, the programmer instantiates one thread for each processor core because there is no advantage to having more threads than CPU cores. With OpenCL, the goal is to exploit parallelism as the finest grain possible and it benefits the programmer to invoke as many work-items as possible regardless of the number of physical processor cores on the target device. As such, when adapting OpenMP code to OpenCL code, it is common to delete the outermost for-loop and replace it by instancing one work-item for every iteration of the outermost loop. In this case, each thread only performs one iteration of the original outermost loop.

Cycle	0	1	2	3	4	5	6	7
Lane 0	it 0, ln 4	it 4, ln 4	it 8, ln 4	it 12, ln 4	it 0, ln 5	it 4, ln 5	it 8, ln 5	it 12, ln 5
Lane 1	it 1, ln 4	it 5, ln 4	it 9, ln 4	it 13, ln 4	it 1, ln 4	it 5, ln 5	it 9, ln 5	it 13, ln 5
Lane 2	it 2, ln 4	it 6, ln 4	it 10, ln 4	it 14, ln 4	it 2, ln 4	it 6, ln 5	it 10, ln 5	it 14, ln 5
Lane 3	it 3, ln 4	it 7, ln 4	it 11, ln 4	it 15, ln 4	it 3, ln 4	it 7, ln 5	it 11, ln 5	it 15, ln 5

Figure 5.1: Pipeline SIMD execution. "it" stands for "iteration number" and "ln" stands for "line number". The four-cycle latency between lines 4 and 5 of iteration 0 is hidden by instructions from other iterations.

OpenMP threads each have independent control flow, while it is often the case for GPU-like coprocessors that each OpenCL work-item within each group of 32 or 64 work-items is mapped to an individual SIMD lane, meaning that their control flow must remain in lockstep or two groups of work-items will diverge and become serialized relative to each other. This means that to achieve maximum performance, all if-statements should evaluate equivalently, and all inner loops must iterate an equal number of times.

One of the other major differences between OpenMP and OpenCL is the amount of extra code required to use it as compared to serial code. A programmer may add OpenMP support to a serial program by adding as few as one additional line of code, while a programmer must add hundreds of additional lines of code to add OpenCL support. Luckily, much of this extra code is *boilerplate*, meaning that it is reusable between different programs.

5.3 OpenCL programming model, idioms, and abstractions

This section briefly summarizes OpenCL terminology, the associated application programming interface (API) functions, and their relevance for both the host and device code.

5.3.1 The host/device programming model

Code intended for execution on the device is referred to as a *kernel*. The kernel performs the computationally- or memory-intensive computations on behalf of the host CPU. OpenCL kernels are written in the C language, augmented with a few special OpenCL-specific types and built-in functions.

An OpenCL programmer must explicitly divide the program into code executed by the *host* CPU and code executed by the coprocessor, or *device*.

The programmer must write special code for that host to interact with the OpenCL runtime environment. The special functions called in this code make up the OpenCL *platform layer*. Specifically, the platform layer is comprised of a set of API functions used to initialize and communicate with the device. The API function interfaces are standardized, meaning that they will work on any OpenCL-compatible device, but their implementations are provided by the target device's vendor. A vendor implementation of the OpenCL platform layer is called a *platform*.

The next several subsections describe a basic set of OpenCL platform functions and their usage. Each of these subsections includes a section that shows the prototypes of the related functions and a section that shows a relevant code snippet from the running example program. When put together, these code snippets will form a complete program that executes an OpenCL implementation of the Horner example from Chapter 2.

To begin, include the necessary header files:

- `stdio.h` for basic console and file I/O.
- `stdlib.h` for random number generation for creating synthetic datasets.
- `CL/cl.h` for the OpenCL platform functions.
- `sys/time.h` for the POSIX `gettimeofday()` function. Linux perf_event is not compatible with coprocessor performance counters, so this code will use wall clock time and OpenCL's built-in profiling functionality to measure kernel performance.

```
#include <stdio.h>

#include <stdlib.h>

#include <CL/cl.h>

#include <sys/time.h>
```

5.3.2 Error checking

OpenCL platform functions use return codes defined in `cl.h` to communicate error codes back to the user in the form of a 32-bit signed integer of type `cl_int`. Unfortunately, OpenCL does not provide any corresponding error reporting functions—like the POSIX function *strerror*() and *perror*() functions—to convert an error code into a human-readable string. As a result, for debugging purposes it is important for the programmer to write one such function as part of the host boilerplate code.

C99 has a somewhat obscure feature called "stringification", in which a preprocessor definition is interpreted by the compiler as a string literal when preceded by a hash mark (#). Using this, the programmer can write a function to convert an OpenCL error definition to a string.

One way to do this is to use a switch statement to map OpenCL error symbols to their corresponding strings. To make this easier, define a preprocessor macro such as the one below:

```
#define CASE_CL_ERROR(NAME) case NAME: return #NAME;
```

…and apply it to each of the error codes listed in `cl.h` to construct a switch statement:

```
const char* opencl_error_to_str (cl_int error) {

    switch(error) {

    CASE_CL_ERROR(CL_SUCCESS)

    CASE_CL_ERROR(CL_DEVICE_NOT_FOUND)

    CASE_CL_ERROR(CL_DEVICE_NOT_AVAILABLE)

    …
```

```
        default:

        return "UNKNOWN ERROR CODE";

    }

}
```

Using this, it is possible to define a preprocessor macro for reporting OpenCL errors back to the user and exiting the program.

For any return code other than CL_SUCCESS, the program will print the error and exit with code 0. In addition to showing the "stringified" error code in the error message, this define will also provide the source file name and approximate line number where the error occurred using the __FILE__ and __LINE__ preprocessor macros.

```
#define CHECK_STATUS(status) \

        if (status != CL_SUCCESS) {\

                fprintf(stderr,\

                "OpenCL error in file %s line %d, error code %s\n",\

                        __FILE__,\

                        __LINE__,\

                        opencl_error_to_str(status));\

                exit(0);\

        }
```

This chapter's example code will invoke this macro after every call to an OpenCL platform function.

5.3.3 Platform layer: Initializing the platforms

OpenCL platform functions begin with "cl" followed by a capital letter, for example: clGetDeviceIDs()and clFinish().

In practice, most calls to the OpenCL platform functions serve one of the following purposes:

- querying the OpenCL runtime for device-specific or kernel-specific information (e.g., determining how many devices are present or determining the maximum number of work-items allowed for a device);
- device memory management (e.g., allocating memory on a device); or
- sending commands to the device (e.g., initiating kernel execution on a device).

This section describes how to obtain a handle to the platforms and query them for information.

Some OpenCL functions require that the host call them twice: once to obtain the size of the requested data structure and again to obtain its data. The initialization section of the example host code calls `clGetPlatformIDs()` to obtain the number of available platforms. Then, using the returned number of platforms, it allocates a correspondingly sized array of type *cl_platform_id* and calls the function again to obtain a list of platform handles.

For example, a theoretical embedded SoC may contain CPUs, GPUs, and an FPGA fabric. In this case, the OpenCL platform layer would include one platform corresponding to the GPU, another platform corresponding to the FPGA fabric, and potentially a third platform to allow OpenCL kernels to execute on the CPU cores. However, in practice, most embedded SoCs today only have one platform.

Once the host obtains the platform handles, it can query them for information such as name, OpenCL version (profile), etc.

Related Functions:

```
cl_int clGetPlatformIDs(cl_uint num_entries,

                        cl_platform_id *platforms,

                        cl_uint *num_platforms)
```

Obtain the list of platforms available. Set the *platforms* argument to NULL to obtain the number of platforms.

```
cl_int clGetPlatformInfo(cl_platform_id platform,

                         cl_platform_info param_name,

                         size_t param_value_size,

                         void *param_value,

                         size_t *param_value_size_ret)
```

Get specific information about the OpenCL platform.

Example Code:

```
cl_platform_id platform_ids[8];

cl_int ret;

size_t length;

char str[1024];
```

```
// query number of platforms

ret = clGetPlatformIDs(0,0,&num_platforms);

CHECK_STATUS(ret);

printf("Number of available platforms: %u\n", num_platforms);

// retrieve handle to platforms, limit to 8

ret = clGetPlatformIDs(num_platforms > 8 ? 8:

        num_platforms,platform_ids,0);

CHECK_STATUS(ret);

// query each platform

for (i = 0; i < num_platforms; i++) {

        ret = clGetPlatformInfo(platform_ids[i],

            CL_PLATFORM_PROFILE,0,0, &length);

CHECK_STATUS(ret);

ret = clGetPlatformInfo(platform_ids[i],

    CL_PLATFORM_PROFILE,

    length>1024?1024:length,&str[0],0);

CHECK_STATUS(ret);

printf("CL_PLATFORM_PROFILE: %s\n",str);

// display the platform version

ret = clGetPlatformInfo(platform_ids[i],

    CL_PLATFORM_VERSION,

    0,0, &length);

CHECK_STATUS(ret);

ret = clGetPlatformInfo(platform_ids[i],

    CL_PLATFORM_VERSION,

    length>1024?1024:length, &str[0], 0);

CHECK_STATUS(ret);

printf("CL_PLATFORM_VERSION: %s\n",str);

ret = clGetPlatformInfo(platform_ids[i],

    CL_PLATFORM_ NAME, 0,0, &length);

CHECK_STATUS(ret);
```

```
ret = clGetPlatformInfo(platform_ids[i],

    CL_PLATFORM_NAME,length>1024?1024:length,

    &str[0], 0);

CHECK_STATUS(ret);

printf("CL_PLATFORM_NAME: %s\n",str);

ret = clGetPlatformInfo(platform_ids[i],

    CL_PLATFORM_VENDOR,0,0,&length);

CHECK_STATUS(ret);

ret = clGetPlatformInfo(platform_ids[i],

    CL_PLATFORM_VENDOR,

    length>1024?1024:length,

    &str[0],0);

CHECK_STATUS(ret);

printf ("CL_PLATFORM_VENDOR: %s\n",str);

ret = clGetPlatformInfo(platform_ids[i],

    CL_PLATFORM_EXTENSIONS,

    0,0, &length);

CHECK_STATUS(ret);

ret = clGetPlatformInfo(platform_ids[i],

    CL_PLATFORM_EXTENSIONS,

    length>1024?1024:length,

    &str[0], 0);

CHECK_STATUS(ret);

printf("CL_PLATFORM_EXTENSIONS: %s\n",str);

}
```

5.3.4 Platform layer: Initializing the devices

This section describes device-specific functions in the platform layer. Once the host has obtained handles to the platforms, it must obtain handles to the devices. Optionally it can query the devices for information.

The example code calls the `clGetDeviceIDs()` and `clGetDeviceInfo()` to obtain handles to the devices associated with each platform.

Related Functions:

```
cl_int clGetDeviceIDs(cl_platform_id platform,
                      cl_device_type device_type,
                      cl_uint num_entries,
                      cl_device_id *devices,
                      cl_uint *num_devices)
```

Obtain the list of devices available on a platform.

```
cl_int clGetDeviceInfo(cl_device_id device,
                       cl_device_info param_name,
                       size_t param_value_size,
                       void *param_value,
                       size_t *param_value_size_ret)
```

Get information about an OpenCL device.

Required Declarations:

```
cl_device_id device;
```

Example Code:

```
ret = clGetDeviceIDs(platform_ids[0],CL_DEVICE_TYPE_ALL,0,0,&num_devices);
CHECK_STATUS(ret);
printf("Number of devices for platform 0: %d\n",num_devices);
for(i=0;i<num_devices;i++) {
    ret =
    clGetDeviceIDs(platform_ids[0],
        CL_DEVICE_TYPE_ALL,num_devices,&device[i],0);
    CHECK_STATUS(ret);
}
for(i=0;i<num_devices;i++) {
    ret = clGetDeviceInfo(device[i], CL_DEVICE_NAME, 0, 0, &length);
  CHECK_STATUS(ret);
```

```
    ret = clGetDeviceInfo(device[i],
        CL_DEVICE_NAME,
        length>1024?1024:length,
        &str[0],0);
    printf("Device NAME: %s\n",str);
}
```

5.3.5 Platform layer: Initializing the context

A *context* is an abstraction on the host that manages host-device interaction and device memory. Every OpenCL function that interacts with the device requires a context. After obtaining a handle to the platform and device(s), the host calls `clCreateContext()` or `clCreateContext-FromType()` to obtain a handle to a corresponding context.

Both functions are similar, but `clCreateContext()` returns a context given associated with a given device handle, while `clCreateContextFromType()` returns a context associated with a given device "type", such as GPU.

Both of these functions return the context through the *properties* argument, passed by reference.

The callback function *pfn_notify* and associated *user_data* are used by the runtime environment to asynchronously report errors to the application, but the programmer can set both to *NULL* if this behavior is not needed.

The example code below uses `clCreateContextFromType()` to request a context handle for a device of type `CL_DEVICE_TYPE_GPU` and then uses the context handle to extract the associated device handle. The program will use the device handle later for discovering the cause of kernel build errors and determining the maximum workgroup size and preferred vector width.

Related Functions:

```
cl_context clCreateContext(cl_context_properties *properties,
                           cl_uint num_devices,
                           const cl_device_id *devices,
                           void (*pfn_notify) (const char *errinfo,
                                               const void *private_info,
                                               size_t cb,
              void *user_data),
```

```
          void *user_data,

          cl_int *errcode_ret)
```

Create an OpenCL context (from a specified device).

```
cl_context clCreateContextFromType(cl_context_properties *properties,

                    cl_device_type device_type,

                    void (*pfn_notify) (const char *errinfo,

                          const void *private_ info,

                          size_t cb,

                          void *user_data),

                    void *user_data,

                    cl_int *errcode_ret)
```

Create an OpenCL context from a device type that identifies the specific device(s) to use.

```
cl_int clReleaseContext (cl_context context)
```

Decrement the context reference count. When the count reaches zero, the OpenCL runtime can unload the context from memory.

Example Code:

```
#define DEVICE 0

cl_context context;

cl_context_properties context_props[] = {

  CL_CONTEXT_PLATFORM,(cl_context_properties)platform_ids[0],0

};

context = clCreateContextFromType(context_props,

        CL_DEVICE_ TYPE_GPU,0,0,&ret);

CHECK_STATUS(ret);

ret = clGetContextInfo(context, CL_CONTEXT_DEVICES,

        0, NULL, &deviceBufferSize);

CHECK_STATUS(ret);

ret = clGetContextInfo(context, CL_CONTEXT_DEVICES,

        deviceBufferSize, &device[DEVICE], NULL);

CHECK_STATUS(ret);
```

5.3.6 Platform layer: Kernel control

All communication between the host and device is handled through a *command queue*. The programmer uses the command queue to set the size of the kernel data set and send input data to the kernel.

The program obtains a handle to a command queue by passing an associated context to `clCreateCommandQueue()`.

When calling `clCreateCommandQueue()`, specify the `CL_QUEUE_PROFILING_ENABLE` option, which will allow the host to collect runtime information.

```
cl_command_queue clCreateCommandQueue(cl_context context,

                cl_device_id device,

                cl_command_queue_ properties properties,

                cl_int *errcode_ret)
```

Create a command queue on a specific device.

```
cl_int clReleaseCommandQueue(cl_command_queue command_queue)
```

Decrement the command_queue reference count.

Example Code:

```
cl_command_queue queue;

queue = clCreateCommandQueue(context,device,

        CL_QUEUE_PROFILING_ENABLE,&ret);

CHECK_STATUS(ret);
```

5.3.7 Platform layer: Kernel compilation

OpenCL kernel code is usually compiled by the host program at runtime. As such, OpenCL uses a *just in time* compilation approach, where instead of the kernel being compiled alongside the host code (as in NVIDIA's CUDA framework), the host code must include a sequence of actions that read the kernel code and compile it using an API call.

The platform layer function that compiles the kernel source code does not take a path to the source code file as one might expect but instead takes a pointer to a zero-terminated character array—a C string—containing the source code. As such, the programmer must use standard system calls to read the kernel source file into a string before calling the compile function.

To do this, open the file (with `fopen()`), determine its size (with a `fseek()`, `ftell()`, `fseek()` sequence), allocate memory for the string (with `malloc()`), then read the contents of the file into the string (with `fread()`). Make sure you allocate one extra character for the string to zero-terminate it before passing the string to the compile function.

To compile the program, call `clCreateProgramWithSource()` to obtain a handle to the program, `clBuildProgram()` to compile the program, and `clCreateKernel()` to create kernel instantiation.

When building, the program can pass the compiler options stored in an *options* string. This example uses "`-cl-fast-relaxed-math`." These options allow the GPU to perform floating-point operations that are not 100% IEEE 754 compliant but achieve higher throughput than if compliance must be guaranteed.

Since the programmer (usually) cannot compile any OpenCL kernels outside of the OpenCL host API, the programmer needs a way to identify any syntax or semantic errors in our kernel source. For this the program can use the `clGetProgramBuildInfo()` along with the device ID of the coprocessor.

Related Functions:

```
cl_program clCreateProgramWithSource (cl_context context,

                                      cl_uint count,

                                      const char **strings,

                                      const size_t *lengths,

                                      cl_int *errcode_ret)
```

Create a program object for a context and loads the source code specified by the text strings in the strings array into the program object.

```
cl_int clBuildProgram (cl_program program,

                       cl_uint num_devices,

                       const cl_device_id *device_list,

                       const char *options,

                       void (*pfn_notify)(cl_program, void *user_data),

                       void *user_data)
```

Build (compile and link) a program executable from the program source or binary.

```
cl_kernel clCreateKernel (cl_program program,

                          const char *kernel_name,

                          cl_int *errcode_ret)
```

Create a kernel object.

```
cl_int clReleaseKernel (cl_kernel kernel)
```

Decrement the kernel reference count.

```
cl_int clGetProgramBuildInfo (cl_program program,
                              cl_device_id device,
                              cl_program_build_info param_name,
                              size_t param_value_size,
                              void *param_value,
                              size_t *param_value_size_ret)
```

Return build information for each device in the program object.

```
cl_int clReleaseProgram (cl_program program)
```

Decrement the program reference count.

Example Code:

```
cl_program program;
cl_kernel kernel;
FILE *myFile;
char *program_source,*log;
size_t file_size, program_size;
const char options[50] = "-cl-fast-relaxed-math\0";
size_t log_length = 0, return_size,
      work_item_sizes[3], max_wg_size[3];
myFile = fopen("horner.cl","r+");
if (!myFile) {
      perror("Cannot open kernel source file");
      exit(0);
}
fseek(myFile,0,SEEK_END);
file_size = ftell(myFile);
fseek(myFile,0,SEEK_SET);
program_source=(unsigned char *)malloc(file_size+1);
```

```
fread((void *)program_source,1,file_size,myFile);
program = clCreateProgramWithSource(context,1,
        &program_source,0,&ret);
CHECK_STATUS(ret);
ret = clBuildProgram(program, 0, 0, options, 0, 0);
fclose(myFile);
program_source[program_size]=0;
if(ret == CL_BUILD_PROGRAM_FAILURE) {
    ret = clGetProgramBuildInfo(program,
        device,CL_PROGRAM_BUILD_LOG,
        0,0,&log_length);
    CHECK_STATUS(ret);
    log=(char *)malloc(log_length);
    ret = clGetProgramBuildInfo(program,device,
        CL_PROGRAM_BUILD_LOG,
        log_length,&log[0],0);
    CHECK_STATUS(ret);
    fprintf(stderr,"OpenCL build error: :%s",log);
    free(log);
    return;
} else
    CHECK_STATUS(ret);
    kernel = clCreateKernel(program, "horner", &ret);
    CHECK_STATUS(ret);
```

5.3.8 Platform layer: Device memory allocation

Desktop and server GPUs typically have physically separated RAM from that of the CPU. Data is exchanged between memories using a peripheral bus such as PCI-express.

Embedded GPUs typically share the same physical memory with the host but may refer to the same memory locations using different addresses because the GPU uses physical addresses while the CPU uses virtual addresses.

Because of this, OpenCL 1.1 and 1.2 require that the host and device allocate shared arrays separately. The programmer allocates host memory statically or on the heap using `malloc()` or `new` and allocates device memory using the platform function `clCreateBuffer()`.

Since the kernel's input data typically originates from host-controlled peripherals such as the disk, network, or camera, the data is copied to the device memory either explicitly using the asynchronous `clEnqueueWriteBuffer()` platform function, or implicitly using the `clCreateBuffer()` function.

OpenCL 2.0 introduced shared virtual memory, in which the management and exchange of data between host and device is abstracted from the programmer, but as of this writing embedded GPUs generally only support earlier version of OpenCL. For example, the ARM Mali-T628 GPU used for this chapter only supports OpenCL 1.1, two versions earlier than OpenCL 2.0.

To allocate memory on the device, the host must create a "memory object", of which there are two types: *buffers* and *images*. Buffers are simple arrays, while images are used to encapsulate data in a device-specific way that facilitates optimizations that are specific to graphical data. Not all devices support images.

To allocate a device buffer, allocate memory on the host and then use the `clCreateBuffer()` function to create a corresponding device buffer.

This example uses the `CL_MEM_COPY_HOST_PTR` option for the two input arrays, `inputBuffer` and `coeffBuffer`, which tells `clCreateBuffer()` to copy the data to the device, avoiding the need to call `clEnqueueWriteBuffer()`

The host must copy the output array, `outputBuffer`, from the device to the host using `clEnqueueReadBuffer()` after the kernel finishes.

Related Functions:

```
cl_mem clCreateBuffer (cl_context context,

                        cl_mem_flags flags,

                        size_t size,

                        void *host_ptr,

                        cl_int *errcode_ret)
```

Create a buffer object.

```
cl_int clReleaseMemObject (cl_mem memobj)
```

Decrement the memory object reference count.

Example Code:

```
#define N 128 << 20      // data set is 128 MB

cl_mem inputBuffer;

cl_mem outputBuffer;

cl_mem coeffBuffer;

cl_uint vecwidth;

float *x, *d;

float coeff[8] = {1.2f,1.4f,1.6f,1.8f,2.0f,2.2f,2.4f,2.6f};

d = (float *)malloc(N);

x = (float *)malloc(N);

for (i=0;i<N/4;i++) x[i]=(float)rand()/(float)RAND_MAX;

inputBuffer = clCreateBuffer(context,
        CL_MEM_READ_ONLY |
        CL_MEM_COPY_HOST_PTR,
        N,x,&ret);
CHECK_STATUS(ret);
coeffBuffer = clCreateBuffer(context,
        CL_MEM_READ_ONLY |
        CL_MEM_COPY_HOST_PTR,
        8 * sizeof(float),coeff,&ret);
outputBuffer = clCreateBuffer(context,
        CL_MEM_WRITE_ONLY |
        CL_MEM_USE_HOST_PTR,
        N,d,&ret);
CHECK_STATUS(ret);
```

5.4 Kernel workload distribution

The next step is to specify parameters for the kernel, assign the kernel's arguments, and dispatch the kernel to the device. As described earlier, an OpenCL thread is called a work item because kernels are typically parallelized by associating each work-item with a data element.

When adapting a serial loop to an OpenCL kernel, it is often the case that each iteration of the original outermost loop is mapped to a work-item. As a result, the outermost loop is deleted and upon dispatch the kernel is assigned one work item for each of the original iterations of the outermost loop.

For example, consider a loop that processes each pixel for a 1920×1080 image:

Kernel:

```
for (i = 0;i < 1080;i++)
  for (j = 0;j < 1920;j++)
  // process pixel (i,j)
```

The OpenCL kernel could be comprised of the inner loop (the $j =$ loop), and the program would dispatch the kernel with 1080 work-items, one for each pixel row:

Kernel:

```
for (j = 0;j < 1920;j++)
  // process pixel (work_item_number,j)
```

Alternatively, the programmer can associate each pixel with a work item and dispatch the kernel with a 2D work item size:

Kernel:

```
// process pixel (work_item_number(0),work_item_number(1))
```

When the host dispatches a kernel, the program assigns the kernel a number of work-items. This is called an *n-dimensional range* (*NDRange*), which is a 1D, 2D, or 3D value that represents how the input or output data is mapped into work-items.

As in OpenMP, the kernel code associated with each thread—or work item—can identify its unique ID for the purpose of adapting its runtime behavior to its own workload, or element of its working set.

The work-items can also be organized into a two-level hierarchy, in which sets of work-items can be divided into equal-sized *workgroups*. All threads within a workgroup can synchronize and access a shared memory space. Work-items in different workgroups cannot communicate.

For example, if the programmer sets NDRange to {64,4,2}, the kernel will be comprised of $64 \times 4 \times 2 = 512$ work-items. If the programmer defines the workgroup size to be {2,2,2} then there will be $512/(2 \times 2 \times 2) = 64$ workgroups.

5.4.1 Device memory

One of the most important differences between CPUs and coprocessor devices such as GPUs, FPGAs, and DSPs is their memory hierarchy. CPUs derive much of their performance from their caches, which typically support rich feature sets such as sophisticated replacement policies, prefetching, victim caches, and coherency with other caches. These features are designed to maximize memory performance for platform agnostic code. Aggressive multi-level caches also allow CPUs to have small general-purpose register files, since compilers can use frequent *register spilling* to exchange register contents with memory without a large performance penalty.

On the other hand, GPUs, FPGAs, and DSPs generally have simple or no caches, relying instead on annotations in the program code that explicitly allocate and manage on-chip memories. These program-controlled on-chip memories are sometimes referred to as *scratchpad memory*, although GPUs sometimes call them *shared memory* since they are also used as a mechanism by which intermediate results can be exchanged between work-items within a workgroup.

On a CPU, the contents of any memory address may be stored in multiple levels of the memory hierarchy at any given time. In other words, the physical location of the data stored at a particular address cannot be determined since the on-chip caches are automatically managed by the hardware.

On a GPU, on-chip memory locations have their own special address ranges. This allows the program to specifically address on-chip memory and to explicitly copy data between on-chip and off-chip memory.

Also, GPUs typically have large register files and their compilers do not spill register values to off-chip memory. The registers serve as a work-item's private memory and must have sufficient capacity to store the highest number of live register values that a work-item will ever need during its execution, multiplied by the number of work-items assigned to the same GPU core.

OpenCL supports programming idioms by which these different memories are referenced. Since different devices have different on-chip memory structures, OpenCL must define a set of generalized abstractions that can be mapped to different device technologies.

OpenCL defines *global memory* as memory accessible by all processor cores. Global memory is usually the off-chip RAM. Global memory has the largest capacity and is globally accessible to all work-items in the kernel but has the highest latency. The OpenCL keyword "`global`" is used as a prefix to specify a pointer that points to global memory.

Despite OpenCL's objective of being an opaque abstraction for programming coprocessor devices, there are some technology-specific elements that exist in the language. These elements have a lineage that traces back to GPUs. One of these is the concept of *constant memory*. Many

GPUs include a memory pathway that is specifically designed for high bandwidth retrieval of read-only graphical texture data that are painted over 3D-rendered objects. This area of the memory space can be initialized by the host but not written by the device. In OpenCL, a pointer declared with the "constant" keyword points to data in this memory space. Constant memory is physically stored in global memory, but it can be optimized for high-bandwidth read access.

In OpenCL, *local memory* refers to program-controlled on-chip scratchpad memory and is specified when declaring a pointer or array using the "local" prefix. Local memory has limited capacity, is shared by all work-items within a single workgroup, and has a lower latency than global memory. Local memory can be allocated at runtime by declaring a local array in the kernel function or in the host by using the clSetKernelArg() function (described below).

The programmer can also declare a variable or small array to be allocated in *private memory* that is private to an individual work item. Private variables are generally mapped to registers.

Table 5.1 summarizes the device memory types for a typical GPU, although in theory, all these memory types are abstractions and can have different meanings on different device technologies.

5.4.2 Kernel parameters

The programmer must set three primary parameters that affect determine how workload is distributed:

- *Number of workgroups (referred to as "NWG")*
  For most GPUs, the unit of workload assigned to processor cores is the workgroup. This means that the programmer must instantiate at least as many workgroups as cores in order to take advantage of multicore parallelism. As described above, the workgroup also has implications for the memory system, since only work-items within the same workgroup

Table 5.1: Summary of device memory types.

Declaration prefix	Where allocated	Capacity	Speed	Sharing	Usage
global	Onboard (off-chip) DRAM memory	Large	Slow	All work-items in all workgroups	Top-level input and output arrays
constant	Onboard (off-chip) DRAM memory	Device-specific	Device-specific	All work-items in all workgroups	Read-only input arrays
shared	On-chip SRAM	Small	Fast	Local to each workgroup	Intermediate arrays
private	On-chip registers	Very small	Very fast	Local to each work item	Intermediate scalars

can share on-chip memory. Having too many workgroups will thus limit data sharing and may also add scheduling overhead.

- *Workgroup size (referred to as "WGS")*
  The workgroup size, or number of work-items per workgroup, affects the number of instructions executed per work-item invocation. Having too few work-items may limit the number of work-items that the GPU can map on parallel SIMD lanes or limit the pool of ready work-items available to hide the latency of other work-items. Having too many work-items might result in work-items executing so few instructions that their dispatch overhead outweighs their performance benefit. The workgroup size has an upper limit as determined by the hardware but can be limited further by register and shared memory usage of the kernel.

- *Work-item vector size (referred to as "VS")*

The programmer can explicitly vectorize the OpenCL kernel, much like as described in Chapter 2 for ARM NEON instructions. This is less necessary for desktop and server GPUs since they are more effective at abstracting the vectorization from the programmer, while embedded GPUs may still benefit from this.

For a simple kernel like the Horner example, the product of NWG × WGS × VS determines the minimal number of elements processed by the kernel. If this number is less than the dataset, the kernel will need a loop.

The programmer can get hints for setting these parameters by invoking certain queries to the platform layer.

For example, the programmer can use `clGetDeviceInfo()` to report the maximum number of work-items supported by the hardware in each of the three workgroup size dimensions (x, y, z):

```
ret = clGetDeviceInfo(device[DEVICE],
    CL_DEVICE_MAX_WORK_ITEM_SIZES,
    3*sizeof(size_t),
    work_item_sizes,&return_size);
CHECK_STATUS(ret);
printf("CL_DEVICE_MAX_WORK_ITEM_SIZES: %d,%d,%d\n",
    work_item_sizes[0], work_item_sizes[1], work_item_sizes[2]);
```

This information varies per device. For example, on the OpenCL platform for the Imagination Technologies PowerVR 544 GPU, the maximum workgroup size is only one. The OpenCL platform for the ARM Mali-T628 reports a maximum size of 256, 256, 256. The OpenCL platform for the NVIDIA K20X GPU (a server GPU) reports 1024, 1024, 64.

The programmer can use `clGetDeviceInfo()` to determine the device's preferred vector width:

```
ret = clGetDeviceInfo(device[DEVICE],

    CL_DEVICE_PREFERRED_VECTOR_WIDTH_FLOAT,

    sizeof(cl_uint),&vecwidth,&return_size);

printf("CL_DEVICE_PREFERRED_VECTOR_WIDTH_FLOAT: \t%d",

    vecwidth);
```

This information also varies per device. The ARM Mali reports four, while the NVIDIA K20X reports one. This implies that the ARM Mali benefits from the explicit vectorization of the kernel while the server GPU can dynamically map scalar operations on individual work-items to the SIMD lanes in the hardware.

The programmer can use `clGetDeviceInfo()` to determine the number of processor cores on the CPU:

```
ret = clGetDeviceInfo(device[DEVICE],

    CL_DEVICE_MAX_COMPUTE_UNITS,

    sizeof(cl_uint),&maxComputeUnits,

    &return_size);

CHECK_STATUS(ret);

printf("CL_MAX_COMPUTE_UNITS:\t%d\n ", maxComputeUnits);
```

The ARM Mali has 4 compute units on each of its two devices, while the NVIDIA K20X has 14 compute units.

Related Functions:

```
cl_int clGetDeviceInfo(cl_device_id device,

                    cl_device_info param_name,

                    size_t param_value_size,

                    void *param_value,

                    size_t *param_value_size_ret)
```

Get information about an OpenCL device.

5.4.3 Kernel vectorization

OpenCL kernel code uses an elegant way to explicitly perform SIMD arithmetic. Instead of intrinsic functions as required for ARM NEON as described in Chapter 2, the OpenCL compiler will automatically generate SIMD instructions for any normal arithmetic operation when one or more operands are of a SIMD type. These SIMD types can be as large as 16 elements.

Consider the following example variable declarations and operations:

```
float4 a,b;

float c;

a = a * b;

b = a * c;
```

The variables *a* and *b* will be 4-element floating-point vectors. This code will result in a being computed as an element-wise vector product of *a* and *b*, that is,

```
a <= {a[3]*b[3], a[2]*b[2], a[1]*b[1], a[0]*b[0]},
```

while *b* will be computed as the product of each element of *b* and the scalar value *c*, that is,

```
b = {a[3]*c, a[2]*c, a[1]*c, a[0]*c}.
```

For variables declared using a SIMD type, individual elements of floating-point vector types can be referenced as:

<name>.s0 (element 0)

<name>.s1 (element 1)

...

<name>.se (element 14)

<name>.sf (element 15)

You can even reference subsets of a vector, using, for example,

<name>.s02 (elements 0 and 2 concatenated)

<name>.s441 (two copies of element 4 concatenated with element 1)

OpenCL includes function primitives that perform vector operations on variables declared using SIMD datatypes, such as *distance()*, *dot()*, and *normalize()*, which compute the distance between two vectors, dot product of two vectors, and the normalized form of a vector, respectively.

In the kernel code there are various functions to determine the number of work-items, number of workgroups, and offsets, such as:

`size_t get_global_id(uint D)`	get global work item number for dimension D
`size_t get_local_id(uint D)`	get local work item number for dimension D
`size_t get_global_size(uint D)`	get global size for dimension D
`size_t get_local_size(uint D)`	get local size for dimension D
`size_t get_global_offset(uint D)`	get global offset for dimension D

Related Functions:

```
cl_int clGetDeviceInfo(cl_device_id device,
        cl_device_info param_name,
        size_t param_value_size,
        void *param_value,
        size_t *param_value_size_ret)
```

Get information about an OpenCL device.

5.4.4 Parameter space for Horner kernel

The input and output arrays of the Horner kernel are 1D, each comprising N bytes, interpreted as an array of $N/4$ floating-point values.

The input array is likely to be too large to associate one element with one work item. In this example there are 32 million elements, and the maximum workgroup size is $256 \times 256 \times 256$ = 16 million. Even if it were possible to associate one element per work item, the program would likely not be able to exploit multicore parallelism.

As such, the programmer must choose the workgroup size (WGS), number of workgroups (NWG), and kernel vector size (VS).

Figure 5.2 shows how each of these parameters affects the hierarchical way the workload associated with the input data is subdivided among the work-items.

The top of the figure shows x, the input array. The array is evenly divided into each of the workgroups, which themselves are divided into work-items. Each work item can optionally process input elements using vector operations and/or a for-loop.

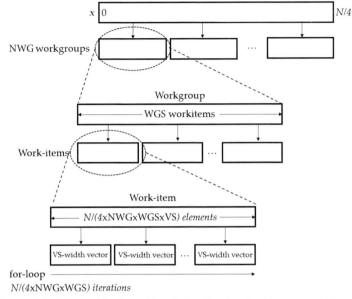

Figure 5.2: Hierarchical workload distribution for the example kernel.

The number of iterations performed by the for-loop is a function of the values N, WGS, NWG, and VS. In other words, if $N/4 <$ NWG $\times$ WGS $\times$ VS, then the for-loop within the work-items balances out the workload by looping through $N/(4 \times$ NWG $\times$ WGS $\times$ VS) iterations.

5.4.5 Kernel attributes

The programmer declares the kernel function using the `kernel` prefix. Between this prefix and the return type of kernel function, the programmer can use the "__*attribute*(())" qualifier to set attributes that can provide hints to the kernel compiler.

For example, consider the following kernel declaration:

```
kernel __attribute((reqd_work_group_size(8,8,1)))

void naive_opencl (global float *x,

    global float *d,

    global float *coeff) {
```

The `reqd_work_group_size` attribute specifies the workgroup size that the programmer must use when dispatching the kernel. This is essentially a promise that the programmer makes to the compiler, which allows the compiler to optimize the code appropriately.

5.4.6 Kernel dispatch

The host typically performs the following steps before and after kernel dispatch:

1. set the kernel arguments (call `clSetKernelArg()`)
2. optionally transfer the input data into the device's memory (call `clEnqueueWriteBuffer()` by referencing the input buffers previously created with `clCreateBuffer()`) (note that the example uses the `CL_MEM_COPY_HOST_PTR` option in `clEnqueueWriteBuffer()`, which allows it to avoid this step)
3. set the workgroup size and number of workgroups and execute the kernel (call `clEnqueueNDRangeKernel()`)
4. transfer the output data to host memory (call `clEnqueueReadBuffer()` by referencing the output buffers previously created with `clCreateBuffer()`)

In Practice:

One potentially confusing aspect of kernel dispatch is the managing of the kernel's input and output arrays. Each of these arrays is referenced by its pointer in host memory (usually obtained from a call to `malloc()`), as well as a corresponding `cl_mem` object that serves as a handle to the corresponding OpenCL buffer (obtained from a call to `clCreateBuffer()`).

The kernel function expects to receive pointers to each of these arrays as arguments, but these pointers will be different from the ones allocated on the host. To reconcile this difference, the host will send the kernel a reference to each corresponding `cl_mem` object.

In other words, the host calls `clSetKernelArg()` for each of the kernel's corresponding arguments. Some of these may be scalars, but for each array argument the host will pass its corresponding `cl_mem` object. Note that the host must pass each argument to `clSetKernelArg()` by reference as a void pointer, but the kernel receives a dereferenced version of each argument. Also note that `clSetKernelArg()` assigns each actual argument value to each of the kernel's formal arguments according to the order in which the formal arguments are listed in the kernel function (see the second argument value of `clSetKernelArg()`, which specifies the formal argument by its relative position in the kernel's argument list).

For example, the arguments of the example kernel prototype:

```
kernel void example_kernel(global float* invals,
        global float* outvals, int n)
```

...could be assigned on the host with:

```
clSetKernelArg(my_kernel, 0, sizeof(cl_mem),
        (void*)&inval_buffer);
```

```
clSetKernelArg(my_kernel, 1, sizeof(cl_mem),
        (void*)&outval_buffer);
clSetKernelArg(my_kernel, 2, sizeof(cl_mem),
        (void*)&n);
```

…where `inval_buffer` and `outval_buffer` are declared as `cl_mem` objects and *n* is declared as *int*.

To dispatch the kernel, the host calls `clEnqueueNDRangeKernel()`, whose arguments specify the workgroup size and number of workgroups.

After the kernel completes execution, the host must call `clEnqueueReadBuffer()` to transfer the kernel's output arrays back to the host.

Related Functions:

```
cl_int clSetKernelArg (cl_kernel kernel,
                        cl_uint arg_index,
                        size_t arg_size,
                        const void *arg_value)
```

Used to set the argument value for a specific argument of a kernel.

```
cl_int clEnqueueWriteBuffer (cl_command_queue command_queue,
                        cl_mem buffer,
                        cl_bool blocking_write,
                        size_t offset,
                        size_t cb,
                        const void *ptr,
                        cl_uint num_events_in_wait_list,
                        const cl_event *event_wait_list,
                        cl_event *event)
```

Enqueue commands to write to a buffer object from host memory.

```
cl_int clEnqueueNDRangeKernel (cl_command_queue command_queue,
                        cl_kernel kernel,
                        cl_uint work_dim,
                        const size_t *global_work_offset,
```

```
                          const size_t *global_work_size,
                          const size_t *local_work_size,
                          cl_uint num_events_in_wait_list,
                          const cl_event *event_wait_list,
                          cl_event *event)
```

Enqueue a command to execute a kernel on a device.

```
cl_int clEnqueueReadBuffer (cl_command_queue command_queue,
                          cl_mem buffer,
                          cl_bool blocking_read,
                          size_t offset,
                          size_t cb,
                          void *ptr,
                          cl_uint num_events_in_wait_list,
                          const cl_event *event_wait_list,
                          cl_event *event)
```

Enqueue commands to read from a buffer object to host memory.

```
cl_int clFinish (cl_command_queue command_queue)
```

Block until all previously queued OpenCL commands in a command queue are issued to the associated device and have completed.

```
cl_int clGetEventProfilingInfo (cl_event event,
                          cl_profiling_info param_name,
                          size_t param_value_size,
                          void *param_value,
                          size_t *param_value_size_ret)
```

Return profiling information for the command associated with event if profiling is enabled.

The following definitions will provide the input size (in bytes), the kernel vector size, the workgroup size (assuming 1D workgroups), the number of workgroups (assuming 1D array of workgroups), and the device number.

In this example, the number of workgroups is maximized by setting to $N/(4 \times VS \times WGS)$. This will cause each work item to perform only one loop iteration.

```
#define N          1024*1024*128
#define VS         4
#define WGS        256
#define NWG        N/(4*VS*WGS)
#define DEVICE     1
```

localSize and globalSize are 1D arrays that specify the workgroup size and number of workgroups to the platform layer.

localSize directly determines the workgroup size, while globalSize determines the total number of work-items. The number of workgroups is thus implied as globalSize/localSize.

```
size_t localSize[1] = {WGS};
size_t globalSize[1] = {NWG*WGS};
struct timeval start, end;
```

Example Code:

```
ret = clSetKernelArg(kernel, 0, sizeof (inputBuffer), &input Buffer);
CHECK_STATUS(ret);
ret = clSetKernelArg(kernel, 1, sizeof (outputBuffer), &outputBuffer);
CHECK_STATUS(ret);
ret = clSetKernelArg(kernel, 2, sizeof (coeffBuffer), &coeffBuffer);
CHECK_STATUS(ret);
```

Since this was the last step before invoking the kernel, timing code to instrument the kernel execution. Note that clEnqueueNDRangeKernel() is asynchronous, meaning that it returns immediately after enqueuing the kernel. The clFinish() function will block until the kernel has completed execution, so the program can assume that the clEnqueueNDRangeKernel() marks the beginning of kernel execution and clFinish() marks the end of kernel execution. Note that this time does not necessarily include the time to transfer the input and output data between the host and device.

```
gettimeofday(&start, NULL);

ret = clEnqueueNDRangeKernel(queue,kernel,1,0,
          globalSize,localSize,0,0,&horner);

CHECK_STATUS(ret);

ret = clFinish(queue);

CHECK_STATUS(ret);

gettimeofday(&end, NULL);

float ndrangeDuration = (end.tv_sec + end.tv_usec * 1e-6) -
          (start.tv_sec + start.tv_usec * 1e-6);

float gflops = (float)(N/4 * 14) / ndrangeDuration / 1.0e9;
```

Since the code enabled profiling support when creating the command queue, the OpenCL runtime will return the kernel's execution time (note that the host code uses its own timing).

```
ret = clGetEventProfilingInfo(horner,

    CL_PROFILING_COMMAND_START,

    sizeof(cl_ulong),&start_t,

    &return_size);

CHECK_STATUS(ret);

ret = clGetEventProfilingInfo(horner,

    CL_PROFILING_COMMAND_END,

    sizeof(cl_ulong),&end_t,

    &return_size);

CHECK_STATUS(ret);

float runtime = (float)(end_t - start_t) / 1.0e9;
```

The kernel must also retrieve the output array of the kernel using clEnqueueReadBuffer() for validation using a CPU-based verification routine as in Chapter 2 (the verify() function is also shown in Section 5.5.1).

Notice the third argument to clEnqueueReadBuffer, blocking_read, which is set to CL_TRUE to prevent the function from returning until the copy completes.

```
ret = clEnqueueReadBuffer (queue,outputBuffer,CL_TRUE, 0,N,d,0,0,0);
CHECK_STATUS(ret);
verify(x,d);
```

And finally deallocate the arrays and shut down the OpenCL runtime:

```
free(x);
free(d);
ret = clReleaseMemObject(coeffBuffer);
CHECK_STATUS(ret);
ret = clReleaseMemObject(inputBuffer);
CHECK_STATUS(ret);
ret = clReleaseMemObject(outputBuffer);
CHECK_STATUS(ret);
ret = clReleaseKernel(kernel);
CHECK_STATUS(ret);
ret = clReleaseProgram(program);
CHECK_STATUS(ret);
ret = clReleaseCommandQueue(queue);
CHECK_STATUS(ret);
ret = clReleaseContext(context);
CHECK_STATUS(ret);
```

5.5 OpenCL implementation of Horner's method: Device code

Begin with the kernel parameters, which must match the corresponding parameters in the host code:

```
#define N      1024*1024*128
#define VS     4
#define WGS    256
#define NWG    N/(4*VS*WGS)
```

The top-level kernel function must have the "kernel" prefix, its name must match the name specified in the clCreateKernel() call, and its arguments must match those specified in the clSetKernelArg() calls:

```
kernel void horner (global float *x, global float *d,

    global float *coeff) {
```

The kernel requires two local variables to hold intermediate values. By default, local variables are private and are allocated in registers.

The first, temp, holds each coefficient and the partial sums when evaluating the polynomial. The other, xtemp, holds the input value, *x*.

Both these variables must match the vector size of the kernel. Thus, these variables are declared differently in five different versions of the kernel, corresponding to vector size 1, 2, 4, 8, and 16:

> For VS = 1
> ```
>    float temp,xtemp;
> ```
> For VS = 2
> ```
>    float2 temp,xtemp;
> ```
> For VS = 4
> ```
>    float4 temp,xtemp;
> ```
> For VS = 8
> ```
>    float8 temp,xtemp;
> ```
> For VS = 16
> ```
>    float16 temp,xtemp;
> ```

Using preprocessor directives, it is possible to avoid having to maintain one version of the kernel code for each vector size:

```
#if VS == 1

        float temp,xtemp;

#elif VS == 2

        float2 temp,xtemp;

#elif VS == 4

        float4 temp,xtemp;

#elif VS == 8

        float8 temp,xtemp;

#elif VS == 16

        float16 temp,xtemp;

#endif
```

Next, the kernel needs to declare integers for both the loop iterator and the start and end indices for which the loop will cover. Note that these variables default to the "private" OpenCL storage class.

Since the kernel will operate over vectors of size VS, all vector load and store operations must assume an element size of $4 \times$ VS. For example, for VS $= 4$, the kernel will operate over 16-byte values, so all indexing operations must be divided by this value.

Declare and initialize these integers as shown below:

```
int i,
    start = get_global_id(0) * N/(4*NWG*WGS*VS),
    end = (get_global_id(0)+1) * N/(4*NWG*WGS*VS);
```

The kernel's main loop, which will iterate if $N/(4 \times \mathrm{NWG} \times \mathrm{WGS} \times \mathrm{VS})$ times, begins:

```
for (i=start;i<end;i++) {
```

The loop body begins by loading the element(s) of *x* into `xtemp`. OpenCL requires the use of special load and store intrinsics for vectors, so use preprocessor commands to differentiate the behavior for a given vector size:

```
#if VS == 1
        xtemp = x[i];
#elif VS == 2
        xtemp = vload2(i,x);
#elif VS == 4
        xtemp = vload4(i,x);
#elif VS == 8
        xtemp = vload8(i,x);
#elif VS == 16
        xtemp = vload16(i,x);
#endif
```

The main computational portion of the loop body can be written in a way that is generalized for any vector size. The code begins by loading VS copies of the first coefficient into `temp`:

```
temp = coeff[0];
```

The OpenCL *mad(a,b,c)* intrinsic is compatible with vector types and performs the operation $a \times b + c$.

This intrinsic can multiply the previous partial sum—initially the first coefficient—by x, add the next coefficient to the sum, and store the result back to temp. Unroll this "loop" to avoid the need for an inner loop:

```
temp = mad(temp,xtemp,coeff[1]);

temp = mad(temp,xtemp,coeff[2]);

temp = mad(temp,xtemp,coeff[3]);

temp = mad(temp,xtemp,coeff[4]);

temp = mad(temp,xtemp,coeff[5]);

temp = mad(temp,xtemp,coeff[6]);

temp = mad(temp,xtemp,coeff[7]);
```

The kernel must store the final value of temp back to the d-array. This line depends on the vector size, so as before, use preprocessor to differentiate the code's behavior depending on the value of VS:

```
#if VS == 1

            d[i] = temp;

#elif VS == 2

            vstore2(temp,i,d);

#elif VS == 4

            vstore4(temp,i,d);

#elif VS == 8

            vstore8(temp,i,d);

#elif VS == 16

            vstore16(temp,i,d);

#endif

}

}
```

As in Chapter 2, when developing and characterizing a tuned kernel implementation, the program should validate the results of a trusted implementation of the same operation.

```c
int verify (float *x,float *d) {
    int i,j;
    float error;
    float *d_test;
    float coeff[8] = {1.2f,1.4f,1.6f,1.8f,2.0f,2.2f,2.4f, 2.6f};
    d_test = (float *)malloc(N);
    if (!d_test) {
        perror("malloc() in verify()");
        return 0;
    }
    for (i=0;i<N/4;i++) {
        d_test[i]=coeff[0];
        for (j=1;j<8;j++) {
            d_test[i]*=x[i];
            d_test[i]+=coeff[j];
        }
        error = fabs(d[i]-d_test[i])/d_test[i];
        if (error > 1.0e-2) {
            printf("verification error,\
                d_test[%d]=%0.2e,\
                d[%d]=%0.2e,\
                error=%0.2f%%\n",
                i,d_test[i],i,d[i],
                error*1.0e2);
            free(d_test);
            return 0;
        }
    }
    printf("results verified\n");
    free(d_test);
    return 1;
}
```

5.6 Performance results

One surprising result from running the example code is that the performance measured using `getttimeofday()` is substantially less—indicating as little as half the performance in Gflops—than the performance measured using OpenCL profiling.

When using gettimeofday(), the program begins measuring immediately before the call to `clEnqueueNDRangeKernel()`, so there is an assumption that the kernel begins execution soon after calling this function. Latency between when the kernel is enqueued and when it begins execution on the device will cause this perceived performance difference.

5.6.1 Parameter exploration

The values of the WGS, NWG, and VS parameters affect kernel performance. To examine the impact of each parameter separately, hold two parameters constant while varying the other.

5.6.2 Number of workgroups

The OpenCL runtime reports that both of the Mali-T628 GPU devices on the ODROID-XU3 board contain four compute units, as reported by `clGetDeviceInfo()` with the `CL_DEVICE_MAX_ COMPUTE_UNITS` option.

The kernel has little potential for load imbalance, having a uniform loop iteration count and lack of if-statements. Given this, it may be reasonable to conclude that there is no advantage to instantiate more than four workgroups, since four workgroups would utilize all available multicore parallelism.

Table 5.2 shows the performance results reported by the OpenCL profiler, with:

- WGS = 256, the maximum number in one dimension for the kernel (as reported by clGet-KernelWorkGroupInfo() with CL_KERNEL_WORK_GROUP_SIZE);
- VS = 4, the preferred vector size for the device (as reported by CL_DEVICE_ PREFERRED_VECTOR_WIDTH_FLOAT); and
- sweeping NWG from 4 to 32,768 (the maximum for $N = 128$ MB).

The results show that performance improves as the number of workgroups is increased. For this test the maximum performance is 15.6 Gflops, achieved with the 32,768 workgroups, which indicates that the number of compute units has no effect on the ideal number of workgroups.

Recall that in Chapter 2, the same kernel executed on four ARM Cortex A15 cores running at 2.23 GHz with the most highly tuned implementation achieved 17.8 Gflops. Note that these results were obtained on the NVIDIA Jetson TK1, which is a larger, more substantial platform than the ODROID-XU3.

Table 5.2: Kernel performance for $N = 128$ MB,
WGS $= 256$, VS $= 4$.

NWG	Kernel FP throughput (Gflops)
4	0.6
2048	5.8
4096	6.3
8192	7.1
16,384	14.4
32,768	15.6

Table 5.3: Kernel performance for $N = 128$ MB,
NWG $= N/(4 \times$ VS $\times$ WGS), VS $= 4$.

WGS	Kernel FP throughput (Gflops)
1	6.9
16	13.8
32	13.9
64	13.8
128	15.3
256	15.6

5.6.3 Workgroup size

Workgroup size affects how effectively the GPU core can hide the latency of instructions from individual work-items.

Table 5.3 shows the performance results as reported by the OpenCL profiler, with:

- NWG $= N/(4 \times$ VS $\times$ WGS), the maximum possible value such that the kernel's for-loop executes only one iteration and the best-performing setting from the previous test;
- VS $= 4$, the preferred vector size for the device (as reported by CL_DEVICE_PREFERRED_VECTOR_WIDTH_FLOAT); and
- sweeping WGS from 1 to 256.

For this test, the maximum performance is again 15.6 Gflops, which is achieved for the maximum workgroup size of 256, matching the same parameters from the last row of the previous table.

5.6.4 Vector size

Regardless of the native width of the GPU's SIMD functional units, using wider vectors in the kernel may provide the GPU architecture more opportunity for exploiting data-level parallelism.

**Table 5.4: Kernel performance for $N = 128$ MB,
NWG $= N/(4 \times VS \times WGS)$, WGS $= 256$.**

VS	Kernel FP throughput (Gflops)
1	4.8
2	9.4
4	15.6
8	15.5
16	14.7

Table 5.4 shows the performance results as reported by the OpenCL profiler, with:

- NWG $= N/(4 \times VS \times WGS)$, which is the maximum possible, such that the kernel's for-loop executes only one iteration;
- WGS $= 256$; the best-performing setting for this parameter was determined by the previous test; and
- sweeping VS from 1 to 16.

The performance exhibits an increasing trend from VS $= 1$ to VS $= 4$ and a decreasing trend from VS $= 4$ to VS $= 16$. The maximum performance is at VS $= 4$ with 15.6 Gflops, achieved with the same parameters as in the previous test.

5.7 Chapter wrap-up

This chapter introduces OpenCL, an openly defined framework for developing and dispatching general-purpose programs to a slave-type coprocessor such as a GPU. OpenCL is adopted by several CPU, GPU, FPGA, and DSP manufacturers, allowing programs written in OpenCL to be portable across a wide range of diverse embedded and high-performance processing technologies.

OpenCL is already well known in the high-performance computing area but is arguably more important for embedded systems, which often rely on coprocessors to meet real-time performance constraints such as real-time video compression for smartphones or computer vision algorithms for robots.

Unlike OpenMP, which only requires a few additional lines of code to convert a serial program into a parallel program, OpenCL is more verbose but it gives the programmer fine-grain control over memory allocation and movement.

Writing OpenCL programs requires code at the platform level and kernel level.

At the kernel level, the programmer must identify the applications' kernels—the loops that account for nearly all execution time—and adapt them for execution on the coprocessor device. This requires that the programmer isolate the loops in separate source files and transform them into an explicitly data-parallel form in which the outermost loop iterations are mapped to hierarchical work-sharing constructs known as workgroups and work-items.

OpenCL kernel code provides many opportunities for optimization, such as explicitly allocating and managing program-controlled on-chip memories, using SIMD intrinsics, and adjusting the granularity of parallelization. OpenCL also provides a mechanism for *parameterizing* kernels—by adjusting workgroup and vector size—to tune to specific architectures.

At the platform level, the programmer must manage the initialization, communication, and synchronization of the devices, allocate device memory, and compile the kernel code at runtime.

This chapter provides a running example in which Horner's method program from Chapter 2 is adapted into the OpenCL framework for an embedded GPU. The code is tested on the ARM Mali-T628 embedded GPU, which achieves an effective performance of 15.6 Gflops.

Exercises

1. Write an OpenCL kernel to measure the actual memory bandwidth of the coprocessor. Use one work item per workgroup with 1024 workgroups. Each work item should use the *vload16()* and *vstore16()* functions to copy a block of data from one location to another. How does the coprocessor's bandwidth compare to that of the host CPU?
2. Plot the performance of the Horner example described in this chapter with WGS = 1, NWG = $N/(4 \times VS \times WGS)$, and VS = $\{1, 2, 4, 8, 16\}$.
3. Change the Horner example such that the coefficient array is allocated in local memory. How does this impact the performance results from Tables 5.2 to 5.4?
4. Use OpenCL to implement the image transformation example from Chapter 3. Use fixed-point datatypes. Write the kernel such that it uses SIMD operations to calculate the interpolated values for 16 destination pixels in parallel. Invoke the kernel for all the pixels simultaneously. Calculate the resultant performance in frames per second and compare to that of your embedded CPU.
5. Use OpenCL to implement the Mandelbrot set generator from Chapter 3. Use floating-point datatypes. Write the kernel such that it calculates the color value for a particular pixel given its coordinates and the x- and y-range. Invoke the kernel for all the pixels simultaneously. Calculate the resultant performance in frames per second and compare to that of your embedded CPU.
6. Use OpenCL to implement the tiled Sobel filter from Chapter 4. Copy the entire frame to the device memory before dispatching the kernel. Begin by processing each output pixel with each work item. Then change the code such that each work item processes one tile. Finally, change the kernel such that it buffers each input tile in local memory before processing it. What is the achieved performance in Gflops in each of these three cases?

Adding PMU support to Raspbian for the generation 1 Raspberry Pi

Chapter Outline

The Linux kernel included in the Raspbian Linux distribution through its December 2014 release does not support for the ARM11 Performance Monitoring Unit through Linux's perf_event API. Fortunately, it is relatively easy to patch the kernel to enable this feature. This patch was developed by Chad Paradis and Vincent M. Weaver of the University of Maine.

To check to see if your kernel supports perf_event, check to see if the directory */sys/bus/event_source/devices* contains any files *except* from "breakpoint" and "software." On the Raspberry Pi, the existence of the symbolic link named "v6" indicates support for perf_event.

To enable support you must make a minor change to two kernel source files and recompile the kernel. Compiling the Linux kernel requires an unreasonable amount of time if performed on the Raspberry Pi itself, so it is best to do this by cross-compiling on a capable Linux workstation.

A.1 Download the Linux kernel and cross-compiler tools

The Raspbian kernel is available for download on GitHub at `https://github.com/raspberrypi/linux.git`. You should download the same kernel version as currently running on your Raspberry Pi. You can check your kernel version using the `uname -a` command on the Raspberry Pi.

This kernel repository is usually several versions ahead of the kernel installed in the latest version of Raspbian, but you can use the "git clone" command to download a specific branch of the source code using a command such as:

```
git clone-branch rpi-3.12.y
```

```
https://github.com/raspberrypi/linux.git
```

You can download the ARM cross-compiler toolchain for Intel-based workstations at `https://github.com/raspberrypi/tools.git`.

A.2 Kernel modifications

In the kernel source code, open the file `arch/arm/mach-bcm2708/bcm2708.c`. At (or around) line 468, add the following code:

```
static struct platform_device bcm2708_pmu_device = {
        .name = "arm-pmu",
        .id = -1, /* Only one */
};
```

In the function bcm2708_init(), after the following line of code:

```
bcm_register_device(&bcm2708_powerman_device);
```

...add:

```
bcm_register_device(&bcm2708_pmu_device);
```

Next, open the file arch/arm/kernel/perf_event_cpu.c. In the `cpu_pmu_request_irq()` function, change the following code:

```
if (irqs < 1) {
        pr_err("no irqs for PMUs defined\n");
        return -ENODEV;
}
```

...to:

```
if (irqs < 1) {
        printk_once("no irqs for PMUs defined, disabling sampled events\n");
        return 0;
}
```

A.3 Building the kernel

On your workstation, define the *CCPREFIX* environment variable to:

"<tools directory root >/`arm-bcm2708/arm-bcm2708-linux-gnueabi/bin/`
`arm-bcm2708-linux-gnueabi-`"

Next, define the *KERNEL_SRC* environment variable to the root of your kernel source code.

Copy and decompress your Raspberry Pi's current kernel build configuration to the kernel source directory with the filename ".config". The kernel configuration is stored in the compressed file /proc/config.gz on the Raspberry Pi.

You can use the "zcat" command to perform the decompression, that is,

```
zcat config.gz > $KERNEL_SRC/.config
```

Change to the root of the kernel source and issue the following command, which will ensure that the .config file is correct. Due to minor version differences between your current kernel and the downloaded kernel, this command may prompt you for a few build options. If so, just push enter to accept the default responses.

```
make ARCH=arm CROSS_COMPILE=${CCPREFIX} oldconfig
```

Use the following command to build the kernel. This step may take a significant amount of time.

```
make ARCH=arm CROSS_COMPILE=${CCPREFIX}
```

Use the following command to build the modules.

```
make ARCH=arm CROSS_COMPILE=${CCPREFIX} modules
```

Finally, on the Raspberry Pi itself, issue the following command in Linux kernel source root. This will install the modules.

```
make modules_install
```

A.4 Installing the kernel

The new kernel image will be located in the kernel source at *arch/arm/boot/zImage*. Copy this file to **/boot/kernel.img** and reboot.

After the reboot, re-check the **/sys/bus/event_source/devices** directory for perf_event support.

NEON intrinsic reference

Chapter Outline

The *arm_neon.h* header file defines 102 data types and 2009 intrinsics that allow the programmer to explicitly encode support for ARM NEON instructions in high-level source code. To use an intrinsic, the programmer needs only to call a specific function, but intrinsics are not normal functions. Each intrinsic is defined as an inline function that acts as a wrapper around a built-in compiler command that forces the compiler's back-end to emit a specific instruction (often along with supporting instructions).

This appendix provides additional details on ARM NEON intrinsics beyond that provided in Chapter 2. Interested readers should refer to the actual header file, located in */usr/lib/gcc/arm-linux-gnueabihf/< version >/include*, as well as ARM's documentation for additional details on NEON programming.

B.1 Vector data types

Tables B.1–B.9 list the types defined in *arm_neon.h*. NEON intrinsics support 64-bit and 128-bit ("*quad*"-size) vectors comprised of signed and unsigned integers and floating-point values.

Intrinsics that use 64-bit (double word) vectors have no suffix, while those that use 128-bit (quad-word) vectors require a *q*-suffix that typically appears after the operation mnemonic and before the element type specifier. For example:

- the `vmul_s8` intrinsic performs a pairwise multiply two 64-bit vectors, each comprised of eight 8-bit signed integers of type *int8x8_t*
- the `vmulq_s8` intrinsic (with the *q*-suffix) performs a pairwise multiply two 128-bit vectors each comprised of sixteen 8-bit signed integers of type *int8x16_t*.

Table B.1: NEON types having 8-bit integer elements.

Signed	Unsigned	Elements	Total Bits
		1D types	
int8x8_t	*uint8x8_t*	8	64
int8x16_t	*uint8x16_t*	16	128
		2D types	
int8x8x2_t	*uint8x8x2_t*	8 × 2	128
int8x8x3_t	*uint8x8x3_t*	8 × 3	192
int8x8x4_t	*uint8x8x4_t*	8 × 4	256
int8x16x2_t	*uint8x16x2_t*	16 × 2	256
int8x16x3_t	*uint8x16x3_t*	16 × 3	384
int8x16x4_t	*uint8x16x4_t*	16 × 4	512

Table B.2: NEON types having 16-bit integer elements.

Signed	Unsigned	Elements	Total Bits
		1D types	
int16x4_t	*uint16x4_t*	4	64
int16x8_t	*uint16x8_t*	8	128
		2D types	
int16x4x2_t	*uint16x4x2_t*	4 × 2	128
int16x4x3_t	*uint16x4x3_t*	4 × 3	192
int16x4x4_t	*uint16x4x4_t*	4 × 4	256
int16x8x2_t	*uint16x8x2_t*	8 × 2	256
int16x8x3_t	*uint16x8x3_t*	8 × 3	384
int16x8x4_t	*uint16x8x4_t*	8 × 4	512

Table B.3: NEON types having 32-bit integer elements.

Signed	Unsigned	Elements	Total Bits
		1D types	
int32x2_t	*uint32x2_t*	2	64
int32x4_t	*uint32x4_t*	4	128
		2D types	
int32x2x2_t	*uint32x2x2_t*	2 × 2	128
int32x2x3_t	*uint32x2x3_t*	2 × 3	192
int32x2x4_t	*uint32x2x4_t*	2 × 4	256
int32x4x2_t	*uint32x4x2_t*	4 × 2	256
int32x4x3_t	*uint32x4x3_t*	4 × 3	384
int32x4x4_t	*uint32x4x4_t*	4 × 4	512

Table B.4: NEON types having 64-bit integer elements.

Signed	Unsigned	Elements	Total Bits
	1D types		
int64x1_t	*uint64x1_t*	1	64
int64x2_t	*uint64x2_t*	2	128
	2D types		
int64x1x2_t	*uint64x1x2_t*	1 × 2	128
int64x1x3_t	*uint64x1x3_t*	1 × 3	192
int64x1x4_t	*uint64x1x4_t*	1 × 4	256
int64x2x2_t	*uint64x2x2_t*	2 × 2	256
int64x2x3_t	*uint64x2x3_t*	2 × 3	384
int64x2x4_t	*uint64x2x4_t*	2 × 4	512

Table B.5: NEON types having 8-bit polynomial elements.

Type	Elements	Total Bits
	Primitive types	
poly8_t	1	8
	1D types	
poly8x8_t	8	64
poly8x16_t	16	128
	2D types	
poly8x8x2_t	8 × 2	128
poly8x8x3_t	8 × 3	192
poly8x8x4_t	8 × 4	256
poly8x16x2_t	16 × 2	256
poly8x16x3_t	16 × 3	384
poly8x16x4_t	16 × 4	512

NEON also supports special integer vectors called polynomials. Polynomial elements are stored in integer format, but bit carries are disabled whenever an arithmetic operation uses polynomial input and output operands. As such all additions are replaced with bitwise XOR operations.

For example, multiplying 3×3 in binary requires the addition of two partial products, 3 (011_2) and 6 (110_2), but when performed as polynomial values the result is 5 (011_2 XOR $110_2 = 101_2$).

NEON also supports small matrix types having up to 16 columns and 4 rows. Variables of these types are only used for special 2D "reordering" operations: transposing, interleaving (zipping), and 2D loads and stores, although their 1D constituent vectors can be used with any NEON operation.

Table B.6: NEON types having 16-bit polynomial elements.

Type	Elements	Total Bits
Primitive types		
poly16_t	1	16
1D types		
poly16x4_t	4	64
poly16x8_t	8	128
2D types		
poly16x4x2_t	4×2	128
poly16x4x3_t	4×3	192
poly16x4x4_t	4×4	256
poly16x8x2_t	8×2	256
poly16x8x3_t	8×3	384
poly16x8x4_t	8×4	512

Table B.7: Other NEON polynomial types.

Type	Elements	Total Bits
Primitive types		
poly64_t	1	64
poly128_t	1	128
1D types		
poly64x1_t	1	64
poly64x2_t	2	128
2D types		
poly64x1x2_t	1×2	128
poly64x1x3_t	1×3	192
poly64x1x4_t	1×4	256
poly64x2x2_t	2×2	256
poly64x2x3_t	2×3	324
poly64x2x4_t	2×4	512

Table B.8: NEON types having 16-bit (half precision) floating-point elements.

Type	Elements	Total Bits
float16x4_t	4	64

Table B.9: NEON types having 32-bit (single precision) floating-point elements.

Type	Elements	Total Bits
Primitive types		
float32_t	1	32
1D types		
float32x2_t	2	64
float32x4_t	4	128
2D types		
float32x2x2_t	2×2	128
float32x2x3_t	2×3	192
float32x2x4_t	2×4	256
float32x4x2_t	4×2	256
float32x4x3_t	4×3	384
float32x4x4_t	4×4	512

B.2 Reading and writing vector variables

There are several methods for reading and writing NEON vector variables outside of the intrinsics. The simplest way is to treat them as any standard C array.

For example:

- Initialize on declaration:

```
int8x8_t a={0,0,2,2,4,4,6,6};
```

- Set as an array:

```
int8x8_t a;

for (i=0;i<8;i++) a[i]=i*2;
```

- Read as an array:

```
for (i=0;i<8;i++) printf("%d ",a[i]);

printf ("\n");
```

As shown below, NEON intrinsics have a suffix that specifies the type and size of their elements. Note the conspicuous lack of 64-bit floating point.

- _s8 signed 8-bit integer
- _u8 unsigned 8-bit integer
- _s16 signed 16-bit integer
- _u16 unsigned 16-bit integer
- _s32 signed 32-bit integer
- _u32 unsigned 32-bit integer

- _p8 8-bit polynomial
- _p16 16-bit polynomial
- _f16 16-bit float
- _f32 32-bit float

Normal, double-word intrinsics assume a 64-bit total width, so the vector size is implied by the element size. For example, an _s8 intrinsic would operate on a 64/8 = 8-element vector. As described above, the "q" suffix specifies a 128 bit vector, so an intrinsic ending with q_s8 would operate on a 128/8 = 16-element vector.

Some intrinsics are used to instance a vector. For example, the vcreate intrinsic maps each 8-bit field from a scalar into the elements of an 8-element vector:

```
// set vector from least significant byte,
// i.e. a[0] 55 0, a[7]5514
a = vcreate_s8(0x0D0C0A0806040200);
```

The vdup intrinsic sets each element to a specified scalar value:

```
int8x16_t b;
a = vdup_n_s8(5); // set all 8 elements to 5
b = vdupq_n_s8(5); // set all 16 elements to 5
```

You can load and store 64-bit and 128-bit vectors using the vld1 and vld1q intrinsics. For example:

```
// declare standard local arrays for
// demonstrating vld and vst
int8_t data_in[64],data_out[64];
// initialize data in the data_in array
for (i=0;i<64;i++) data_in[i]=i;
// load 64 bits, or eight elements of 8-bit values
// into vector variable a
a = vld1_s8(data_in);
// print the elements in vector variable a
for (i=0;i<8;i++) printf("%d ",a[i]); printf ("\n");
// store the contents of vector variable a into output array
vst1_s8(data_out,a);
// print the output array
for (i=0;i<8;i++) printf("%d ",data_out[i]); printf ("\n");
```

NEON supports loading and storing vectors with a stride of two, three, and four elements with the *vld* and *vst* intrinsics.

One way to interpret the behavior of the *vld4* intrinsic is that it treats the input array as a row-major matrix with $64/n$ rows and 4 columns, where n is the bit width of the type suffix, while the intrinsic returns the data in transposed order.

The code below uses the *vld4_s8* intrinsic to load data from the *data_in* array as declared and initialized above. The returned variable, *c*, is declared as an 8×4 array. The vld4 intrinsic loads four double words (64 bits each, 256 bits total), but also applies a stride of four elements to each of the four 8×1 vectors given by *c*.

```
int8x8x4_t c;

c=vld4_s8(data_in);

for (i=0;i<8;i++)

        for (j=0;j<4;j++) printf("%d ",c.val[j][i]);

printf ("\n");
```

The vld4_s4 works in a similar way but in reverse. There are also 2- and 3-stride versions of both the *vld* and *vst* instructions.

B.3 Vector element manipulation

Several intrinsics are available for manipulating elements within a vector.

Reversing:

Vector elements can be reversed using the *vrev* intrinsic, for example:

```
// reverse the eight elements in vector variable a

b=vrev64_s8(a);
```

Combining:

A range of elements from two vectors can be extracted and combined using the *vext* intrinsic. For example if the state of the *a* and *b* vectors are the following:

$a = \{0, 1, 2, 3, 4, 5, 6, 7\}$

$b = \{8, 9, 10, 11, 12, 13, 14, 15\}$

The following intrinsic call will extract the last five elements from *a* and first three elements from *b*:

```
b=vext_s8(a,b,3);
```

Setting the new state of vector *b* to:

$b = \{3, 4, 5, 6, 7, 8, 9, 10\}$

Transposing:

The *vtrn* intrinsic takes two vectors, interprets them as a set of 2 × 2 matrixes, transposes the matrices, and then returns the result as a 2D vector type having two rows.

As before, assume the *a* and *b* vectors are initialized as follows:

$a = \{0, 1, 2, 3, 4, 5, 6, 7\}$

$b = \{8, 9, 10, 11, 12, 13, 14, 15\}$

The following intrinsic call will interpret these vectors as four 2×2 matrices and transpose them. The result is returned as an *int8x2_t* type.

```
c=vtrn_s8(a,b);
```

$c = \{\{0, 8, 2, 10, 4, 12, 6, 14\},$

$\{1, 9, 3, 11, 5, 13, 7, 15\}\}$

Interleaving:

The *vzip* intrinsic takes two input vectors and interleaves them. The result is returned as a two-row vector type.

For example, assume *a* and *b* are initialized as before:

$a = \{0, 1, 2, 3, 4, 5, 6, 7\}$

$b = \{8, 9, 10, 11, 12, 13, 14, 15\}$

The following intrinsic call will return the following value of *c*:

```
c=vzip_s8(a,b);
```

$c = \{\{0, 8, 1, 9, 2, 10, 3, 11\},$

$\{4, 12, 5, 13, 6, 14, 7, 15\}\}$

The *vuzip* intrinsic takes two vectors and returns the even-numbered elements in one vector and the odd-numbered elements in another vector.

Starting with the same input vectors as above:

$a = \{0, 1, 2, 3, 4, 5, 6, 7\}$

$b = \{8, 9, 10, 11, 12, 13, 14, 15\}$

The following intrinsic call will return the following value as an *int8x2_t* type:

```
c=vuzp_s8(a,b);
```

$c = \{\{0, 2, 4, 6, 8, 10, 12, 14\},$

$\{1, 3, 5, 7, 9, 11, 13, 15\}\}$

Gather:

The *vtbl* intrinsic performs a "gather" operation, which takes two vectors and interprets the second vector as a set of indices to load a set of corresponding elements from the first vector. If any of the values of the second vector are out of range, vtbl inserts zeroes at their corresponding positions in the return vector. A related intrinsic, vtblx, performs the same operation but treats out of range values in the second vector differently. In for these, vtbx copies the original values from the first vector.

Assume *a* and *b* are initialized as follows:

$a = \{0, 1, 2, 3, 4, 5, 6, 7\}$

$b = \{0, 0, 2, 2, 4, 4, 6, 6\}$

Passing *a* and *b* to vtbl will return the following value of *c*.

```
b=vtbl1_s8(a,b);
```

$c = \{8, 8, 10, 10, 12, 12, 14, 14\}$

Combining:

The *vcombine* intrinsic concatenates two vectors, where the result vector is twice the width of the input vectors.

Assume two 8-element vectors *a* and *b* with the following values:

$a = \{0,0,2,2,4,4,6,6\};$

$b = \{8,8,10,10,12,12,14,14\};$

The following intrinsic call will return the following 16-element vector:

```
c=vcombine_s8(a,b);
```

$c = \{0, 0, 2, 2, 4, 4, 6, 6, 8, 8, 10, 10, 12, 12, 14, 14\}$

B.4 Optimizing floating-point code with NEON intrinsics

Inline assembly does not include its own set of special data types, but the NEON intrinsics are more "type-aware" in that they expect their inputs to be NEON vector variables passed by value and their outputs are given as return values.

The need for these special vector variables complicates the process by which NEON support is added to existing code that uses standard C-style arrays, but luckily the compiler is able to reinterpret standard arrays as NEON vector pointers. However, this requires that NEON code include frequent typecasting, making the code appear more cluttered and less readable.

To demonstrate how existing floating-point code can be enhanced with NEON intrinsics, this appendix examine a simple implementation for matrix inversion using Gaussian elimination.

This method begins by concatenating the input matrix, shown as matrix A below, with the identity matrix, shown below it:

$$A = \begin{bmatrix} 1 & 2 & 3 & 1 \\ 2 & 1 & 4 & 1 \\ 5 & 6 & 2 & 1 \\ 7 & 6 & 3 & 2 \end{bmatrix}$$

$$\begin{array}{c} R0 \\ R1 \\ R2 \\ R3 \end{array} \left[\begin{array}{cccc|cccc} 1 & 2 & 3 & 1 & 1 & 0 & 0 & 0 \\ 2 & 1 & 4 & 1 & 0 & 1 & 0 & 0 \\ 5 & 6 & 2 & 1 & 0 & 0 & 1 & 0 \\ 7 & 6 & 3 & 2 & 0 & 0 & 0 & 1 \end{array} \right]$$

Gaussian elimination performs successive row transformations on the concatenated matrix having the objective of transforming the left-side of the concatenated matrix—the original A matrix—into the identity and the right side into the inverted form of A.

This requires three discrete steps. The first step is to convert the matrix into triangular form, in which the transformations systematically set each element of the bottom triangle to zeroes beginning with the lower-left element and then each element along each upper-left to lower-right diagonal as shown below.

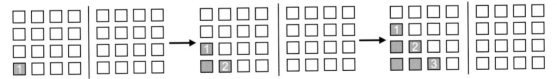

For the purpose of this simple example, assume that the original A matrix contains no zero elements. This allows the matrix to be converted to triangular form using the following row transformations:

1. set element (3,0) to zero $R3 \leftarrow R3 + (-A_{3,0}/A_{2,0})R2$
2. set element (2,0) to zero $R2 \leftarrow R2 + (-A_{2,0}/A_{1,0})R1$
3. set element (3,1) to zero $R3 \leftarrow R3 + (-A_{3,1}/A_{2,1})R1$
4. set element (1,0) to zero $R1 \leftarrow R1 + (-A_{1,0}/A_{0,0})R0$
5. set element (2,1) to zero $R2 \leftarrow R2 + (-A_{2,1}/A_{1,1})R1$
6. set element (3,2) to zero $R3 \leftarrow R3 + (-A_{3,2}/A_{2,2})R1$

This gives the following result:

$$
\begin{array}{c}
\text{R0} \\
\text{R1} \\
\text{R2} \\
\text{R3}
\end{array}
\left[
\begin{array}{cccc|cccc}
1.0 & 2.0 & 3.0 & 1.0 & 1.0 & 0 & 0 & 0 \\
0 & -3.0 & -2.0 & -1.0 & -2.0 & 1.0 & 0 & 0 \\
0 & 0 & -10.3 & -2.7 & -2.3 & -1.3 & 1.0 & 0 \\
0 & 0 & 0 & 0.9 & 1.2 & -1.0 & -1.2 & 1.0
\end{array}
\right]
$$

Assuming the input matrix is stored in row-major order in array *a* and the identity matrix is stored in array *b*, the code that performs this is as follows:

```
for (i=3;i>0;i--) {

    for (j=0;j<(4-i);j++) {

        coeff = -a[(i+j)*4+j]/a[((i+j)-1)*4+j];

        for (k=0;k<4;k++) {

         b[(i+j)*4+k]+= coeff * b[((i+j)-1)*4+k];

         a[(i+j)*4+k]+= coeff * a[((i+j)-1)*4+k];

        }

    }

}
```

gcc 4.8.2 does not generate any NEON SIMD instructions when compiling this code, even when requesting maximum optimization and explicitly specifying their target architecture and NEON support (using the *-O3 -mfpu = neon -march = armv7-a* switches).

The programmer can replace the entire innermost loop (the *k*-loop) with two 4-wide (quad) VMLAQ (multiply-accumulate quad) intrinsics, using:

```
*((float32x4_t *)(&b[(i+j)*4])) =

            vmlaq_f32(*((float32x4_t *)&b[(i+j)*4]),

                *((float32x4_t *)(&b[((i+j)-1)*4])),

                vdupq_n_f32(coeff));

*((float32x4_t *)(&a[(i+j)*4])) =

            vmlaq_f32(*((float32x4_t *)(&a[(i+j)*4])),

                *((float32x4_t *)(&a[((i+j)-1)*4])),

                vdupq_n_f32(coeff));
```

Notice that the *a*- and *b*-arrays must be referenced, cast as float32x4_t pointers, and then dereferenced for both the vector inputs and outputs. Also, the *coeff* scalar value must be converted from a scalar to a vector using the duplicate (vdupq) intrinsic.

The next step of the Gaussian elimination is to further refine the matrix by setting each element in the upper triangle to zero using a similar approach:

1. set element (2,3) to zero $\quad R2 \leftarrow R2 + (-A_{2,3}/A_{3,3})R3$
2. set element (1,2) to zero $\quad R1 \leftarrow R1 + (-A_{1,2}/A_{2,2})R2$
3. set element (1,3) to zero $\quad R1 \leftarrow R1 + (-A_{1,3}/A_{3,3})R3$
4. set element (0,1) to zero $\quad R0 \leftarrow R0 + (-A_{0,1}/A_{1,1})R1$
5. set element (0,2) to zero $\quad R0 \leftarrow R0 + (-A_{0,2}/A_{2,2})R2$
6. set element (0,3) to zero $\quad R0 \leftarrow R0 + (-A_{0,3}/A_{3,3})R3$

This gives the following result:

$$
\begin{array}{c}
R0 \\ R1 \\ R2 \\ R3
\end{array}
\left[
\begin{array}{cccc|cccc}
1.0 & 0 & 0 & 0 & -0.6 & 0.3 & 0 & 0.1 \\
0 & -3.0 & 0 & 0 & -0.9 & 0.7 & -0.8 & 0.5 \\
0 & 0 & -10.3 & 0 & 1.1 & -4.3 & -2.5 & 2.9 \\
0 & 0 & 0 & 0.9 & 1.2 & -1.0 & -1.2 & 1.0
\end{array}
\right]
$$

This can be performed with the following loop nest:

```
for (i=2;i>=0;i--) {

    for (j=i+1;j<4;j++) {

        coeff = -a[i*4+j]/a[j*4+j];

        for (k=0;k<4;k++) {

            b[i*4+k]+=coeff * b[j*4+k];

            a[i*4+k]+=coeff * a[j*4+k];

        }

    }

}
```

Again the innermost loop (k-loop) can be replaced with two NEON intrinsics:

```
*((float32x4_t *)(&b2[i*4])) =

            vmlaq_f32(*((float32x4_t *)(&b2[i*4])),

    *((float32x4_t *)(&b2[j*4])),

            vdupq_n_f32(coeff));

*((float32x4_t *)(&a2[i*4])) =

            vmlaq_f32(*((float32x4_t *)(&a2[i*4])),

    *((float32x4_t *)(&a2[j*4])),

            vdupq_n_f32(coeff));
```

As a final step, divide each row by its diagonal value to complete the transition of the matrix into the identity matrix:

1. set element (0,0) to one $R0 \leftarrow R0/A_{0,0}$
2. set element (1,1) to one $R1 \leftarrow R1/A_{1,1}$
3. set element (2,2) to one $R2 \leftarrow R2/A_{2,2}$
4. set element (3,3) to one $R3 \leftarrow R3/A_{3,3}$

This gives the following result:

$$
\begin{array}{c}
R0 \\
R1 \\
R2 \\
R3
\end{array}
\left[
\begin{array}{cccc|cccc}
1.0 & 0 & 0 & 0 & -0.6 & 0.3 & 0 & 0.1 \\
0 & 1.0 & 0 & 0 & 0.3 & -0.2 & 0.3 & -0.2 \\
0 & 0 & 1.0 & 0 & -0.1 & 0.4 & 0.2 & -0.3 \\
0 & 0 & 0 & 1.0 & 1.3 & -1.1 & -1.3 & 1.1
\end{array}
\right]
$$

This can be performed with the following code:

```
for (i=0;i<4;i++) for (j=0;j<4;j++) b[i*4+j] /= a[i*4+i];
```

B.5 Summary of NEON instrinsics

NEON intrinsics begin with the letter "*v*" and follow the following naming scheme:

$$v\{\,prefix\,\}\{\,operation\,\}\{\,modifier\,\} - \{\,operand\ type\,\}\{\,operand\ width\,\}$$

The *prefix* is optional and, depending on the intrinsic, is used to specify one of the available rounding and saturating modes.

The *operation* is a mnemonic usually named the same or similar to the intrinsic's associated instruction.

The *modifier* is optional and is used for intrinsics that do not use standard 64-bit operands and results.

The *operand type* and *width* defines the datatype of each vector element.

B.5.1 Prefix

The set of allowable *prefix* values depends on the operation. Example prefixes include:

- *h* (halving): shifts each output element one bit to the right
- *d* (doubling): shifts each output element by one bit to the left
- *r* (rounding): rounds each output element (used with the *hn* modifier)

- *rh* (rounding halving): shifts each output element one bit to the right and rounds
- *q* (saturate): sets each output element to its maximum value on overflow or minimum value on underflow
- *qd* (saturating doubling): saturates and doubles
- *qrd* (saturating, rounding, and doubling): saturates, rounds, and doubles

B.5.2 Operation

NEON operations can be grouped into several basic categories:

Arithmetic:

- *add, sub, mul*: add, subtract, multiply
- *mla, mls*: multiply-accumulate, multiply-subtract
- *padd, padal*: adds (or add and accumulate) each adjacent pair of elements from each input vector *recpe, rsqrte*: reciprocal estimate, reciprocal square root estimate (can be fp)
- *abs, neg*: absolute value and negate (can be fp)
- *fma*: fused multiply-accumulate
- *fms*: fused multiply-subtract

Bit manipulation:

- *shl, shr*: shift left, shift right (logical?)
- *sra*: and accumulate. Each vector element is shift independently.
- *sra*
- *sli, sri*: shift left insert, shift right insert. Bits are not shifted across element boundaries. Each element is shifted independently. [do these support the prefixes??]
- *and* (Bitwise AND), *vbic* (Bit Clear), *veor* (Bitwise Exclusive OR), *vorn* (Bitwise OR NOT), and *vorr* (Bitwise OR): bitwise logical operations between two registers, and place the results in the destination register
- *mov, mvn*: move, move negate
- *cls*, *clz*, *cnt*: count leading sign bits, count leading zeros, count set bits
- *vbif*, *vbit*, *vbsl*: bitwise insert if true, bitwise insert if false, bitwise select; copies bits from the source operands into the destination.

Comparison:

- *ceq, cge, cgt, cle, clt*: compare equal, greater-than-or-equal, greater-than, less-than, less-than-or-equal
- *tst*: performs a bitwise logical AND between the corresponding elements in both vectors, if the result of the AND is not zero, sets the output element to all ones, otherwise sets the output element all zeros

- *abd, aba*: absolute difference, absolute difference and accumulate
- *max, min*: sets each output element to the maximum or minimum of the each of the two corresponding elements
- *pmin, pmax*: sets each output element to the maximum or minimum of each of the adjacent pairs of elements in both vectors
- *ceq, cge, cgt, cle, clt*: compare equal, greater-than-or-equal, greater-than, less-than, less-than-or-equal

B.5.3 Modifier

By default the intrinsic will use a 64-bit input and output width, implying that the vector size is 64/(*operand width*). The following modifiers are available:

- *q* specifies 128 bit input and output width.
- *l* specifies a 64-bits input width but generates a 128-bit output width.
- *w* allows the operation to accept one operand that is 128 bits wide and a second operand that is 64 bits wide operands and generate a result that is 128 bits wide.
- *hn* stores the high half of each result element (implies half-width result elements).
- *q* specifies 128 bit input and output width.
- *l* specifies a 64-bits input width but generates a 128-bit output width.
- w allows the operation to accept a 128-bit and 64-bit operands and generate a 128-bit result.
- *hn* stores the high half of each result element (implies half-width result elements).

B.5.4 Operand type and width

operand width is one of:

- s8, s16, s32: signed integer
- u8, u16, u32: unsigned integer
- p8: polynomial integer
- f16, f32: floating point

OpenCL reference

Chapter Outline

This appendix provides a reference for the most common features of OpenCL versions 1.1 and 1.2. These are older versions of OpenCL but are the most likely to be supported on embedded GPUs at the time of this writing.

Annotations throughout the appendix note any differences between OpenCL versions 1.1 and 1.2 where appropriate.

This appendix is intended only as a quick reference; it provides only a brief summary of the relevant information. For more a more thorough description of any feature, the reader should refer to the official OpenCL documentation.

Much of this information is from Khronos Group OpenCL documentation, available at the Khronos Group website at https://www.khronos.org.

C.1 Platform layer

The platform layer includes a set of functions called by the host to query coprocessor capabilities and instantiate communication channels to the device, called *contexts*. This section lists the most commonly used of these.

```
cl_int clGetPlatformIDs (cl_uint num_entries,
                         cl_platform_id *platforms,
                         cl_uint *num_platforms)
```

Obtain the list of platforms available.

This function retrieves the number of available platforms (if platforms *is NULL) or retrieves handles to the actual platforms themselves (if* num_platforms *contains a value or NULL).*

```
cl_int clGetPlatformInfo (cl_platform_id platform,
                          cl_platform_info param_name,
                          size_t param_value_size,
                          void *param_value,
                          size_t *param_value_size_ret)
```

param_name: CL_PLATFORM_{PROFILE, VERSION},
        CL_PLATFORM_{NAME, VENDOR, EXTENSIONS}

Get specific information about the OpenCL platform.

This function retrieves information regarding the available platform(s), such as the version of OpenCL and set of extensions supported. This is most useful for writing portable OpenCL applications, allowing the application to adapt to the capabilities of the available resources.

```
cl_int clGetDeviceIDs (cl_platform_id platform,
                       cl_device_type device_type,
                       cl_uint num_entries,
                       cl_device_id *devices,
                       cl_uint *num_devices)
```

device_type: CL_DEVICE_TYPE_{ACCELERATOR, ALL, CPU},
        CL_DEVICE_TYPE_{CUSTOM, DEFAULT, GPU}

Obtain the list of devices available on a platform.

This function retrieve device handle(s). Every OpenCL application must call this function in order to access a device.

```
cl_int clGetDeviceInfo (cl_device_id device,
                        cl_device_info param_name,
                        size_t param_value_size,
                        void *param_value,
                        size_t *param_value_size_ret)
```

param_name: CL_DEVICE_{NAME, VENDOR, PROFILE, TYPE},

CL_DEVICE_NATIVE_VECTOR_WIDTH_{CHAR, INT},

CL_DEVICE_NATIVE_VECTOR_WIDTH_{LONG, SHORT},

CL_DEVICE_NATIVE_VECTOR_WIDTH_{DOUBLE, HALF},

CL_DEVICE_NATIVE_VECTOR_WIDTH_FLOAT,

CL_DEVICE_PREFERRED_VECTOR_WIDTH_{CHAR, INT},

CL_DEVICE_PREFERRED_VECTOR_WIDTH_{LONG, SHORT},

CL_DEVICE_PREFERRED_VECTOR_WIDTH_{DOUBLE, HALF},

CL_DEVICE_PREFERRED_VECTOR_WIDTH_FLOAT,

CL_DEVICE_PREFERRED_INTEROP_USER_SYNC,

CL_DEVICE_ADDRESS_BITS,

CL_DEVICE_AVAILABLE,

CL_DEVICE_BUILT_IN_KERNELS,

CL_DEVICE_COMPILER_AVAILABLE,

CL_DEVICE_{DOUBLE, HALF, SINGLE}_FP_CONFIG,

CL_DEVICE_ENDIAN_LITTLE,

CL_DEVICE_EXTENSIONS,

CL_DEVICE_ERROR_CORRECTION_SUPPORT,

CL_DEVICE_EXECUTION_CAPABILITIES,

CL_DEVICE_GLOBAL_MEM_CACHE_{SIZE, TYPE},

CL_DEVICE_GLOBAL_MEM_{CACHELINE_SIZE, SIZE},

CL_DEVICE_HOST_UNIFIED_MEMORY,

CL_DEVICE_IMAGE_MAX_{ARRAY, BUFFER}_SIZE,

CL_DEVICE_IMAGE_SUPPORT,

CL_DEVICE_IMAGE2D_MAX_{WIDTH, HEIGHT},

CL_DEVICE_IMAGE3D_MAX_{WIDTH, HEIGHT, DEPTH},

CL_DEVICE_LOCAL_MEM_{TYPE, SIZE},

```
CL_DEVICE_MAX_{READ, WRITE}_IMAGE_ARGS,

CL_DEVICE_MAX_CLOCK_FREQUENCY,

CL_DEVICE_MAX_COMPUTE_UNITS,

CL_DEVICE_MAX_CONSTANT_{ARGS, BUFFER_SIZE},

CL_DEVICE_MAX_{MEM_ALLOC, PARAMETER}_SIZE,

CL_DEVICE_MAX_SAMPLERS,

CL_DEVICE_MAX_WORK_GROUP_SIZE,

CL_DEVICE_MAX_WORK_ITEM_{DIMENSIONS,SIZES},

CL_DEVICE_MEM_BASE_ADDR_ALIGN,

CL_DEVICE_OPENCL_C_VERSION,

CL_DEVICE_PARENT_DEVICE,

CL_DEVICE_PARTITION_AFFINITY_DOMAIN,

CL_DEVICE_PARTITION_MAX_SUB_DEVICES,

CL_DEVICE_PARTITION_{PROPERTIES, TYPE},

CL_DEVICE_PLATFORM,

CL_DEVICE_PRINTF_BUFFER_SIZE,

CL_DEVICE_PROFILING_TIMER_RESOLUTION,

CL_DEVICE_QUEUE_PROPERTIES,

CL_DEVICE_REFERENCE_COUNT,

CL_DEVICE_VENDOR_ID,

CL_{DEVICE, DRIVER}_VERSION
```

Get information about an OpenCL device.

This function retrieves specific information regarding the architecture of the device. Advanced OpenCL applications may use this information to automatically adjust kernel parameters. For example, the kernel's tile size could theoretically be customized according to the device's cache size (CL_DEVICE_GLOBAL_MEM_CACHE_SIZE)*.*

```
cl_context clCreateContext

    (const cl_context_properties *properties,

            cl_uint num_devices,

            const cl_device_id *devices,

            void (CL_CALLBACK* pfn_notify)

                (const char *errinfo,
```

```
                    const void *private_info, size_t cb,

                    void *user_data),

                    void *user_data,

                    cl_int *errcode_ret)
```

properties: `NULL or CL_CONTEXT_PLATFORM,`

           `CL_CONTEXT_INTEROP_USER_SYNC,`

           `CL_CONTEXT_{D3D10, D3D11}_DEVICE_KHR,`

           `CL_CONTEXT_ADAPTER_{D3D9, D3D9EX, DXVA}_KHR,`

           `CL_GL_CONTEXT_KHR,`

           `CL_CGL_SHAREGROUP_KHR,`

           `CL_{EGL, GLX}_DISPLAY_KHR,`

           `CL_WGL_HDC_KHR`

Creates an OpenCL context.

This function retrieves a context. Every OpenCL application must call this function or `clCreateContextFromType()` *in order to access the device.*

```
    cl_context clCreateContextFromType

        (const cl_context_properties *properties,

                    cl_device_type device_type,

                    void (CL_CALLBACK *pfn_notify)

                        (const char *errinfo,

                        const void *private_ info, size_t cb,

                        void *user_data),

                    void *user_data,

                    cl_int *errcode_ret)
```

properties: See clCreateContext

Create an OpenCL context from a device type that identifies the specific device(s) to use.

This function retrieves a context. Every OpenCL application must call this function or `clCreateContext()` *in order to access the device.*

```
    cl_int clReleaseContext (cl_context context)
```

Decrement the context reference count.

This function is typically called in the "cleanup" code before an application terminates.

```
cl_int clGetContextInfo (cl_context context,
                         cl_context_info param_name,
                         size_t param_value_size,
                         void *param_value,
                         size_t *param_value_size_ret)
```

param_name: `CL_CONTEXT_REFERENCE_COUNT,`

`CL_CONTEXT_{DEVICES, NUM_DEVICES, PROPERTIES},`

`CL_CONTEXT_D3D10_PREFER_SHARED_RESOURCES_KHR,`

`CL_CONTEXT_D3D11_PREFER_SHARED_RESOURCES_KHR`

Query information about a context.

This function retrieves information about a context, although the usefulness of this information is limited.

C.2 Memory types

Coprocessor devices such as GPUs, DSPs, and FPGAs contain specialized program-controlled on-chip memories. Programs can use these memories to allocate application data whose locality is particularly suited to the target memory's organization.

These memories may hold input or output tiles (such as when using the tiling approach described in Chapter 4) or serve as an extended register file for intermediate values that never need to be read to written to off-chip memory (such as for storing partial sums when summing an array of numbers).

OpenCL defines four abstract classes of memory according to a set of constraints regarding how each is accessed and allocated. Since the device vendor determines the implementation of these memories, OpenCL does not include any guidelines on how their usage affects performance. As such, it is up to the programmer on how and when to use these memories.

Generally speaking, all the kernel's input data originates from global memory, and all the kernel's outputs will ultimately be stored in global memory.

All function local variables default to private memory, and are usually reserved for scalars such as loop iterators and temporaries for index calculations.

Local memory is typically used as a replacement for cache for devices that lack caches. As such, kernels often contain a loop whose body begins by copying a block of input data into a small array declared in local memory, process it, and then write it back to global memory.

Table C.1: OpenCL buffer types, from the perspective of the host and kernel.

	Global	Constant	Local	Private
Host	Dynamic allocation, read/write access	Dynamic allocation, read/write access	Dynamic allocation, no access	No allocation, no access
Kernel	No allocation, read/write access	Static allocation, read-only access	Static allocation, read/write access	Static allocation, read/write access

Table C.1 lists the four types of memories in which buffers (arrays) can be allocated in the OpenCL device architecture. Each type of memory has different allocation and access restrictions on the host and device.

C.2.1 Global memory

Global memory can only be allocated on the host using the **clCreateBuffer()** function. The host sends a pointer to each global buffer to the kernel through the kernel function arguments using the clSetKernelArg() function.

Global buffers are generally used to send input data to the kernel (in which the host writes data using clEnqueueWriteBuffer()) and to retrieve output data from the kernel (in which the kernel reads it using clEnqueueReadBuffer()).

Since global memory buffers are normally allocated in off-chip memory, it generally has the highest access time.

C.2.2 Constant memory

Constant memory is allocated on the host and its pointers are sent to the kernel the same way as with global memory. To define a buffer as being allocated in constant memory, "global const" or "constant" prefix must precede the corresponding kernel arguments.

Unlike global memory, the kernel can statically allocate and initialize constant arrays by declaring a local array variable using the "constant" prefix.

Constant memory is read-only in the kernel but is generally stored in off-chip memory. Some devices include special caches for constant memory.

C.2.3 Local memory

The host can allocate buffers in local memory and send their corresponding pointers to the kernel using the same method as global and constant memory. In this case, the corresponding buffer name must include the "*local*" prefix in the kernel argument list. Also, when setting this parameter using clSetKernelArg() the host must specify NULL for the arg_value argument, because the host cannot initialize local buffers.

The kernel can statically allocate and initialize local arrays by declaring a local array variable using the "*local*" prefix.

Local memory is generally stored in fast on-chip memory and the contents of local buffers are shared among all work-items in each workgroup.

C.2.4 Private memory

The host cannot allocate buffers in private memory. The kernel can allocate and initialize buffers in private memory by specifying the "`private`" prefix for variable declarations. Buffers stored in private memory are generally stored in registers and are private to each work-item.

C.3 Buffer management

The host allocates global, constant, and local memory buffers using the `clCreateBuffer()` function. The host can subsequently read and write the buffer, most commonly using `clEnqueueWriteBuffer()` and `clEnqueueReadBuffer()`. There are also several more specialized functions for reading and writing buffers.

For example, `clEnqueueReadBufferRect()` writes a rectangular buffer, one that is not stored contiguously in host memory but instead comprised of a series of separated contiguous data blocks. `clEnqueueFillBuffer()` allows an arbitrary data pattern to be copied to a buffer. `clEnqueueCopyBuffer()` copies data from one buffer to another. `clEnqueueMapBuffer()` allows a memory region on the host to be mapped to a buffer, in which updates to either the host's mapped region on the device's buffer will be visible by the other entity.

```
cl_mem clCreateBuffer (cl_context context,

                       cl_mem_flags flags,

                       size_t size,

                       void *host_ptr,

                       cl_int *errcode_ret)
```

flags: CL_MEM_READ_WRITE,

CL_MEM_{WRITE, READ}_ONLY,

CL_MEM_HOST_NO_ACCESS,

CL_MEM_HOST_{READ, WRITE}_ONLY,

CL_MEM_{USE, ALLOC, COPY}_HOST_PTR

The following flags are available in OpenCL 1.2:

CL_MEM_COPY_HOST_WRITE_ONLY,

CL_MEM_COPY_HOST_READ_ONLY,

CL_MEM_COPY_HOST_NO_ACCESS

Creates a buffer object.

The programmer must be careful when using this function, since its usage may depend on whether the host and device share a physical memory. For example, the programmer shouldn't use the CL_MEM_USE_HOST_PTR *option for devices on add on cards that have separate memories from the host CPU.*

Also, some options, such as CL_MEM_COPY_HOST_PTR, *will cause the OpenCL runtime to automatically copy the data into the device's memory, meaning that the programmer does not need to call* clEnqueueWriteBuffer() *for the corresponding array.*

```
cl_int clEnqueueReadBuffer (cl_command_queue command_queue,

                            cl_mem buffer,

                            cl_bool blocking_read,

                            size_t offset,

                            size_t size,

                            void *ptr,

                            cl_uint num_events_in_wait_list,

                            const cl_event *event_wait_list,

                            cl_event *event
```

Enqueue commands to read from a buffer object to host memory.

The name of this function can potentially be confusing. "Read" is from the perspective of the host, so this function is normally applied to an output array of the kernel. In other words, the programmer refers to the output array as a read buffer, since it will be eventually read by the host.

```
cl_int clEnqueueReadBufferRect (cl_command_queue command_queue,

                                cl_mem buffer,

                                cl_bool blocking_read,

                                const size_t *buffer_origin,

                                const size_t *host_origin,

                                const size_t *region,

                                size_t buffer_row_pitch,

                                size_t buffer_slice_pitch,

                                size_t host_row_pitch,

                                size_t host_slice_pitch,

                                void *ptr,
```

```
                        cl_uint num_events_in_wait_list,

                        const cl_event *event_wait_list,

                        cl_event *event)
```

Enqueue commands to read from a rectangular region from a buffer object to host memory.

This function is necessary for copying a subregion of a 2D array to the host. This isn't necessary when copying an entire 2D array having the elements of its major dimension stored consecutively since such an array occupies a contiguous block of memory and can thus be copied with clEnqueueReadBuffer()*.*

```
    cl_int clEnqueueWriteBuffer (cl_command_queue command_queue,

                        cl_mem buffer,

                        cl_bool blocking_write,

                        size_t offset,

                        size_t size,

                        const void *ptr,

                        cl_uint num_events_in_wait_list,

                        const cl_event *event_wait_list,

                        cl_event *event)
```

Enqueue commands to write to a buffer object from host memory.

The name of this function can potentially be confusing. "Write" is from the perspective of the host, so this function is normally applied to an input array of the kernel. In other words, the programmer refers to the output array as a write buffer, since it is written by the host prior to being sent to the device.

```
    cl_int clEnqueueWriteBufferRect (cl_command_queue command_queue,

                        cl_mem buffer,

                        cl_bool blocking_write,

                        const size_t *buffer_origin,

                        const size_t *host_origin,

                        const size_t *region,

                        size_t buffer_row_pitch,

                        size_t buffer_slice_pitch,

                        size_t host_row_pitch,

                        size_t host_slice_pitch,
```

```
                        const void *ptr,

                        cl_uint num_events_in_wait_list,

                        const cl_event *event_wait_list,

                        cl_event *event)
```

Enqueue commands to write a rectangular region to a buffer object from host memory.

```
cl_int clEnqueueFillBuffer (cl_command_queue command_queue,

                        cl_mem buffer,

                        const void *pattern,

                        size_t pattern_size,

                        size_t offset,

                        size_t size,

                        cl_uint num_events_in_wait_list,

                        const cl_event *event_wait_list,

                        cl_event *event)
```

Enqueues a command to fill a buffer object with a pattern of a given pattern size. **[OpenCL 1.2 only]**

This function can be used to initialize a buffer on the device.

```
cl_int clEnqueueFillImage (cl_command_queue command_queue,

                        cl_mem image,

                        const void *fill_color,

                        const size_t *origin,

                        const size_t *region,

                        cl_uint num_events_in_wait_list,

                        const cl_event *event_wait_list,

                        cl_event *event)
```

Enqueues a command to fill an image object with a specified color. **[OpenCL 1.2 only]**

This function can be used to initialize an image object on the device.

```
cl_int clEnqueueCopyBuffer (cl_command_queue command_queue,

                        cl_mem src_buffer,

                        cl_mem dst_buffer,
```

```
                         size_t src_offset,

                         size_t dst_offset,

                         size_t size,

                         cl_uint num_events_in_wait_list,

                         const cl_event *event_wait_list,

                         cl_event *event)
```

Enqueues a command to copy a buffer object to another buffer object.

This function is similar to the Linux memcpy() *function for source and destination arrays in the device global memory.*

```
    cl_int clEnqueueCopyBufferRect (cl_command_queue command_queue,

                         cl_mem src_buffer,

                         cl_mem dst_buffer,

                         const size_t *src_origin,

                         const size_t *dst_origin,

                         const size_t *region,

                         size_t src_row_pitch,

                         size_t src_slice_pitch,

                         size_t dst_row_pitch,

                         size_t dst_slice_pitch,

                         cl_uint num_events_in_wait_list,

                         const cl_event *event_wait_list,

                         cl_event *event)
```

Enqueues a command to copy a rectangular region from the buffer object to another buffer object.

This function is the rectangular version of clEnqueueCopyBuffer().

```
    void *clEnqueueMapBuffer (cl_command_queue command_queue,

                         cl_mem buffer,

                         cl_bool blocking_map,

                         cl_map_flags map_flags,

                         size_t offset,

                         size_t size,
```

```
                              cl_uint num_events_in_wait_list,

                              const cl_event *event_wait_list,

                              cl_event *event,

                              cl_int *errcode_ret)
```

map_flags: CL_MAP_{READ, WRITE},

        CL_MAP_WRITE_INVALIDATE_REGION **[OpenCL 1.2 only]**

Enqueues a command to map a region of the buffer object given by buffer into the host address space and returns a pointer to this mapped region.

This function allows an array in host memory and an array in device memory to be linked, such that updates to one array will update the other.

```
    cl_int clRetainMemObject (cl_mem memobj)
```

Increments the memory object reference count.

This function prevents an OpenCL buffer from being deleted by the runtime.

```
    cl_int clReleaseMemObject (cl_mem memobj)
```

Decrements the memory object reference count.

This function is typically called during program cleanup to free all OpenCL buffers.

```
    cl_int clSetMemObjectDestructorCallback (cl_mem memobj,

                              void (CL_CALLBACK *pfn_notify)

                                (cl_mem memobj, void *user_data),

                              void *user_data)
```

Registers a user callback function that will be called when the memory object is deleted and its resources freed.

This function allows the program to determine when a buffer is deleted.

```
    cl_int clEnqueueUnmapMemObject (cl_command_queue command_queue, cl_mem memobj,

                                  void *mapped_ptr,

                                  cl_uint num_events_in_wait_list,

                                  const cl_event *event_wait_list,

                                  cl_event *event)
```

Enqueues a command to unmap a previously mapped region of a memory object.

This function reverses the operation performed by clEnqueueMapBuffer().

```
cl_int clEnqueueMigrateMemObjects (cl_command_queue command_queue,
                                   cl_uint num_mem_objects,
                                   const cl_mem *mem_objects,
                                   cl_mem_migration_flags flags,
                                   cl_uint num_events_in_wait_list,
                                   const cl_event *event_wait_list,
                                   cl_event *event)
```

flags: CL_MIGRATE_MEM_OBJECT_HOST,

   CL_MIGRATE_MEM_OBJECT_CONTENT_UNDEFINED

Enqueues a command to indicate which device a set of memory objects should be associated with. **[OpenCL 1.2 only]**

One of the improvements of OpenCL 1.2 over 1.1 was a set of functionalities designed for systems with multiple devices. This function associates buffers with a specific device.

```
cl_int clGetMemObjectInfo (cl_mem memobj, cl_mem_info param_name,
                           size_t param_value_size, void *param_value,
                           size_t *param_value_size_ret)
```

param_name: CL_MEM_{TYPE, FLAGS, SIZE, HOST_PTR},

   CL_MEM_{MAP, REFERENCE}_COUNT,

   CL_MEM_OFFSET,

   CL_MEM_CONTEXT,

   CL_MEM_ASSOCIATED_MEMOBJECT,

   CL_MEM_{D3D10, D3D11}_RESOURCE_KHR,

   CL_MEM_DX9_MEDIA_ADAPTER_TYPE_KHR,

   CL_MEM_DX9_MEDIA_SURFACE_INFO_KHR

Used to get information that is common to all memory objects (buffer and image objects).

This function is useful for recovering the host address associated with an OpenCL buffer.

```
cl_mem clCreateImage (cl_context context,

                      cl_mem_flags flags,

                      const cl_image_format *image_format,

                      const cl_image_desc *image_desc,

                      void *host_ptr,

                      cl_int *errcode_ret)
```

Creates a 1D image, 1D image buffer, 1D image array, 2D image, 2D image array, or 3D image object. **[OpenCL 1.2 only]**

This function creates an image object. This replaced the OpenCL 1.1 function clCreateImage2D().

```
cl_mem clCreateImage2D (cl_context context,

                        cl_mem_flags flags,

                        const cl_image_format *image_format,

                        size_t image_width,

                        size_t image_height,

                        size_t image_row_pitch,

                        void *host_ptr,

                        cl_int *errcode_ret)
```

Creates a 2D image object. **[OpenCL 1.1 only]**

This function creates an image object. This was replaced in OpenCL 1.2 with clCreateImage().

```
cl_mem clCreateImage3D (cl_context context,

                        cl_mem_flags flags,

                        const cl_image_format *image_format,

                        size_t image_width,

                        size_t image_height,

                        size_t image_depth,

                        size_t image_row_pitch,

                        size_t image_slice_pitch,

                        void *host_ptr,

                        cl_int *errcode_ret)
```

Creates a 3D image object. **[OpenCL 1.1 only]**

This function creates an image object. This was replaced in OpenCL 1.2 with
`clCreateImage()`.

C.4 Programs and compiling

OpenCL kernels can compiled at runtime using `clCreateProgramWithSource()` and
`clBuildProgram()` (or `clCompileProgram()` and `clLinkProgram()`) or offline using
`clCreateProgramWithBinary()`.

Either way, the kernel code is stored in separate file from the host object code, so the host
must explicitly read the kernel code before dispatching it onto the device for execution.

After this, the program is associated with a kernel using a function such as `clCreateKer-`
`nel()`, arguments are set using `clSetKernelArg()`, and invoked using a function such as
`clEnqueueNDRangeKernel()`.

```
cl_program clCreateProgramWithSource (cl_context context,

                                      cl_uint count,

                                      const char **strings,

                                      const size_t *lengths,

                                      cl_int *errcode_ret)
```

Creates a program object for a context, and loads the source code specified by the text strings
in the strings array into the program object.

*Using this function as part of a "just-in-time" compilation method is perhaps the most
common method to compile a kernel in OpenCL. Since different devices often have different
binary interfaces, this approach provides an obvious advantage in portability. Its drawback
is that it compiles the kernel source code every time the program is executed, adding performance overhead that degrades the overall benefit from coprocessor acceleration.*

```
cl_program clCreateProgramWithBinary (cl_context context,

                                      cl_uint num_devices,

                                      const cl_device_id *device_list,

                                      const size_t *lengths,

                                      const unsigned char **binaries,

                                      cl_int *binary_status,

                                      cl_int *errcode_ret)
```

Creates a program object for a context, and loads specified binary data into the program object.

This function allows the loading of pre-compiled kernels. Many OpenCL platform implementations don't offer a standalone (offline) compiler. In this case, the programmer needs to write his or her own program that compiles the kernel, extract the binary using clGetProgramInfo()*, and save it to a file.*

```
cl_program clCreateProgramWithBuiltInKernels (cl_context context,
                                              cl_uint num_devices,
                                              const cl_device_id *device_list,
                                              const char *kernel_names,
                                              cl_int *errcode_ret)
```

Creates a program object for a context, and loads the information related to the built-in kernels into a program object.

This function allows vendors to offer pre-made kernels to programmers.

```
cl_int clRetainProgram (cl_program program)
```

Increments the program reference count.

This function prevents a program object from being deleted by the runtime.

```
cl_int clReleaseProgram (cl_program program)
```

Decrements the program reference count.

This function is typically used in the program's "cleanup" code to de-allocate a program.

```
cl_int clBuildProgram (cl_program program,
                       cl_uint num_devices,
                       const cl_device_id *device_list,
                       const char *options,
                       void (CL_CALLBACK *pfn_notify) (cl_program program,
                       void *user_data), void *user_data)
```

Builds (compiles and links) a program executable from the program source or binary.

This function compiles a kernel. The programmer can specify a callback function to notify the program when the compile is complete.

```
cl_int clCompileProgram (cl_program program,
                         cl_uint num_devices,
                         const cl_device_id *device_list,
                         const char *options,
                         cl_uint num_input_headers,
                         const cl_program *input_headers,
                         const char **header_include_names,
                         void (CL_CALLBACK *pfn_notify) (cl_program program,
                             void *user_data),
                         void *user_data)
```

Compiles a program's source for all the devices or a specific device(s) in the OpenCL context associated with program. **[OpenCL 1.2 only]**

This function compiles a program without linking. Typically it is used together with `clLinkProgram()`.

```
cl_program clLinkProgram (cl_context context,
                          cl_uint num_devices,
                          const cl_device_id *device_list,
                          const char *options,
                          cl_uint num_input_programs,
                          const cl_program *input_programs,
                          void (CL_CALLBACK*pfn_notify) (cl_program program,
                              void *user_data),
                          void *user_data,
                          cl_int *errcode_ret))
```

Links a set of compiled program objects and libraries for all the devices or a specific device(s) in the OpenCL context and creates an executable. **[OpenCL 1.2 only]**

This function links a compiled program. Typically it is used together with `clCompileProgram()`.

```
cl_int clUnloadCompiler (void)
```

Allows the implementation to release the resources allocated by the OpenCL compiler. **[OpenCL 1.1 only]**

This function is a hint to the runtime that it can unload the compiler, although calling this function doesn't prevent the program from performing further compiles.

This function is replaced with `clUnloadPlatformCompiler()` *in OpenCL 1.1.*

```
cl_int clUnloadPlatformCompiler (cl_platform_id platform)
```

Allows the implementation to release the resources allocated by the OpenCL compiler for platform. **[OpenCL 1.2 only]**

This function is a hint to the runtime that it can unload the compiler, although calling this function doesn't prevent the program from performing further compiles.

This function replaced `clUnloadCompiler()` *from OpenCL 1.0.*

```
cl_int clGetProgramInfo (cl_program program,
                         cl_program_info param_name,
                         size_t param_value_size,
                         void *param_value,
                         size_t *param_value_size_ret)
```

param_name: `CL_PROGRAM_REFERENCE_COUNT,`

      `CL_PROGRAM_{CONTEXT,NUM_DEVICES, DEVICES},`

      `CL_PROGRAM_{SOURCE, BINARY_SIZES, BINARIES},`

      `CL_PROGRAM_{NUM_KERNELS, KERNEL_NAMES}` **[OpenCL 1.2 only]**

Returns information about the program object.

This function is useful for obtaining kernel object code for platform implementations that don't provide a standalone (offline) kernel compiler.

```
cl_int clGetProgramBuildInfo (cl_program program,
                              cl_device_id device,
                              cl_program_build_info param_name,
                              size_t param_value_size,
                              void *param_value,
                              size_t *param_value_size_ret)
```

param_name: `CL_PROGRAM_BINARY_TYPE,`

      `CL_PROGRAM_BUILD_{STATUS, OPTIONS, LOG}`

Returns build information for each device in the program object. **[OpenCL 1.2 only]**

Using this function to retrieve the list of potential warnings and errors from the kernel build is a virtual necessity when using just-in-time compilation, since otherwise it's very inconvenient for the programmer to identify and fix errors in the kernel source.

Compile options

The kernel compiler accepts options that are familiar to programmers that use gcc. There are some options that allow the programmer to relax accuracy requirements for the device's floating-point units in order to achieve higher performance.

Preprocessor: (`-D` processed in order listed in `clBuildProgram()` or `clCompileProgram()`)

`-D` name

`-D` name = definition

`-I` dir

Math intrinsics: `-cl-single-precision-constant`

　　　　　　　`-cl-denorms-are-zero`

　　　　　　　`-cl-fp32-correctly-rounded-divide-sqrt`

Optimization options: `-cl-opt-disable`

　　　　　　　`-cl-mad-enable`

　　　　　　　`-cl-no-signed-zeros`

　　　　　　　`-cl-finite-math-only`

　　　　　　　`-cl-unsafe-math-optimizations`

　　　　　　　`-cl-fast-relaxed-math`

Warning request/suppress: `-w`

　　　　　　　`-Werror`

Control OpenCL C language version: `-cl-std=CL1.1` // OpenCL 1.1 specification

　　　　　　　`-cl-std=CL1.2` // OpenCL 1.2 specification

Query kernel argument information: `-cl-kernel-arg-info`

Link options

Library linking options: `-create-library`

`-enable-link-options`

Program linking options: `-cl-denorms-are-zero`

`-cl-no-signed-zeroes`

`-cl-unsafe-math-optimizations`

`-cl-finite-math-only`

`-cl-fast-relaxed-math`

C.5 Kernel functions

The kernel functions allow the programmer to prepare the kernel's parameters and arguments prior to kernel execution.

```
cl_kernel clCreateKernel (cl_program program,

                          const char *kernel_name,

                          cl_int *errcode_ret)
```

Creates a kernel object.

When using this function, be sure that the `kernel_name` *string matches the kernel function name in the .cl source code file. Otherwise the kernel will fail to execute.*

```
cl_int clCreateKernelsInProgram (cl_program program,

                                 cl_uint num_kernels,

                                 cl_kernel *kernels,

                                 cl_uint *num_kernels_ret)
```

Creates kernel objects for all kernel functions in a program object.

This function allows the programmer to obtain kernel objects for all the functions in a program declared with "`kernel`," *as opposed to obtain only one kernel by name as in* `clCreateKernel()`.

```
cl_int clRetainKernel (cl_kernel kernel)
```

Increments the kernel object reference count.

This function prevents a kernel from being de-allocated by the runtime.

```
cl_int clReleaseKernel (cl_kernel kernel)
```

Decrements the kernel reference count.

This function is typically used in the program's "cleanup" code to de-allocate a kernel.

```
cl_int clSetKernelArg (cl_kernel kernel,
                       cl_uint arg_index,
                       size_t arg_size,
                       const void *arg_value)
```

Used to set the argument value for a specific argument of a kernel.

This function is used to set the kernel arguments before execution, since the kernel can't be called directly from the host program. This function is used in virtually all OpenCL programs.

```
cl_int clGetKernelInfo (cl_kernel kernel,
                        cl_kernel_info param_name,
                        size_t param_value_size,
                        void *param_value,
                        size_t *param_value_size_ret)
```

param_name: CL_KERNEL_FUNCTION_NAME,
            CL_KERNEL_NUM_ARGS,
            CL_KERNEL_REFERENCE_COUNT,
            CL_KERNEL_{ATTRIBUTES, CONTEXT, PROGRAM}

Returns information about the kernel object.

This function can be used to obtain information such as function name or program object from a kernel object.

```
cl_int clGetKernelWorkGroupInfo (cl_kernel kernel,
                                 cl_device_id device,
                                 cl_kernel_work_group_info param_name,
                                 size_t param_value_size,
                                 void *param_value,
                                 size_t *param_value_size_ret)
```

param_name: CL_KERNEL_GLOBAL_WORK_SIZE,

     CL_KERNEL_[COMPILE_]WORK_GROUP_SIZE,

     CL_KERNEL_{LOCAL, PRIVATE}_MEM_SIZE,

     CL_KERNEL_PREFERRED_WORK_GROUP_SIZE_MULTIPLE

Returns information about the kernel object that may be specific to a device.

The kernel compiler is able to determine from the kernel source information such as its maximum workgroup size and local memory size. For example, the register requirement of a kernel may prevent it from executing with the device's maximum workgroup size. This function allows the platform layer to determine this information prior to having to set the execution parameters such as workgroup size.

```
cl_int clGetKernelArgInfo (cl_kernel kernel,

                    cl_uint arg_indx,

                    cl_kernel_arg_info param_name,

                    size_t param_value_size,

                    void *param_value,

                    size_t *param_value_size_ret)
```

param_name: CL_KERNEL_ARG_{ACCESS, ADDRESS, TYPE}_QUALIFIER,

     CL_KERNEL_ARG_NAME,

     CL_KERNEL_ARG_TYPE_NAME

Returns information about the arguments of a kernel. **[OpenCL 1.2 only]**

This function can retrieve the kernel's arguments after they are set.

C.6 Command queue functions

The OpenCL command queue is the method by which the host controls the device(s). The host can use the command queue to send simple, in-order commands to the device, or it can configure the command queue as being an *out-of-order queue*, which allows it to construct complex *task graphs*.

A task graph is comprised of nodes representing kernels and uses events to control when each kernel executes according to the data dependencies as defined by the graph's arcs.

The command queue can contain *commands*, which execute code or exchange data with buffers. Commands are kernels, tasks, native kernels, read buffers, or write buffers.

The commands queue can also contain *synchronization primitives*, which enforce ordering between the execution of commands on the device (and host, in the case of native kernels). Synchronization primitives include events, markers, and barriers.

Events allow commands to wait for the completion of another command or commands. Each of the functions that enqueue commands:

- `clEnqueueReadBuffer()`,
- `clEnqueueWriteBuffer()`,
- `clEnqueueReadImage()`,
- `clEnqueueWriteImage()`,
- `clEnqueueMapBuffer()`,
- `clEnqueueMapImage()`,
- `clEnqueueNDRangeKernel()`,
- `clEnqueueTask()`, and
- `clEnqueueNativeKernel()`,

…have arguments named `event_wait_list` and `event`. `event_wait_list` is an array of event objects that must trigger before the task executes. `event` is event object that triggers than the command completes.

Markers are synchronization primitives that the host can enqueue that do nothing but trigger an event after all previously enqueued commands (in program order) have completed.

Barriers are synchronization primitives that the host can enqueuer that do nothing but require that all commands enqueued before the barrier (in program order) have completed before any of the commands enqueued after.

```
cl_command_queue clCreateCommandQueue (cl_context context,

                                       cl_device_id device,

                                       cl_command_queue_properties properties,

                                       cl_int *errcode_ret)
```

properties: `CL_QUEUE_PROFILING_ENABLE`,
       `CL_QUEUE_OUT_OF_ORDER_EXEC_MODE_ENABLE`

Create a command-queue on a specific device.

This function creates a command queue and only has two options. `CL_QUEUE_PROFILING_ENABLE` *allows the host to gather performance information.* `CL_QUEUE_OUT_OF_ORDER_EXEC_MODE_ENABLE` *allows commands to be dequeued out-of-order. In this case, the host must also use events, markers, and barriers to determine execution order.*

```
cl_int clRetainCommandQueue (cl_command_queue command_queue)
```

Increments the command_queue reference count.

This function prevents a command queue from being de-allocated by the runtime.

```
cl_int clReleaseCommandQueue (cl_command_queue command_queue)
```

Decrements the command_queue reference count.

This function is typically used in the program's "cleanup" code to de-allocate a command queue.

```
cl_int clGetCommandQueueInfo (cl_command_queue command_queue,

                              cl_command_queue_info param_name,

                              size_t param_value_size,

                              void *param_value,

                              size_t *param_value_size_ret)

        param_name: CL_QUEUE_CONTEXT,

                    CL_QUEUE_DEVICE,

                    CL_QUEUE_REFERENCE_COUNT,

                    CL_QUEUE_PROPERTIES
```

Query information about a command-queue.

This function is typically used to retrieve the context or device associated with a command queue.

```
cl_int clEnqueueNDRangeKernel (cl_command_queue command_queue,

                               cl_kernel kernel,

                               cl_uint work_dim,

                               const size_t *global_work_offset,

                               const size_t *global_work_size,

                               const size_t *local_work_size,

                               cl_uint num_events_in_wait_list,

                               const cl_event *event_wait_list,

                               cl_event *event)
```

Enqueues a command to execute a kernel on a device.

This is arguably the most important function in the OpenCL platform layer, since it instructs the device to execute a kernel with an NDRange.

```
cl_int clEnqueueTask (cl_command_queue command_queue,

                      cl_kernel kernel,

                      cl_uint num_events_in_wait_list,

                      const cl_event *event_wait_list,

                      cl_event *event)
```

Enqueues a command to execute a kernel on a device.

This function is the same as clEnqueueNDRangeKernel() *but only executes one work-item, i.e., equivalent to calling* clEnqueueNDRangeKernel() *with work_dim = 1, global_work_offset = NULL, global_work_size[0] set to 1, and local_work_size[0] set to 1.*

```
cl_int clEnqueueNativeKernel (cl_command_queue command_queue,

                             void (*user_func)(void *),

                             void *args, size_t cb_args,

                             cl_uint num_mem_objects,

                             const cl_mem *mem_list,

                             const void **args_mem_loc,

                             cl_uint num_events_in_wait_list,

                             const cl_event *event_wait_list,

                             cl_event *event)
```

Enqueues a command to execute a native C/C++ function not compiled using the OpenCL compiler.

This function enqueues a kernel that executes on the host and trigger and be triggered by events.

```
cl_event clCreateUserEvent (cl_context context,

                            cl_int *errcode_ret)
```

Creates a user event object.

This function instantiates an event object.

```
cl_int clSetUserEventStatus (cl_event event,

                             cl_int execution_status)
```

Sets the execution status of a user event object.

This function can trigger an event manually, as opposed to from the completion of command, or earlier than it would otherwise.

```
cl_int clWaitForEvents (cl_uint num_events,

                            const cl_event *event_list)
```

Waits on the host thread for commands identified by event objects to complete.

This function forces the host to wait for a specific event.

See also: clGetEventInfo(), clSetEventCallback()

```
cl_int clGetEventInfo (cl_event event,

                          cl_event_info param_name,

                          size_t param_value_size,

                          void *param_value,

                          size_t *param_value_size_ret)
```

param_name: CL_EVENT_COMMAND_{QUEUE, TYPE},

CL_EVENT_{CONTEXT, REFERENCE_COUNT},

CL_EVENT_COMMAND_EXECUTION_STATUS

Returns information about the event object.

This function retrieves information relating to an event. It is useful for polling, as opposed to blocking with clWaitForEvents(), *when waiting for an event to trigger.*

See also: clWaitForEvents(), clSetEventCallback()

```
cl_int clSetEventCallback (cl_event event,

                              cl_int command_exec_callback_type,

                              void (CL_CALLBACK *pfn_event_notify)

                                 (cl_event event,

                                  cl_int event_command_exec_status,

                                  void *user_data),

                              void *user_data)
```

Registers a user callback function for a specific command execution status.

This function registers a callback function to notify the host when an event triggers.

See also: clWaitForEvents(), clGetEventInfo()

    cl_int clRetainEvent (cl_event event)

Increments the event reference count.

This function prevents and event from being deleted by the runtime.

    cl_int clReleaseEvent (cl_event event)

Decrements the event reference count.

This function is typically called in the "cleanup" code before an application terminates.

    cl_int clEnqueueMarker (cl_command_queue command_queue,

                    cl_event *event)

Enqueues a marker command. **[OpenCL 1.1 only]**

The order the marker is enqueued, in relation to the enqueued commands, determines the set of commands that, when complete, trigger the marker.

    cl_int clEnqueueBarrier (cl_command_queue command_queue)

A synchronization point that enqueues a barrier operation. **[OpenCL 1.1 only]**

This function ensures that all commands enqueued before the barrier complete earlier than those before.

    cl_int clEnqueueWaitForEvents (cl_command_queue command_queue,

                    cl_uint num_events,

                    const cl_event *event_list)

Enqueues a wait for a specific event or a list of events to complete before any future commands queued in the command-queue are executed. **[OpenCL 1.1 only]**

This synchronization primitive prevents any commands enqueued after this primitive to wait until all the specified events have triggered.

    cl_int clEnqueueMarkerWithWaitList

        (cl_command_queue command_queue,

                    cl_uint num_events_in_wait_list,

                    const cl_event *event_wait_list,

                    cl_event *event)

Enqueues a marker command which waits for either a list of events to complete, or all previously enqueued commands to complete. **[OpenCL 1.2 ONLY]**

This synchronization primitive triggers and event after all the specified events have triggered.

```
cl_int clEnqueueBarrierWithWaitList
        (cl_command_queue command_queue,
                            cl_uint num_events_in_wait_list,
                            const cl_event *event_wait_list,
                            cl_event *event)
```

A synchronization point that enqueues a barrier operation. **[OpenCL 1.2 ONLY]**

This function prevents any commands enqueued afterward from executing until either all previously enqueued commands completed or all the specified events have triggered. This synchronization can also trigger its own event.

```
cl_int clGetEventProfilingInfo (cl_event event,
                            cl_profiling_info param_name,
                            size_t param_value_size,
                            void *param_value,
                            size_t *param_value_size_ret)
```

param_name: CL_PROFILING_COMMAND_QUEUED,
            CL_PROFILING_COMMAND_{SUBMIT, START, END}

Returns profiling information for the command associated with event if profiling is enabled.

This function is typically used to retrieve the time in which a command is queued, submitted, starts execution, or completes execution.

```
cl_int clFlush (cl_command_queue command_queue)
```

Issues all previously queued OpenCL commands in a command-queue to the device associated with the command-queue.

This function flushes all blocking enqueue commands, which include those that enqueue or dequeue buffers, images, mapbuffers, etc.

```
cl_int clFinish (cl_command_queue command_queue)
```

Blocks until all previously queued OpenCL commands in a command-queue are issued to the associated device and have completed.

This function is typically used to block the host until all commands in a command queue have completed.

C.7 Vector and image data types

As shown in Table C.2, OpenCL includes a set of special types. Of these have different names depending on if the declaration is made on the host or kernel code.

The vector and image types are useful for explicitly vectorizing code. OpenCL generally allows for vectors of up to length 16. Individual elements of a vector element can be accessed by adding a ".s*n*" suffix after the variable, where *n* is a hexadecimal number

Table C.2: OpenCL types.

Kernel Type	Description	Host Type (If Applicable)
char*n*	8-bit signed	cl_char*n*
uchar*n*	8-bit unsigned	cl_uchar*n*
short*n*	16-bit signed	cl_short*n*
ushort*n*	16-bit unsigned	cl_ushort*n*
int*n*	32-bit signed	cl_int*n*
uint*n*	32-bit unsigned	cl_uint*n*
long*n*	64-bit signed	cl_long*n*
ulong*n*	64-bit unsigned	cl_ulong*n*
float*n*	32-bit float	cl_float*n*
double*n*	64-bit float	cl_double*n*
image2d_t	2D image handle	
image3d_t	3D image handle	
image2d_array_t	2D image array	
image1d_t	1D image handle	
image1d_buffer_t	1D image buffer	
image1d_array_t	1D image array	
sampler_t	Sampler handle	
event_t	Event handle	
bool*n*	Boolean vector	
half*n*	16-bit float, vector	
quad, quad*n*	128-bit float, vector	
complex_half, complex_half*n*	16-bit complex, vector	
imaginary_half, imaginary_half*n*	16-bit imaginary, vector	
complex_float, complex_float*n*	32-bit complex, vector	
imaginary_float, imaginary_float*n*	32-bit imaginary, vector	
complex_double, complex_double*n*	64-bit complex, vector	
imaginary_double, imaginary_double*n*	64-bit imaginary, vector	
complex_quad, complex_quad*n*	128-bit complex, vector	
imaginary_quad, imaginary_quad*n*	128-bit imaginary, vector	
float*nxm*	*nxm* matrix of 32-bit floats	
double*nxm*	*nxm* matrix of 64-bit floats	

from 0 to f (or F). Multiple elements can be combined by adding multiple indices after the ".s" suffix, for example ".s02".

C.8 Attributes

When dispatching a kernel using `clEnqueueNDRangeKernel()`, the programmer may specify the number of work-items without specifying the number of workgroups (by setting the `local_work_size` argument to NULL). In this case, the OpenCL implementation will determine how to break the number of global work-items into appropriate workgroup instances. In this case, the programmer can provide workgroup and vector size information to the kernel in the form of attributes, as shown below.

Kernel attributes

```
__attribute__(vec_type_hint(type))
```

```
__attribute__((work_group_size_hint(X, Y, Z)))
```

```
__attribute__((reqd_work_group_size(X, Y, Z)))
```

OpenCL also allows for declared variables to be given attributes for alignment, packing, and endianness.

Type attributes

```
__attribute__((aligned(n)))
```

```
__attribute__((aligned))
```

```
__attribute__((packed))
```

```
__attribute__((endian(host)))
```

```
__attribute__((endian(device)))
```

```
__attribute__((endian))
```

C.9 Constants

OpenCL defines a list of single-precision floating-point constants as defined in Table C.3. Each constant that ends with "_F" has a corresponding double precision version without the "_F" suffix and half precision by replacing with the "_H" suffix, when supported by the OpenCL implementation.

Table C.3: OpenCL constants.

Constant	Description
MAXFLOAT	Value of maximum noninfinite single-precision floating-point number
HUGE_VALF	Positive float expression, evaluates to $+$ infinity
HUGE_VAL	Positive double expression, evaluates to $+$ infinity
INFINITY	Constant float expression, positive or unsigned infinity
NAN	Constant float expression, quiet NaN.
M_E_F	Value of e
M_LOG2E_F	Value of $\log_2 e$
M_LOG10E_F	Value of $\log_{10} e$
M_LN2_F	Value of $\log_e 2$
M_LN10_F	Value of $\log_e 10$
M_PI_F	Value of π
M_PI_2_F	Value of $\pi/2$
M_PI_4_F	Value of $\pi/4$
M_1_PI_F	Value of $1/\pi$
M_2_PI_F	Value of $2/\pi$
M_2_SQRTPI_F	Value of $2/\sqrt{\pi}$
M_SQRT2_F	Value of $\sqrt{2}$
M_SQRT1_2_F	Value of $1/\sqrt{2}$

C.10 Built-in functions

OpenCL provides a set of built-in functions available for use in kernel code. Some of these functions are standard mathematical primitives and many of these accept vector operands. Others are utility functions for work-item identification and vector loads and stores.

C.10.1 Integer functions

Table C.4 list the integer functions. These functions accept vector operands.

C.10.2 Floating-point functions

Table C.5 lists the floating-point functions. Most of these functions accept vector operands.

C.10.3 Vector functions

OpenCL kernels should always use explicit vector load and store functions to exchange data between vector variables and arrays (Table C.6).

Table C.4: Built-in functions.

`abs(x)`	$\lvert x \rvert$ (unsigned)
`abs_diff(x)`	$\lvert x - y \rvert$ without overflow (unsigned)
`add_sat(x,y)`	$x + y$ and saturate the result
`hadd(x,y)`	$(x + y) >> 1$ without overflow
`rhadd(x,y)`	$(x + y + 1) >> 1$
`clamp(x,minval,maxval)`	$\min(\max(x,minval),maxval)$ min and max can be vectors or scalars
`clz(x)`	Number of leading 0-bits in x
`mad_hi(a,b,c)`	$\text{mul\_hi}(a,b) + c$
`mad_sat(a,b,c)`	$a * b + c$ and saturates the result
`max(x,y)`	y if $x < y$ else x y can be a vector or scalar
`min(x,y)`	y if $y < x$ else x y can be a vector or scalar
`mul_hi(x,y)`	high half of $x * y$
`rotate(v,i)`	rotate v by i bits
`sub_sat(x,y)`	$x - y$ and saturate the result
`popcount(x)`	Number of one-zero bits in x
`short[n] upsample(char[n] hi, uchar[n] lo)`	result$[i]$ = ((short)hi$[i]$ << 8) | lo$[i]$
`ushort[n] upsample(uchar[n] hi, uchar[n] lo)`	result$[i]$ = ((ushort)hi$[i]$ << 8) | lo$[i]$
`int [n] upsample(short[n] hi, ushort[n] lo)`	result$[i]$ = ((int)hi$[i]$ << 16) | lo$[i]$
`uint[n] upsample(ushort[n] hi, ushort[n] lo)`	result$[i]$ = ((uint)hi$[i]$ << 16) | lo$[i]$
`long [n] upsample(int[n] hi, uint[n] lo)`	result$[i]$ = ((long)hi$[i]$ << 32) | lo$[i]$
`ulong[n] upsample(uint[n] hi, uint[n] lo)`	result$[i]$ = ((ulong)hi$[i]$ << 32) | lo$[i]$
`mad24(x,y,z)`	Multiply 24-bit integer values x, y, add 32-bit int. result to 32-bit int. z
`mul24(x,y)`	Multiply 24-bit integer values x and y

Table C.5: Built-in floating-point functions.

Trigonometry functions	
`sin(x), cos(x), tan(x),`	Basic trigonometry functions
`asin(x), acos(x), atan(x),`	Inverse trigonometry functions
`sinh(x), cosh(x), tanh(x),`	Hyperbolic trigonometry functions
`asinh(x), acosh(x), atanh(x),`	Inverse hyperbolic trigonometry functions
`sinpi(x), cospi(x), tanpi(x),`	Basic trigonometry functions, result divided by pi
`asinpi(x), acospi(x), atanpi(x)`	Inverse trigonometry functions, result divided by pi
`atan2(x,y)`	Tangent of x/y
`atan2pi(x,y)`	atan2(x,y)/pi
Logarithms, exponentiation, and power functions	
`log(x), log2(x), log10(x),`	Logarithm base e, 2, and 10
`log1p(x),`	$\ln(1.0 + x)$

Continued

Table C.5: Built-in floating-point functions.—cont'd

`logb(x)`, `ilogb(x)`	Exponent of x as float, integer
`exp(x)`, `exp2(x)`, `exp10(x)`,	Exponentiation, base e, 2, and 10
`expm1(x)`	$e^x - 1.0$
`pow(x,y)`, `pown(x,y)`, `powr(x,y)`	Computes x^y
`rootn(x,y)`	$x^{1/y}$
`ilogb(x)`	Extract exponent
`ldexp(x,n)`	$x * 2^n$
`frexp(x, *exp)`	Extract mantissa and exponent
`modf(x, *iptr)`	Decompose floating-point number
Geometric functions	
`cbrt(x)`	Cube root of x
`hypot(x,y)`	Square root of $x^2 + y^2$
`cross(p0,p1)`	Cross product (vector size 3 or 4)
`distance(p0,p1)`	Vector distance
`dot(p0,p1)`	Dot product
`length(p)`	Normal vector length 1
`normalize(p)`	Normalize
`fast_distance(p0,p1)`	Vector distance
`fast_length(p)`	Vector length
`fast_normalize(p)`	Normal vector length 1
Rounding operations	
`ceil(x)`, `floor(x)`	Ceiling, floor
`rint(x)`	Round to nearest even integer
`copysign(x,y)`	x changed to sign of y
`erf(x)`, `erfc(x)`	Error function, complementary error function
`fabs(x)`,	Absolute value
`fdim(x)`	Positive difference between x and y
Multiply accumulate	
`fma(a,b,c)`, `mad(a,b,c)`	Multiply accumulate
Max/min functions	
`fmax(x,y)`, `fmin(x,y)`	Maximum, minimum
`maxmad(x,y)`, `minmad(x,y)`	Maximum, minimum magnitude of x and y
Division operations	
`fmod(x,y)`,	Floating-point modulo of x and y
`fract(x)`	Fractional portion of x
`remainder(x,y)`	Remainder of x and y
`remquo(x,y,*quo)`	Remainder and quotient of x and y
`tgamma(x)`	Gamma function
`lgamma(x)`	Log gamma
`nextafter(x,y)`	Next representable floating-point value after x in the direction of y

Table C.6: Vector load and store functions.

`vloadn (offset, *p)`	Load vector of size *n*
`vload_half(offset, *p)`	Load half precision floating-point value
`vload_halfn (offset, *p)`	Load vector of half precision f.p. values
`vstoren (offset, *p)`	Store vector of size *n*
`vstore_half(offset, *p)`	Store half precision floating-point value
`vstore_halfn (offset, *p)`	Store vector of half precision f.p. values

Table C.7: Work-item functions.

`get_work_dim()`	Number of dimensions
`get_global_size(D)`	Number of global work-items in dimension D
`get_global_id(D)`	Global work-item number in dimension D
`get_local_size(D)`	Number of local work-items in dimension D
`get_local_id(D)`	Local work-item ID in dimension D
`get_num_groups(D)`	Number of workgroups in dimension D
`get_group_id(D)`	Workgroup ID
`get_global_offset(D)`	Global offset in dimension D

Table C.8: Work-item synchronization.

`barrier(flags)`	All work-items within a workgroup must execute this before any can continue
`mem_fence(flags)`	Orders loads and stores of a work-item executing a kernel
`read_mem_fence(flags)`	Orders memory loads
`write_mem_fence(flags)`	Orders memory stores

C.10.4 Work-item functions

OpenCL kernels can be dispatched as a 1-, 2-, and 3-dimensional array of work-items. The array of work-items can optionally be subdivided into a 1-, 2-, or 3-dimensional array of workgroups (when `clEnqueueNDRangeKernel()` is called with the `local_work_size` argument set to a non-NULL value).

Kernel workload distribution is governed by the ability for each work-item to self-identify itself within this coordinate system. A work-item's global ID is calculated irrespective of its position within a workgroup, while its local ID is calculated relative to its location within its workgroup (Table C.7).

Work-items within a workgroup can be synchronized with a barrier operation and their memory operations ordered (Table C.8).

C.10.5 Relational functions

OpenCL provides a set of functions for comparing vector variables.

`isequal(x,y)`	Basic comparison operations, returns vector
`isnotequal(x,y)`	
`isgreater(x,y)`	
`isgreaterequal(x,y)`	
`isless(x,y)`	
`islessequal(x,y)`	
`islessgreater(x,y)`	
`isfinite(x)`	Tests each element for special floating-point values
`isinf(x)`	
`isnan(x)`	
`isnormal(x)`	
`isordered(x,y)`	
`  isunordered(x,y)`	
`signbit(x)`	Returns sign bit of each element
`any(x)`	Tests if MSB of any element is 1
`all(x)`	Tests if all MSB of all elements is 1
`bitselect(a,b,c)`	Each bit of result is corresponding bit of a if corresponding bit of c is 0. Otherwise it is the corresponding bit of b.
`select(a,b,c)`	For each component of a vector type, result$[i]$ = if MSB of $c[i]$ is set ? $b[i]$: $a[i]$. For scalar type, result = c ? b : a.

C.10.6 Atomic functions

Atomic operations allow shared memory locations to be read, modified, and updated in a way that is not interruptible, allowing work-items to perform certain primitive shared memory operations without a critical section lock.

Note that OpenCL 1.1 and 1.2 do not include any locking functions for kernels, but one can be built using the atomic exchange function.

`atomic_add(*p,val)`	Read, add, store Integers only
`atomic_sub(*p,val)`	Read, subtract, and store Integers only
`atomic_xchg(*p,val)`	Read, swap, and store Returns the value swapped out from *p
`atomic_inc(*p)`	Read, increment, and store Integers only
`atomic_dec(*p)`	Read, decrement, and store Integers only
`atomic_cmpxchg(*p,cmp,val)`	Read, store only if memory contents match cmp
`atomic_min(*p,val)`	Read, store min(*p,val) Integers only
`atomic_max(*p,val)`	Read, store max(*p,val) Integers only
`atomic_and(*p,val)`	Read, store (*p & val) Integers only
`atomic_or(*p,val)`	Read, store (*p | val) Integers only
`atomic_xor(*p,val)`	Read, store (*p ^ val) Integers only

C.10.7 Conversions

OpenCL supports C99-style typecasting, but also has conversion extensions to support saturation and rounding modes.

`a = convert_T_R(b):`   convert to type T with rounding mode R

`a = convert_T_sat_R`   convert to type T with saturation and rounding mode R

where R is one of

- `_rte (to nearest even)`
- `_rtz (toward zero)`
- `_rtp (toward + infinity)`
- `_rtn (toward - infinity)`

Index

Note: Page numbers followed by *f* indicate figures and *t* indicate tables.